Business Intelligence with MicroStrategy Cookbook

Over 90 practical, hands-on recipes to help you build
your MicroStrategy business intelligence project,
including more than a 100 screencasts

Davide Moraschi

ADMIRAL
ACADEMY
CARDIFF

[PACKT] enterprise
PUBLISHING
professional expertise distilled

BIRMINGHAM - MUMBAI

Business Intelligence with MicroStrategy Cookbook

First published: October 2013

Production Reference: 1231013

Published by Packt Publishing Ltd.
Livery Place
35 Livery Street
Birmingham B3 2PB, UK.

ISBN 978-1-78217-975-7

www.packtpub.com

Cover Image by Davide Moraschi (davidem@eurostrategy.net)

Credits

Author

Davide Moraschi

Reviewers

Fernando Carlos Rivero Esqueda

Chandana Koritala

Acquisition Editor

Pramila Balan

Lead Technical Editor

Madhuja Chaudhari

Technical Editors

Manan Badani

Hardik B. Soni

Pankaj Kadam

Nadeem N. Bagban

Copy Editors

Alfida Paiva

Gladson Monteiro

Adithi Shetty

Kirti Pai

Tanvi Gaitonde

Brandt D'Mello

Project Coordinator

Apeksha Chitnis

Proofreader

Linda Morris

Indexer

Rekha Nair

Production Coordinator

Conidon Miranda

Cover Work

Conidon Miranda

Foreword

Information is the most important competitive force shaping the business landscape today. Companies that harness information well are more efficient because they manage their resources with less waste. They are more nimble because they can sense what is happening in the market more keenly and quickly. The other major economic factors, land, labor, and capital are important, but after 300 years of the Industrial Age experience, their use has been reduced to commoditized best practices. Companies and products are no longer distinguished by innovative uses of land, labor, or capital. But when you find an organization that creates marketing strategies based on deep customer insight, or manages inventory using predictive analytics, or sets prices dynamically based on fine-grained demand variations, then you have found an organization that is outperforming its competitors. In this new information age, information is king.

The power of information is becoming greater every year. Our digital world is being "instrumented" at an unprecedented level. Computing is everywhere and it is capturing everything—every transaction, every website visit, every image viewed, every product shipped, every container stacked, and every product scanned. Businesses are drowning in opportunities to exploit so much data. They are limited only by the ingenuity of the information professionals whose job it is to tame it and business professionals who consume it.

MicroStrategy technology was created to tackle the biggest challenges in business intelligence, that is, to analyze the largest datasets with the most sophisticated analytics, and to empower the largest business user populations to consume and manipulate it. To this day, MicroStrategy is widely recognized as one of the most powerful analytic technologies available. MicroStrategy technology is like a nuclear power plant generating information energy for millions of business consumers. But like a nuclear power-plant, it is entirely dependent on skilled professionals to run it.

Mr. Moraschi's excellent book is designed to bring information proficiency to a whole new generation of information producers and business people whose jobs increasingly revolve around information, and not just IT professionals. The brilliance of this book is that it blends both concepts and mechanics into one narrative. Readers learn about the structure and terminology that underlie information engineering, and then learn the mechanics of how to use MicroStrategy to turn that information into insight. At a macro level, this is an important book because it will accelerate information literacy in business professionals. At a personal level, it is important because it can propel people into new and prosperous careers in information.

Mark S. LaRow

Executive Vice President of Products, MicroStrategy

About the Author

Davide Moraschi is a Business Intelligence contractor and trainer. He is a MicroStrategy Certified Engineering Principal, specialized in healthcare data. Born in Italy and married to a Japanese woman, he now lives in what is probably the hottest city in Europe, Seville. He speaks English, Spanish, and fluent SQL.

Since the early nineties he's been working as a Database Developer and BI specialist for multinational companies (Microsoft, Novartis) or public institutions like the European Commission.

He's the author of the blog `http://blog.eurostrategy.net`, and an active member of the MicroStrategy group on LinkedIn.

He can be reached at `davidem@eurostrategy.net`.

SELECT 'Acknowledgments' FROM DUAL;

I would like to thank my family and everyone who contributed to make this book a reality, the people at Packt Publishing: Pramila Balan, Apeksha Chitnis, Veena Manjrekar, Madhuja Chaudhari, and Hardik B. Soni.

My grateful acknowledgement to Francisco Rodriguez at MicroStrategy for his support and for giving me the opportunity to meet many people at the company and receive invaluable feedback about the content of the chapters.

I also want to express sincere gratitude to Manuel Miguel Martínez Jiménez and Juan Ramón Cuesta Escoresca for lending me their beloved iPads.

About the Reviewers

Fernando Carlos Rivero Esqueda is a Mexican Engineer living and working in Seattle, WA. Fernando earned both his BS in Electronic Systems and his MS in Information Technology Management from the ITESM (Monterrey Institute of Technology in Mexico); later while living in the US, he received honors in MBA from the University of Massachusetts, Amherst. He speaks three languages: Spanish (his native language), English, and Italian.

Fernando has more than 12 years of experience working with the MicroStrategy platform. He has spent 9 years working for MicroStrategy and 3 years for a business partner as a Regional Director. His experience, combined with solid technical skills in Business Intelligence, has bestowed him with the highest certification that a MicroStrategy Professional could attain: The MicroStrategy Certified Engineering Principal (MCEP) title. During his career, he has gained international exposure working in the United States, Mexico, Colombia, Venezuela, and El Salvador.

His professional career outside of the Business Intelligence world includes working for his alma mater's academia for 5 years and starting up his own multimedia, memorabilia, photography, and video production company, Ememories (`www.EMemories.net`).

Fernando, who is also a passionate amateur pianist, enjoys circuits, computers, graphic design, and databases; but mostly he loves his wife and being a father of four busy little boys and one more still in mom's womb.

> I would like to thank my wife and children for their patience while I was reviewing this book. Thank you mom and dad for your love and protection. Thank you my beloved family. Thank you God for everything you have given me.

Chandana Koritala works as a Sr. Business Intelligence Consultant at Smartbridge. She is a MicroStrategy Certified Developer accredited by MicroStrategy University. She has more than 6 years of experience in design, development, testing, and deploying reporting solutions. She is adept at dimensional modeling, data profiling, ETL architecture design and implementation, and OLAP cubes development. Prior to working on Business Intelligence, she created custom mobile applications using XCode, Objective C, and Java for Android, iPad and iPhone devices. She is an experienced web developer and designer too. You can follow her on Twitter `@ckoritala1`.

www.PacktPub.com

Support files, eBooks, discount offers and more

You might want to visit www.PacktPub.com for support files and downloads related to your book.

Did you know that Packt offers eBook versions of every book published, with PDF and ePub files available? You can upgrade to the eBook version at www.PacktPub.com and as a print book customer, you are entitled to a discount on the eBook copy. Get in touch with us at service@packtpub.com for more details.

At www.PacktPub.com, you can also read a collection of free technical articles, sign up for a range of free newsletters and receive exclusive discounts and offers on Packt books and eBooks.

http://PacktLib.PacktPub.com

Do you need instant solutions to your IT questions? PacktLib is Packt's online digital book library. Here, you can access, read and search across Packt's entire library of books.

Why Subscribe?

- ▶ Fully searchable across every book published by Packt
- ▶ Copy and paste, print and bookmark content
- ▶ On demand and accessible via web browser

Free Access for Packt account holders

If you have an account with Packt at www.PacktPub.com, you can use this to access PacktLib today and view nine entirely free books. Simply use your login credentials for immediate access.

Instant Updates on New Packt Books

Get notified! Find out when new books are published by following @PacktEnterprise on Twitter, or the *Packt Enterprise* Facebook page.

To my wife, Tomoko. Thanks for everything.

Table of Contents

Preface

The MicroStrategy Analytics Platform™ enables leading organizations to analyze vast amounts of data and distribute actionable business insight throughout the enterprise. It delivers reports and dashboards, enables users to conduct ad hoc analysis, and share their insights anywhere, anytime. The MicroStrategy Mobile App Platform™ lets organizations rapidly build information-rich applications that combine multimedia, transactions, analytics, and custom workflows.

In this book, we will make a journey from the initial setup to Big Data passing through the construction of the project, the design of interactive dashboards, and the visual data discovery.

Join us on this self-paced trip and follow the tracks of more than 90 recipes, which lead to the creation of a complete Business Intelligence project with MicroStrategy Suite.

What this book covers

Chapter 1, *Getting Started with MicroStrategy*, covers the installation of training environments, complete with sample data, MicroStrategy Suite, metadata, and ODBC connections. Operating system and web server configuration are also covered.

Chapter 2, *The First Steps in a MicroStrategy Project*, explains the creation of a project: how to connect to a data warehouse, the use of tables as data sources, and how to create logical views with SELECT statements.

Chapter 3, *Schema Objects – Attributes*, shows the creation of the first objects: attributes and hierarchies, and how attributes relate to each other (parent-child relationship). We create our first report during this chapter.

Chapter 4, *Objects – Facts and Metrics*, covers the numbers: the use of aggregation functions, how to filter on metrics, the creation of level metrics, and a basic "previous month" transformation.

Chapter 5, Data Display and Manipulation – Reports, treats the design and manipulation of reports in the desktop application. Drill, page-by, custom subtotals, and conditional formatting are shown with practical tips and real-life examples.

Chapter 6, Data Analysis and Visualization – Graphs, covers the graphical part of data analysis, showing how to create compelling graphs with the use of the most common options. Advanced charting techniques like dual axis are demonstrated too.

Chapter 7, Analysis on the Web – Documents and Dashboards, shows how to port the project to the Web, set up the server, and create documents and interactive dashboards for consumption in the Internet browser.

Chapter 8, Dynamic Selection with Filters and Prompts, explains the usage of different filtering techniques and how to use dynamic selections to customize reports. It also explains the use of moving dates in filters.

Chapter 9, Mobile BI for Developers, covers the installation and configuration of mobile Business Intelligence. It shows how to design ad hoc reports and documents for the iPad, using linked documents and info windows.

Chapter 10, Mobile BI for Users, covers the most common scenarios for mobile usage and gives insights and tips on how to consume data (and ask for help) from the user's perspective.

Chapter 11, Consolidations, Custom Groups, and Transformations, explains advanced techniques and objects to solve specific reporting requirements, such as different aggregations, creating banded reports, or month-to-date and year-to-date running sums.

Chapter 12, In-Memory Cubes and Visual Insight, covers the latest In-Memory technology to create Visual Insight dashboards and self-service data discovery from the web interface. It demonstrates the usage of the new network graph visualization.

Chapter 13, MicroStrategy Express, introduces the SaaS version of MicroStrategy self-service data discovery tool and dashboards. It shows how to upload data or connect to on-premises and cloud-based databases to design interactive panels and visualizations without support from the IT personnel.

Appendix A, Solution to Exercises, gives answers to all the questions and exercises of the book.

Appendix B, Where to Look for Information, is a collection of useful resources, blogs, books, and discussion groups to network with fellow BI developers.

Appendix C, Cloudera Hadoop, explains how to connect from MicroStrategy to one of the most commonly used platforms for Big Data. The distribution used is CH4 with Impala.

Appendix D, HP Vertica, demonstrates the connection to a common platform for columnar databases, the Vertica engine by HP. The distribution used is the Community Edition, freely available from the vendor site.

What you need for this book

To make the most of this book, you need to have a virtualization environment with a 32-bit Windows 2008 R2 installed. I am using VMware workstation in the screencasts. The installation of the operating system is not covered by the book, which starts with the setup of a local SQL Server.

Adobe Flash is used in some examples and a PDF reader is needed to use the product documentation.

The use of a modern browser with support for HTML5 is mandatory during *Chapter 13, MicroStrategy Express*.

Who this book is for

This book is intended for Business Intelligence developers who want to expand their reach and add a leading data analysis product to their toolset.

This is also for experienced database developers or administrators, and for everyone who wants to learn how to use one of the most widely used platforms for reporting, dashboarding, and data discovery on the market.

ANSI SQL language familiarity is required. No previous knowledge of MicroStrategy is needed.

Conventions

In this book, you will find a number of styles of text that distinguish between different kinds of information. Here are some examples of these styles, and an explanation of their meaning.

Code words in text, database table names, folder names, filenames, file extensions, pathnames, dummy URLs, user input, and Twitter handles are shown as follows: "Click on **Save and Close** naming the report `01 Countries list`."

Any command-line input or output is written as follows:

```
ALTER TABLE DimDate ADD CalendarYearMonth VARCHAR(7)
go
 UPDATE DimDate SET CalendarYearMonth = CONVERT(VARCHAR(7),
FullDateAlternateKey, 111)
go
exit
```

New terms and **important words** are shown in bold. Words that you see on the screen, in menus or dialog boxes for example, appear in the text like this: "Click on the **Schema Objects | Facts** folder. Right-click on the right pane and select **New | Fact**."

Warnings or important notes appear in a box like this.

Tips and tricks appear like this.

Reader feedback

Feedback from our readers is always welcome. Let us know what you think about this book—what you liked or may have disliked. Reader feedback is important for us to develop titles that you really get the most out of.

To send us general feedback, simply send an e-mail to feedback@packtpub.com, and mention the book title via the subject of your message.

If there is a topic that you have expertise in and you are interested in either writing or contributing to a book, see our author guide on www.packtpub.com/authors.

Customer support

Now that you are the proud owner of a Packt book, we have a number of things to help you to get the most from your purchase.

Downloading the example code

You can download the example code files for all Packt books you have purchased from your account at http://www.packtpub.com. If you purchased this book elsewhere, you can visit http://www.packtpub.com/support and register to have the files e-mailed directly to you.

Errata

Although we have taken every care to ensure the accuracy of our content, mistakes do happen. If you find a mistake in one of our books—maybe a mistake in the text or the code—we would be grateful if you would report this to us. By doing so, you can save other readers from frustration and help us improve subsequent versions of this book. If you find any errata, please report them by visiting http://www.packtpub.com/submit-errata, selecting your book, clicking on the **errata submission form** link, and entering the details of your errata. Once your errata are verified, your submission will be accepted and the errata will be uploaded on our website, or added to any list of existing errata, under the Errata section of that title. Any existing errata can be viewed by selecting your title from http://www.packtpub.com/support.

Piracy

Piracy of copyright material on the Internet is an ongoing problem across all media. At Packt, we take the protection of our copyright and licenses very seriously. If you come across any illegal copies of our works, in any form, on the Internet, please provide us with the location address or website name immediately so that we can pursue a remedy.

Please contact us at `copyright@packtpub.com` with a link to the suspected pirated material.

We appreciate your help in protecting our authors, and our ability to bring you valuable content.

Questions

You can contact us at `questions@packtpub.com` if you are having a problem with any aspect of the book, and we will do our best to address it.

1

Getting Started with MicroStrategy

In this chapter, we will cover:

- ▸ Installing SQL Server 2012 Express LocalDB
- ▸ Installing SQL Server Native Client 11.0
- ▸ Installing SQL Server 2012 Command Line Utilities
- ▸ Setting up the AdventureWorks DW sample database
- ▸ Installing the .NET Framework 4.0 and the 4.0.2 update
- ▸ Checking whether IIS is enabled and working
- ▸ Installing MicroStrategy Suite
- ▸ Registering the MicroStrategy License
- ▸ Metadata and data warehouse
- ▸ Creating ODBC DSN for metadata and data warehouse
- ▸ Modifying the logon account for the Intelligence Server
- ▸ Creating the metadata, and configuring the Intelligence Server
- ▸ Opening the MicroStrategy Desktop application

Introduction

This book is intended for **Business Intelligence** (**BI**) developers who want to expand their knowledge in a technology that is in huge demand at the moment, and for advanced data analysts who are evaluating different technologies. In this first chapter, we will start by downloading and installing the software and a well-known sample SQL Server database. You do not need to be a SQL rock star to read this book, yet some concepts, such as foreign keys or many-to-many relationships, are taken for granted.

Having previous basic knowledge about dimensional modeling (fact tables and dimensions) will also help the comprehension.

The chapters are ordered by increasing difficulties, and each one builds on the top of the preceding, so the learning is progressive; you'll get the most out of it, if you follow the recipes one after the other.

You may already have a working MicroStrategy environment; if so, you can just install the example database and skip the rest of this chapter. However, I suggest using a dedicated installation to follow the recipes; it would be easier and cleaner.

These initial recipes may seem too easy for the more experienced BI specialists, I apologize for that; I only want to be sure that starting from *Chapter 2, The First Steps in a MicroStrategy Project*, everyone has a common setup.

The operating system installation is outside the scope of this book; nevertheless, it is of vital importance that the machine where you will be doing the exercises is correctly configured and loaded with everything we will need. Throughout the course of this book, I will use Windows 2008 Web Server SP2; I have a VMware virtual machine with 2 GB RAM and two cores. The operating system is 32 bits. You may follow the whole book with a 64-bit software, but the examples and the instructions are written and tested on a 32-bit system. While this is a very small setup for a BI machine, it is enough to start.

Installing SQL Server 2012 Express LocalDB

We will use Microsoft SQL Server for our practice; there are several versions out there both free and commercial. I selected the LocalDB because it's the one with less memory footprint and yet, has a complete set of features.

Getting ready

You will need to download some software prior to installation:

- ▶ Microsoft .NET Framework 4.0 available at `http://at5.us/Ch1U3`

- ▶ Update 4.0.2 for Microsoft .NET Framework 4.0 (as in Microsoft article *KB2544514*) available at `http://at5.us/Ch1U4`

- ▶ SQL Server 2012 Express LocalDB available at `http://at5.us/Ch1U5`

- ▶ SQL Server Native Client 11.0 available at `http://at5.us/Ch1U6`

- ▶ SQL Server 2012 Command Line Utilities available at `http://at5.us/Ch1U7`

- ▶ AdventureWorks DW Database creation scripts available at `http://at5.us/Ch1U8`

Download all these files and put them in a folder, for example, `C:\install\`.

How to do it...

The setup is very straightforward, in a command prompt window do the following:

1. Install the SQL Server 2012 Express LocalDB engine by running:

   ```
   C:\install\SqlLocalDB.MSI
   ```

2. Accept the agreement and click your way out through the **Next** button; no special attention other than clicking on **Continue** to allow the user account control permission to install. The setup will take one minute, if not seconds, and it's very simple.

How it works...

We are using a stripped down version of Microsoft SQL Server 2012 database. This LocalDB engine features almost everything from the full-fledged product but runs as a user application, not as a service like its major siblings do. It is important to remember this detail because only the currently logged on user will be able to connect to the database instance.

LocalDB has very low memory requirements and guarantees quick data access on small machines.

There's more...

Check the successful outcome by issuing in a command prompt:

```
sqllocaldb info
```

The system will answer with the version number:

```
v11.0
```

which is also the name of the default instance.

You can watch a screencast of this operation at:
  ▶ `http://at5.us/Ch1V1`

Installing SQL Server Native Client 11.0

After installing the SQL engine, we need to load the last version of the client in order to access the local instance.

Getting ready

You need to have completed the previous recipe to continue.

How to do it...

Here's how to run the installation, in a command prompt window:

1. Install SQL Server Native Client 11.0 by running:

    `C:\install\sqlncli.msi`

2. Leave the default components selected for installation and click on **Next** until the end. As before, give the user account control permission to continue.

How it works...

We are forced to install this version of the client, as previous native clients are not able to connect to the LocalDB engine.

There's more...

Check successful outcome by clicking on **Start | Administrative Tools | Data Sources (ODBC)**. Click on **Continue** if prompted, and in the **ODBC Data Source Administrator** window, select the **Drivers** tab. You should find among the last rows in this list both **SQL Server** and **SQL Server Native Client 11.0**.

You can watch a screencast of this operation at:
  ▶ `http://at5.us/Ch1V2`

Installing SQL Server 2012 Command Line Utilities

The command-line utilities are needed to run SQL sentences and scripts onto the database instance. You may feel more comfortable with the full SQL Server Management Studio Express, which is also free to download and use. For simplicity, and not to overload the machine, I will be using only the command line during the recipes.

Getting ready

You need to have completed the previous recipe to continue.

How to do it...

As in the previous recipes, execute the following steps in a command prompt window:

1. Install SQL Server 2012 Command Line Utilities by running:

   ```
   C:\install\SqlCmdLnUtils.msi
   ```

2. Accept the agreement, allow permission if prompted, and click on **Next** until the end.

There's more...

Check successful outcome with the following command:

```
sqlcmd -S (localdb)\v11.0
```

This should connect to the default instance of SQL Server. It may take a while as the SQL Server instance is loaded on demand, so when you issue this command for the first time, Windows actually has to run the `sqlservr.exe` executable. From the second time, the instance will be loaded faster.

 You can watch a screencast of this operation at:
   ▶ http://at5.us/Ch1V3

Setting up the AdventureWorks DW sample database

Now that the instance is up and running, we can load the data into it. First, we'll create a database that will be populated with sample data.

Getting ready

You need to have completed the previous recipe to continue, and then unzip the `AdventureWorks 2008R2 Data Warehouse.zip` file into the folder `C:\install\`, so that you will end up with a folder named `AdventureWorks 2008R2 Data Warehouse` containing a series of SQL script files; the main being named `instawdwdb.sql`.

How to do it...

Before running this script we need to modify it, in order to specify the name of the source folder containing the CSV files and the name of the destination folder that will store the resulting database:

1. Create a directory named `C:\datawarehouse`; this will be the location of our database.

2. Open in Notepad the file `instawdwdb.sql` and modify lines 36 and 37 so that they look like:

    ```
    :setvar SqlSamplesDatabasePath    "C:\datawarehouse\"
    :setvar SqlSamplesSourceDataPath
    "C:\install\AdventureWorks 2008R2 Data Warehouse\"
    ```

     The two hyphens at the beginning of the lines (comment marks) have been removed and the path to data folder and source scripts folder have been modified, they both include the trailing backslash.

3. Save the file and close Notepad.

4. Open a command prompt and enter the following command:

    ```
    sqlcmd -S (localdb)\v11.0 -i "C:\install\
    AdventureWorks 2008R2 Data Warehouse\instawdwdb.sql"
    ```

     This command must be written all in one line and including the double quotes.

How it works...

The script will create the database and all the needed tables. Then will import the CSV data files into the tables to populate them with data. The script will lastly exit the `sqlcmd` command interface.

There's more...

In order to check if everything was installed correctly, we will perform a couple of very simple SQL queries on the database:

1. Open the `sqlcmd` utility again:

   ```
   sqlcmd -S (localdb)\v11.0
   ```

2. At the `1>` prompt, write the following instructions each on its own line, followed by the *Enter* key:

   ```
   use AdventureWorksDW2008R2

   go

   select count(1) from FactInternetSales

   go

   select count(1) from DimCustomer

   go

   exit
   ```

The database will respond with the number of rows in the main fact table and the customer dimension table, `60398` and `18484` respectively.

Congratulations, you correctly installed the data warehouse source database!

 You can watch a screencast of this operation at:
  ▸ `http://at5.us/Ch1V4`

Exercise 1

From the sqlcmd utility execute the queries to count the number of records in the following tables: `FactCurrencyRate`, `FactResellerSales`, `DimGeography`, `DimDate`, and `DimCurrency`. Note down the numbers.

Installing the .NET Framework 4.0 and the 4.0.2 update

One main software requirement for the setup of MicroStrategy suite is the .NET Framework 4.0, and the update 4.0.2 as in the Microsoft article *KB2544514*.

How to do it...

In a command prompt window, complete the following steps:

1. Run the command:

    ```
    C:\install\dotNetFx40_Full_x86_x64.exe
    ```

2. Accept the license agreement and watch the blue progress bars filling up slowly. This can take a while; you may have a coffee if you need. When it's finished, run:

    ```
    C:\install\NDP40-KB2544514-x86-x64.exe
    ```

3. One accept button (the license agreement) and two more blue progress bars to go. If you're prompted to reboot, please do so.

How it works...

The .NET Framework is a requirement for the MicroStrategy Web and several add-on utilities.

 You can watch a screencast of this operation at:

> ▸ `http://at5.us/Ch1V5`

Checking whether IIS is enabled and working

Since we're using Windows 2008 Web Server, we speak about roles; so we need to be sure that the web role is enabled with all the required features for the platform setup to run smoothly.

Getting ready

You need to have completed the previous recipe to continue.

How to do it...

Use the following steps to check if the required features are enabled:

1. Open the Server Manager (**Start | Administrative Tools | Server Manager**) and scroll to the **Roles Summary** pane.

2. Click on the **Add roles** link, you will see the **Add Roles Wizard** window; click on **Next**.

3. Select **Web Server (IIS)** and click on **Add Required Features** in the pop-up message box; now click on **Next** and then on **Next** again.

4. In the **Select Role Services** page, carefully check the following if not selected already:

    ❏ In the **Application Development** group:

      ASP.NET (add required role services if prompted)

      ASP

    ❏ In the **Security** group:

      Basic Authentication

      Windows Authentication

5. Click on **Next**, then on **Install**, and when finished click on **Close**.

How it works...

These role features enable MicroStrategy Web ASP.NET pages and the ability to use Windows authentication when connecting to the Intelligence Server through the Web.

There's more...

Check the successful outcome by opening Internet Explorer and typing `http://localhost/` in the address bar. You should see the IIS7 welcome logo.

 You can watch a screencast of this operation at:
  ▶ `http://at5.us/Ch1V6`

Installing MicroStrategy Suite

Now that the prerequisites are in place, we can go on with the platform setup.

Getting ready

You need to have completed all the previous recipes to continue.

When you download the MicroStrategy Suite, it can be installed in two different versions: the full-featured 30 days evaluation or the free reporting suite.

The difference between the two is that with the former you have the complete suite with administration tools, unlimited users, the option to use more than one processor, and more; while the second is a free version with limited users, no administrator tools, and one CPU limit.

We will be using the latter, throughout this book, and only cover the features available in the free one.

Prior to downloading and installing the software we need to register on the MicroStrategy website. Please provide a real company e-mail address as the registration process won't allow you to use `@hotmail` or `@gmail` addresses or any other well-known free e-mail service. Once you're registered, you will receive a message in your inbox with a license number.

MicroStrategy installation archive can be found at:

- Free Reporting Suite at `http://at5.us/Ch1U1`
- Evaluation version at `http://at5.us/Ch1U2`

You only need to download one of the two and unzip the archive into a folder, for example, `C:\install\`.

How to do it...

You need to have administrator rights to install the suite:

1. You should have extracted the contents of the **MSTR_93_GA_WindowsFullzip** archive into `C:\install\`, so run the executable:

   `C:\install\MICROSTRATEGY.exe`

2. In the welcome window, click on **Install Software** and then on **Begin MicroStrategy Platform Installation**. If a **User Account Control** dialog pops up, click on **Allow**.

3. The **MicroStrategy-InstallShield Wizard** appears asking you to choose a language for the setup, accept the default English and click on **OK**.

4. You will find yourself in front of yet another welcome page; politely click on **Next** and agree to the following warning message saying that the print spooler and remote registry service will be shut down during the setup (they will restart when you reboot the machine).

5. Now accept the license agreement and click on **Next**.

6. In the **Customer Information** window, fill your username, company, and paste the license number you received via e-mail.

7. Click on **Next**, which will bring you to the **Choose Destination Location** page, accept the defaults and click on **Next** again.

8. Here you have the features selection list; depending if you used the free license or the evaluation key you will be presented with more or less choices. Simply accept the defaults and click on **Next** (if you receive a warning about a missing PDF reader disregard it, for now we do not need this feature).

9. Click on **Yes**, the web server will be stopped and restarted.

10. Then click on **Yes** again, the setup will enable the web service extensions in IIS for us.

11. On the **MicroStrategy Health Center Setting** page, accept the defaults and click on **Next**.

12. On the **Server Activation** page, click on **Next**; fill in the **Name**, **Location**, and **Use** fields. Then click on **Next**.

13. On the following page you must select the first option: **I am an employee of the licensed company.**, otherwise you won't be allowed to continue. All the fields in the **Installer Information** group are mandatory except **State**, so be patient and fill in them all.

14. Lastly, you may choose to request an activation code, which will be sent to your e-mail. Please do so unless you're behind a corporate firewall which in some cases may prevent the operation to complete.

15. Review the summary information and click on **Install**.

16. The full install may last anywhere between 5 and 40 minutes depending on the hard drive speed—time for a break.

17. At the end of the progress bar, read the `Readme` file if you want, and click on **Yes**, reboot the machine when prompted.

There's more...

Check the successful outcome—after the server reboots, the **Configuration Wizard** window will appear. We will use it in a while but not just yet; you can click on **Exit** now or simply leave it in the background while going on to the next recipe.

Also, look at the Windows taskbar. You may see a warning balloon message popping and saying that the operating system has blocked some startup programs; click on the **Blocked Startup Programs** icon and let it run the executable `MASvcMgr`, now you will see the server manager icon with a green check mark meaning the Intelligence Server is running. Good job!

If you chose not to request an activation code, you may use the software for seven days before it stops working.

[You can watch a screencast of this operation at:
    ▸ `http://at5.us/Ch1V7`]

Registering the MicroStrategy License

The license needs to be activated for the software to continue working after the seven days grace period. There is a tool in the suite to help with the registration process, named `License Manager`.

Getting ready

You need to have completed the previous recipe to continue.

How to do it...

We will be now registering the MicroStrategy License:

1. Click on **Start | All Programs | MicroStrategy | License Manager**.

2. In the main window, select the tab named **License Administration**; the first option **Activate Server Installation** should be already selected. Click on **Next**.

3. In the following page, ensure that the radio button **Generate Activation File and Request Activation Code** is selected and click on **Next** and then on **Next** again, until you come to the page where you should enter all the details about your company and contacts.

4. The e-mail address is important to receive the activation code. Click on **Next**.

5. Select **Yes, I want to request an Activation Code now** and hit **Next**. You will shortly receive an e-mail message.

6. Click on **Done** to return to the beginning of the license administration process and start again with the **Activate Server Installation** radio button selected.

7. Click on **Next**, and this time select the option **Server Activation using Activation Code**.

8. In the textbox underneath, paste the code you received by e-mail and click on **Next**, and then click on **OK**, then on **Done**, and then on the **Exit** button.

Congratulations, you have registered the MicroStrategy License. Reboot the machine or restart the following services: `MicroStrategy Intelligence Server` and `World Wide Web Publishing Service`.

There's more....

The free license allows you to use the software with up to 10 named users, with the only limitation that some utilities are missing. With this edition you can build a complete BI solution for a small to mid-size company on a very low budget.

The Evaluation version has no user limitation, and all the utilities, but will expire after 30 days.

 You can watch a screencast of this operation at:
  ► `http://at5.us/Ch1V8`

Metadata and data warehouse

These are two key concepts in every BI project with MicroStrategy so we'd better have them clear since the beginning.

Metadata is data about data (what?). Ok, let's say that in the metadata you won't find any customer names or sales figures or any other fact, you'll just find information about the columns where this data come from, the datatype, and several other details about how to create the customer entity, for example, how does it relate to other elements in the project and where it is stored, plus the definition of all the reports.

While the data warehouse is the real source of the facts and dimensions that you will analyze. So, in principle, metadata and data warehouse are different databases and/or different instances; they may even reside in different hardware (and usually are, for example, in cluster production environments).

It is easy to deduce that the metadata is relatively small compared to the data warehouse, which is usually a huge, daily refreshed, historical storage with lots of records.

So `AdventureWorksDW2008R2`, which we just created, will be our "huge" 78 MB data warehouse; while we still do not have a storage for the metadata. Given that we are in a single-user training environment, we can use the same SQL Server instance for the metadata, but we'll create a new database to hold it.

Getting ready

You need to have completed the previous recipe to continue.

How to do it...

In a command prompt window:

1. Bring up the `sqlcmd` command utility once again with:

   ```
   sqlcmd -S (localdb)\v11.0
   ```

2. And when the `1>` prompt appears, type this (each command in its own line and followed by the *Enter* key):

   ```
   create database metadata
   go
   exit
   ```

How it works...

The `create database metadata` instruction will generate the `metadata.mdf` file. Both databases will be accessible from the same instance named `v11.0`.

There's more...

In SQL Server, the `go` command is the default end of the batch instruction. Other databases use different commands.

You can watch a screencast of this operation at:

▶ `http://at5.us/Ch1V9`

Creating ODBC DSN for metadata and data warehouse

Now that we have two databases, we need to tell MicroStrategy how to find and how to connect to them. Being in a Windows world, all the connections are done through ODBC, 32-bit ODBC to be correct.

You should be aware of this if you happen to install MicroStrategy on 64-bit Windows—the connectivity tier runs on 32 bits, the ODBC drivers are 32-bit drivers, and you won't find them in the default 64-bit ODBC Administrator (hint: look in the SysWOW64 folder).

Getting ready

You need to have completed the previous recipe to continue.

How to do it...

We will create the two DSN:

1. Click on **Start | Administrative Tools | Data Sources (ODBC)** and select the **System DSN** tab.

2. You will find some DSNs already created for you by the setup; we need to create two more (yes, you're right: one for the metadata and one for the data warehouse).

3. Click on the **Add...** button, scroll down the list to select **SQL Server Native Client 11.0** and click on **Finish**.

4. In the **Create a New Data Source to SQL Server** window, type these values:

   ❏ **Name**: metadata

   ❏ **Server**: (localdb)\v11.0

5. Click on **Next** and then on **Next** again.

6. Click the checkbox labeled **Change the default database to** and in the drop-down list underneath, select **metadata**. Leave all the remaining default values and click on **Next** and on **Finish**.

7. Click on **Test Data Source...** and look at the message: if it says **TESTS COMPLETED SUCCESSFULLY!**, you're good to go. Click on **OK** and then on **OK** again.

8. Repeat all the steps to create another DSN to the data warehouse, this time with the following values:

   ❏ **Name**: datawarehouse

   ❏ **Server**: (localdb)\v11.0

   ❏ **Change the default database to**: **AdventureWorksDW2008R2**

How it works...

Every interaction with the relational DBMS is done through ODBC. MicroStrategy ships with a list of out-of-the-box drivers for the most common databases. Nevertheless, you may use other ODBC drivers if so you wish, provided that they work in 32 bits.

There's more...

In our recipes, we will connect to a SQL Server instance, so we need to use the Microsoft provided Native ODBC. If, for example, you use Oracle in your BI environment, you will find the provided Oracle Wire driver being very convenient and light-weight. The company behind the shipped drivers is DataDirect.

 You can watch a screencast of this operation at:
▶ `http://at5.us/Ch1V10`

Modifying the logon account for the Intelligence Server

As said before, the SQL Server LocalDB engine runs as a user application, hence it is only accessible from the currently logged on user. We will now modify the credentials of the MicroStrategy Intelligence Server so that it can connect to the database instance that is running in the user context.

I'm hearing the screams of the security-wise system administrators: of course, you wouldn't want to do this in a production environment as it can pose serious security risks, but here we are in a training environment.

Getting ready

If the current user has no password, create one before proceeding.

How to do it...

Follow these steps to modify the startup account for the Intelligence Server:

1. In **Start | Run** dialog, type `services.msc`.
2. This will open the **Services** console; scroll down to find **MicroStrategy Intelligence Server**, it is now executing with **Local System** credentials, double-click on the service.

3. Select the **Log On** tab and click on the **This account** radio button.

4. Then type your current username and password in the corresponding text fields below.

5. Now click on **OK** to close the dialog box.

6. A message will warn you that the user has been granted the right to log on as a service. Click on **OK** and then on **OK** again at the second warning telling you that you should restart the service. We'll do it in a moment.

7. Right-click on the **MicroStrategy Intelligence Server** service and select **Restart** from the context menu that appears.

How it works...

Most of the services in Windows run with a special account called **Local System**. In our case, the Intelligence Server service must be able to connect to a SQL Server instance that is running under the currently connected user context. This is why we need to run the Intelligence Server as "ourselves", so that it can see the database instance.

There's more...

Restarting the Intelligence Server service will take some time, in case of any error the service won't restart; you probably mistyped the password or the username; double check and retry. Please keep in mind that Windows will not allow blank-password users to log on as a service.

 You can watch a screencast of this operation at:
  ▶ `http://at5.us/Ch1V11`

Creating the metadata and configuring the Intelligence Server

The metadata consists of a series of tables that MicroStrategy uses to store information about projects and the objects that build up those projects. In one of the previous recipes, we created the empty metadata database and now we will start populating it.

Getting ready

You need to have completed the previous recipe to continue.

How to do it...

To create the metadata, do the following:

1. You should already have the configuration wizard open in the background; if you closed it, you can find it in **Start | All Programs | MicroStrategy**. Click on **Configuration Wizard** to run it.

2. In the first page of the wizard, the first option should already be selected, so click on **Next**.

3. In this phase of the project, we're not interested in the history list or statistics, so we uncheck the corresponding checkboxes and leave just the first one checked. Then click on **Next**.

4. Now we are telling the wizard where to look for the metadata database, you should have a list of all the system DSNs present in the machine, select the **metadata** DSN that we created before, click on **Next** and on **Finish**.

5. The wizard starts creating and populating metadata tables. When the process is completed, click on **Close** to go back to the starting page of the wizard.

6. The second option **Configure Intelligent Server** should be automatically selected, click on **Next** and again select the **metadata** DSN from the drop-down list and click on **Next**.

7. When you're prompted for the username and password leave everything as default, the **Administrator** user still has no password, and click on **Next**.

 This **Administrator** user here has nothing to do with the operating system. It's the MicroStrategy metadata administrator.

8. Watch the wizard as it tries to connect to the recently created metadata and when the **Server Definitions** page appears just hit **Next** and **Next** again, as we will use all the default settings.

9. In the **SSL Configuration** page, leave the checkbox unchecked; click on **Next** and on **Finish**.

10. The Intelligence Server is stopping and restarting with the new configuration. Once the process terminates, click on **Close** and then on **Exit**.

We're ready to start up the Desktop application.

How it works...

The Intelligence Server definition is stored in the metadata. The wizard populates the tables with default values such as the server port and the administrator password. The Intelligence Server service then, reads the metadata when starting up, to retrieve all this information. There can be only one active metadata at a time. You may have different versions of it, but only one in use. To switch from one metadata to another, you need to run the configuration wizard again.

There's more...

Needless to say, the backup of the metadata is very important. If you lose this database, you lose every project in it.

You could also create a metadata in an MS Access database, if you want. For small projects or demos, this helps moving it around just by copying the MDB file.

You can watch screencasts of this operation at:

▸ http://at5.us/Ch1V12
▸ http://at5.us/Ch1V13

Opening the MicroStrategy Desktop application

The platform is all set. We now have a brand new MicroStrategy Server up and running, but we don't have any projects yet.

This may be a good time to save your work and store a backup of the Windows machine, just in case. If you are running a virtual environment, a snapshot of the VM would be perfect.

The MicroStrategy Desktop application is the development tool to generate projects, objects, reports, and so on. It is also used to explore and manage the objects that reside in the metadata. From now on, we'll spend the major part of our time in this IDE.

It's not difficult to get used to the interface as it is fairly simple, much like the Windows Explorer you have folders on the left and details on the right.

Getting ready

You need to have completed the previous recipe to continue.

How to do it...

Let's open the Desktop application:

1. Go to **Start | All Programs | MicroStrategy | Desktop** and click on the **Desktop** icon.

2. Double-click on the line named **MicroStrategy Analytics Modules**, which was created by the setup and you'll be prompted for the metadata credentials; remember? The user is **Administrator** with no password.

3. The first time you connect, a message will remind you that no project is there, click on **OK**. We'll create one in a moment.

4. When you enter the **MicroStrategy Analytics Modules** (we call this a project source) for the first time, you'll be watching a window like the one in the following screen capture:

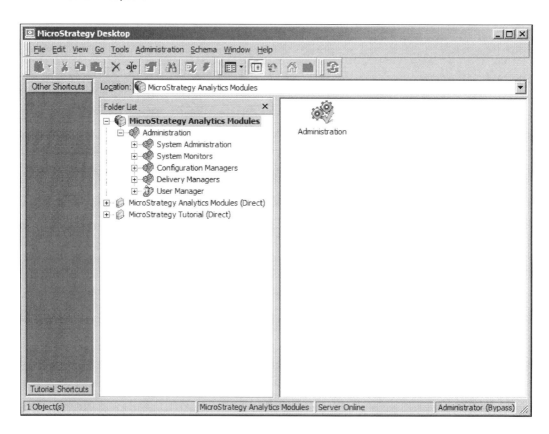

5. Unfold the Administration folder and click on **User Manger** on the left pane. Then double-click on **Everyone** on the right pane. You will see there is only a user in this group.

6. Double-click on the **Administrator** user icon to open the User Editor.

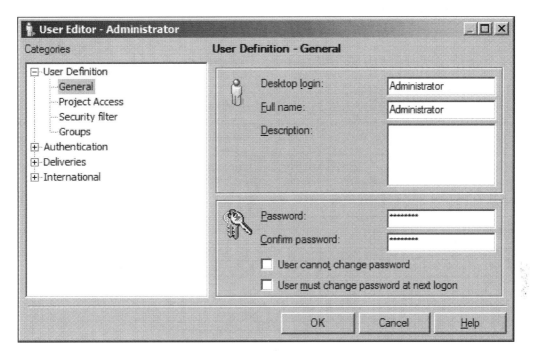

7. Here, you can manage all the details of a user such as full name, login, password, or permission to see projects and which features the user has access to. There are two text fields for password with asterisks, type a new password here and confirm. Then close the editor by clicking on **OK**.

8. Exit the Desktop application and open it again. This time you will be prompted for credentials to enter the **MicroStrategy Analytics Modules**, type Administrator and the password you just created.

How it works...

At the top-most level of the folder tree in MicroStrategy Desktop application there are the project sources, think of them as a shortcut to the Metadata. A project source is just a way for MicroStrategy to know where the Intelligence Server is running and how to connect to it.

The Administration folder is where all the administrative tasks are performed in the Desktop application, and you can see this because you've entered the application with an admin account.

There's more...

There are two types of project source, two-tiers (Direct) and three-tiers (Intelligence Server). Two-tiered project sources connect directly to the metadata database, while three-tiered first connect to an Intelligence Server, which in turn connects to the metadata.

Now that the administrative account is secured, if you forget this password, all of your work will be lost. Ouch! Really? Yes, exactly, please remember: there is no way known to humans to recover a metadata lost password. Only MicroStrategy Support can do this: I never dared to ask them to, so please take my work and be sure not to forget it.

 You can watch a screencast of this operation at:

> `http://at5.us/Ch1V14`

See also

> The *Creating an empty project* recipe in *Chapter 2, The First Steps in a MicroStrategy Project*

2

The First Steps in a MicroStrategy Project

In this chapter, we will cover:

- ▶ Creating an empty project
- ▶ Setting up a data warehouse connection and selecting tables
- ▶ Modifying a table structure
- ▶ Using logical tables to create custom views
- ▶ Generating constants with SELECT statements

Introduction

At this point, you should have a testing machine ready-to-use with all the samples in place. In the previous chapter, we have learned how to install SQL Server and the MicroStrategy platform. In this chapter, we start creating the **schema objects** that represent the building blocks of our BI project.

Schema objects are the metadata components that are logically closer to the physical structure of the database; they are used to create more complex elements (applications or public objects) that will later form reports and documents. Facts and tables, for example, are schema objects. Also attributes, which we'll cover in *Chapter 3, Schema Objects – Attributes*, are schema objects.

The first schema objects that we need to identify are the tables holding our facts and dimensions.

 We will use the sample database AdventureWorks, which is about a sport gear shop. The size of the data is limited but the overall structure of the tables is quite interesting and covers a number of use cases that you will find in real-life BI projects. All the recipes in this book use that database.

To get acquainted with the tables and their relationships, please download this diagram with the full database schema at `http://at5.us/Ch2U1`. Due to its size, it would be useful to print it out on A3 size paper.

The schema is quite complete and contains information about primary and foreign keys. I wish all of my jobs would start with a clear picture like this...

Downloading the example code

You can download the example code files for all Packt books you have purchased from your account at `http://www.packtpub.com`. If you purchased this book elsewhere, you can visit `http://www.packtpub.com/support` and register to have the files e-mailed directly to you.

Creating an empty project

The first step in a MicroStrategy BI application is creating an empty project. An Intelligence Server can host many projects. Projects can be copied from one Intelligence Server to another. Think of a project as a way to keep all the related objects together. A project must have at least one connection to get data from the data warehouse.

Getting ready

You need to have completed the previous chapter to continue.

How to do it...

In this first recipe we'll create a project:

1. Open **Start | All Programs | MicroStrategy | Desktop** menu and click on the **Desktop** icon.

2. Log in with `Administrator` and the corresponding password and right-click on the topmost folder named **MicroStrategy Analytics Modules**.

3. From the context menu that appears, select **Create New Project...**.

4. In the **Project Creation Assistant**, click on **Create project**.

5. Type a name in the first textbox, for example, COOKBOOK and click on **OK**. We accept all the defaults for now. Once the wizard terminates creating the project, you're back to the **Project Creation Assistant**.

6. Click on **OK** and then on **OK** again when the information message appears.

7. Double-click on the project icon and look at the folders that are contained in it. You will see that there is one named **Schema Objects** and another one named **My Personal Objects**.

8. Expand the **Schema Objects** folder and click on **Tables**. Our journey starts here.

How it works...

A project is nothing more than rows in a table of the metadata. If you're curious, you can have a look at the metadata database with `sqlcmd`, the main table is called `DSSMDOBJINFO`. Be careful not to tamper with it, you may lose a little more than one hour of work.

There's more...

If you're not happy with the project name, you may change it with the *F2* key just like renaming a file or a folder.

Just out of curiosity, if you want to see more behind-the-scene objects, you can click on the **Tools | Desktop Preferences** menu and select the **Browsing** category in the **Desktop Preferences** dialog.

Check the **Display hidden objects** box, this will show more folders that were not visible before, such as the profiles or the project templates.

You can watch a screencast of this operation at:
  ▸ `http://at5.us/Ch2V1`

Setting up a data warehouse connection and selecting tables

At the core of a data warehouse, there are facts and dimensions. They can be organized in star schemas, snowflake schemas; they can be more or less complex, and to some extent undocumented. This is not a book about dimensional modeling and discussing how a database layout works better than other is out of scope. Some common sense rules always apply: consistent column naming can be useful (`user_id`, `iduser`, `user_code`, `key_user`, `yetanotheruserid`, you name it...), constraints on tables help to pull the strings and find a way into unexplored databases. `NOT NULL` fields also come in handy.

I personally had my share of good and bad data. I always remember a development team manager who once asked me, "Why do you need primary keys, anyway?" I looked around and thought, "This must be a candid camera..."

If you are drowning in a very complex DB and want some relief, you can go to `http://at5.us/Ch2U2` and read about the Directive 595, it may be a real story after all.

In the course of this book, I will use several editors that MicroStrategy Desktop offers. It is also worth mentioning that there is another way to add tables and create objects, with a tool named **Architect**; it has the same capabilities and a more visual interface. You can find instructions about Architect in the product documentation.

Getting ready

You need to have completed the previous recipe to continue.

How to do it...

First, we create a connection to the data warehouse and then select the source tables:

1. From the **Schema** menu, select **Warehouse Catalog...**.

2. The **Warehouse Database Instance** dialog box pops up. This is because we have not specified a connection yet. Click on the **New...** button.

3. Say Hello to the **Database Instance Wizard** welcome page and click on **Next**.

4. In the following page, type a name in the first textbox, since this is our only data warehouse, we simply put `datawarehouse`.

5. Select the type of RDBMS that you are using from the **Database type** drop-down list, in our case **Microsoft SQL Server 2012**. Then click on **Next**.

6. Now it's the ODBC turn, find the **datawarehouse** DSN we created in the previous chapter and select it.

7. Now since we are using the current Windows user to validate onto SQL Server, check the **Use network login id (Windows authentication)** checkbox and leave the **Database login** and **Password** fields empty. Click on **OK** when you see the warning message, click on **Next** and then on **Finish**.

8. Back to the **Warehouse Database Instance** dialog. Now we have a database instance for the project and can continue. Click on **OK**.

9. This is the **Warehouse Catalog** window: a list of all the tables available in our source system.

10. Right-click on **DimCustomer**, for example, and select **Show Sample Data...**.

11. This is a quick way to have a glimpse at the contents of the tables. Only the first 100 rows will be returned, enough to have an idea of what the table is about.

12. Holding down the *Ctrl* key, select **DimCustomer** and **FactInternetSales** and with the little arrow **>** button, move them to the right.

13. Click on the **Save and Close** button. By default, the comments box will pop up, check **Do not show this screen in the future** and click on **OK**.

14. You should be back in the **Tables** folder, from the **View** menu select **Refresh (F5)** to see the two tables we just selected. Then from the **Schema** menu, click on **Update Schema (Ctrl + U)**.

How it works...

When you select the tables from the left pane list, MicroStrategy reads the definition of all the columns and stores the information inside the metadata, creating the first schema objects (tables). The objects that we see in the **Tables** folder are the logical representations of the underlying database and hold no data, just information about the columns and the datatype; if the physical table in the data warehouse changes, this information must be updated (more on this later). It is important to select all the tables that are useful for the project, not less, not more. It doesn't make sense to have 500 tables in the project if we only use 10. It just complicates the design and slows down the Desktop application.

There's more...

While you have the **Warehouse Catalog** window open:

1. Click on **Options...** and select **Read Settings** from the **Categories** list.

2. Enable **Read the table Primary and Foreign Keys**.

3. Enable **Count the number of rows for all tables when reading the database catalog**.

4. Unfold the **View** category, and select **Table Row Counts** then enable **Display the number of rows per table**.

5. Under the **Schema** category, select **Automatic Mapping** and click on **Do not map schema objects to the new tables**.

6. Click on **OK** and you're back in the **Warehouse Catalog** window. Click on the top-left button with a lightning icon: this will refresh the list of the tables and display the row count for each one.

Notice that, as expected, the fact tables have far more rows than the dimension ones. This is important when you don't have any database documentation and the table names do not make sense. Reading primary and foreign keys from the database helps identifying the parent-child relationship between tables in case you want to use the automatic discovery features of Architect.

Exercise 2

Now that you know how to add tables to the metadata, go on and add:

- `DimDate`

- `DimGeography`

- `DimProduct`, `DimProductSubcategory`, and `DimProductCategory`

- `DimSalesTerritory`

Remember to update the schema.

Exercise 3

Looking at the full database schema diagram, can you tell the type of relationship that links one table to another?

Which table is parent and which is child?

Would you say that this data warehouse is normalized or denormalized?

 You can watch screencasts of this operation at:
- `http://at5.us/Ch2V2`
- `http://at5.us/Ch2V3`

Modifying a table structure

Like it or not, database tables change. Due to upgrades in source systems, mergers and acquisitions, or simply because of a shift in the project management, we suddenly find that an SKU or a customer ID is not there anymore. Let alone systems in continuous development where the database seems to have a life of its own and morphs every now and then into different shapes. We all know how difficult it is to go back and test every ETL script and every report to see if they still return reliable data.

Sometimes changes happen without notice, you come to the office on a Monday morning to see that the CFO has a different color..., then you realize that something went wrong.

There is no vaccine for this, other than carefully documenting everything and hope for the best. Let's see how to refresh our table structure information using the **Warehouse Catalog** window.

Getting ready

You need to have completed the previous recipe and exercises to continue.

How to do it...

First of all, we will modify the structure of the `DimDate` table to add a column with the month's description:

1. In command prompt type:

    ```
    sqlcmd -S (localdb)\v11.0 -d AdventureWorksDW2008R2
    ```

2. Once the `1>` prompt appears, type:

    ```
    ALTER TABLE DimDate ADD CalendarYearMonth VARCHAR(7)
    go
    UPDATE DimDate SET CalendarYearMonth = CONVERT(VARCHAR(7),
    FullDateAlternateKey, 111)
    go
    exit
    ```

3. Now go to the **Warehouse Catalog** window and right-click on the table `DimDate` in the right pane and select **Show Sample Data**.

4. See that there is a new column at the end named `CalendarYearMonth` with the format YYYY/MM.

5. Click on **Close** and right-click again on `DimDate`, then select **Update Structure**.

6. Now click on **Save and Close** to exit this window, MicroStrategy will write the changes to the metadata.

7. Update the schema.

How it works...

It's very important to keep the metadata consistent with the latest information about the structure of the database, especially when changing the datatypes or when columns are removed from data warehouse tables.

 You can watch a screencast of this operation at:
    ▶   `http://at5.us/Ch2V4`

Using logical tables to create custom views

Logical tables are schema objects that are somehow similar to SQL views. They are not a representation of an existing table but a `SELECT` statement that returns a series of columns. There are cases in the course of a BI project when you need the data to be in a different shape than in the source tables, so you have two choices: modify the data warehouse or create logical tables.

Sometimes access to the data warehouse is simply out of the question, or it takes weeks, or the paperwork needed to approve the modification is just not worth it.

To be clear, whenever possible, I prefer changing the data warehouse over creating logical tables because there may be other applications that use that data and it's probably wise to have a common base for every app, but I resort to logical tables for cases like the one in this recipe when I need the data to be prefiltered for a specific purpose.

Getting ready

Look at the `DimEmployee` table in the database diagram. See that it has an arrow pointing to itself, what does that mean? Yes, it's the dreaded recursive relationship that OLTP designers like so much.

Think about a plane: it has wings, tail, fuselage, and more. Each part can be further divided into components: the wing has flaps, engines, and this goes on until the smallest pieces like bolts or wires. Each piece is used to build a bigger one, so it has a parent-child relationship to the part it composes.

Since it is not possible to create a table for every level of detail, OLTP applications use a single recursive table to model this situation, so that every record in that table has a predecessor, which in turn has another predecessor. And this is good, I mean, from the OLTP developer standpoint.

Here, in the `DimEmployee` table, we have `EmployeeKey`, which is the primary key and `ParentEmployeeKey`, which is a foreign key to the same table's primary key. Another example is the `DimAccount` table (`AccountKey` and `ParentAccountKey`).

MicroStrategy is not able to aggregate numbers with this type of dimension tables, so we need to unroll them somehow. In this recipe, we will create different logical tables for each employee level, and we do this because we know there is a finite number of levels in the company hierarchy.

In more complex cases like the parts of the plane, unfortunately, we don't know how many levels we would need to create beforehand, and hence this solution may not be applicable.

You can find the SELECT statement for this recipe in the companion code file.

How to do it...

Follow these steps to create a logical table:

1. Go to the **Schema Objects | Tables** folder, right-click in the right pane and from the context menu select **New | Logical Table**.

2. In the Table Editor, there is a big textbox that says **Click here to type a SQL statement**, click on it and paste this code:

   ```
   select EmployeeKey, ParentEmployeeKey, SalesTerritoryKey,
   FirstName, LastName, DepartmentName from DimEmployee where
   ParentEmployeeKey is null
   ```

3. In the area below, you see an empty grid with **Column object**, **Data Type**. Click on the **Add** button to create an empty line.

4. In the **Column Object** field, type the exact name of the first field that the SELECT returns, EmployeeKey, and leave datatype Integer as default.

5. Click again on the **Add** button and do the same for the second field ParentEmployeeKey leaving the datatype Integer.

6. Do the same for SalesTerritorykey.

7. The remaining fields `FirstName`, `LastName`, and `DepartmentName` are `NVarChar`, so add them as before but change the datatype from `Integer` to `NVarChar`.

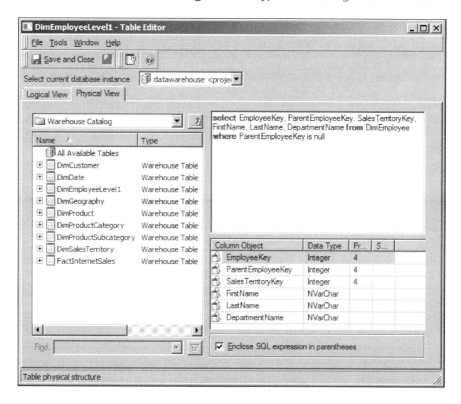

8. When you have completed all the fields, click on **Save and Close** and type a table name, for example, `DimEmployeeLevel1`. The definition is saved into the metadata.

9. Update the schema.

How it works...

MicroStrategy will store the SQL definition of the logical tables, the field names, and the datatype in the metadata. To the MicroStrategy developer, these will be like real tables with no difference from the standard ones.

In the `DimEmployeeLevel1` logical table, we are selecting only the employees who have no boss (`ParentEmployeeKey` is null), that is, the CEO of the company; in the second level, we need to filter the employees whose boss belongs to the group of `DimEmployeeLevel1`.

Going down the levels is just a matter of nesting Matrioska-style subqueries: the employees of Level 3 have a boss in Level 2 and so on until Level 5. There is no Level 6 in this company.

If you've played around with the database, you may have noticed that the FactInternetSales table does not have a foreign key to the employee dimension, that's understandable as those are direct sales. The FactResellerSales table, on the other end, has an EmployeeKey column that relates to the employee dimension.

There's more...

It's worth noting that in the **FactResellerSales** table, we have records with a Level 3 EmployeeKey and records with a Level 4 EmployeeKey. This means that Mr. Jiang—North American Sales Manager—has sold some products, and the people reporting to him also have sold items. This complicates a little bit when you want to report, for example, the total of Mr. Jiang's group sales.

A common solution in these cases is to clone Mr. Jiang and all the Level 3 people who make sales, duplicating them in the Level 4 table. Using the same Level 3 primary key values in both Level 4 EmployeeKey and Level 4 ParentEmployeeKey, they would be treated as Level 4 employees reporting to themselves at Level 3.

Exercise 4

Now repeat this recipe steps to do the same for the lower levels, using the following SQL sentences:

Logical table name	SQL code
DimEmployeeLevel2	select EmployeeKey, ParentEmployeeKey, SalesTerritoryKey, FirstName, LastName, DepartmentName from DimEmployee where ParentEmployeeKey in (select EmployeeKey from DimEmployee where ParentEmployeeKey is null)

Logical table name	SQL code
DimEmployeeLevel3	select EmployeeKey, ParentEmployeeKey, SalesTerritoryKey, FirstName, LastName, DepartmentName from DimEmployee where ParentEmployeeKey in (select EmployeeKey from DimEmployee where ParentEmployeeKey in (select EmployeeKey from DimEmployee where ParentEmployeeKey is null))
DimEmployeeLevel4	select EmployeeKey, ParentEmployeeKey, SalesTerritoryKey, FirstName, LastName, DepartmentName from DimEmployee where ParentEmployeeKey in (select EmployeeKey from DimEmployee where ParentEmployeeKey in (select EmployeeKey from DimEmployee where ParentEmployeeKey in (select EmployeeKey from DimEmployee where ParentEmployeeKey is null)))

Logical table name	SQL code
DimEmployeeLevel5	select EmployeeKey, ParentEmployeeKey, SalesTerritoryKey, FirstName, LastName, DepartmentName from DimEmployee where ParentEmployeeKey in (select EmployeeKey from DimEmployee where ParentEmployeeKey in (select EmployeeKey from DimEmployee where ParentEmployeeKey in (select EmployeeKey from DimEmployee where ParentEmployeeKey in (select EmployeeKey from DimEmployee where ParentEmployeeKey is null))))

You can watch the screencasts of these operations at:
- ▶ http://at5.us/Ch2V5
- ▶ http://at5.us/Ch2V6

Generating constants with SELECT statements

During the development of a BI project, sometimes we need to use values which do not necessarily come from tables; these can be constants such as Data refreshed at or Today. The logical tables come in very handy for this purpose.

Getting ready

You can find the SELECT statement for this recipe in the companion code file.

How to do it...

To create a logical table that returns the current date as a constant, do the following:

1. Go to the **Schema Objects | Tables** folder and right-click on an empty space in the right pane. From the context menu, choose **New | Logical Table**.

2. In the SQL statement text area, paste this sentence:

```
select DATEADD(day, DATEDIFF(day, 0, GETDATE()), 0)
DateValue
```

3. Add one **Column Object** and name it `DateValue`, and select **Date** from **Data Type**.

4. Click on **Save and Close** and name it `Today`.

5. Update the schema.

How it works...

We created a very simple table with one row and one column. This table will always return the current date at midnight; it is useful to filter records based on moving dates, or simply to display it in a report header. Moreover, since the table has only one row, we can join it anywhere without creating dangerous Cartesian products. Even with a CROSS JOIN, it will always multiply the results by one.

There's more...

In SQL Server constants are generated with a SELECT statement without the FROM clause. If you want to display Eat at Joe's, it's as simple as:

```
select "Eat at Joe's"
```

(Sorry, blinking font not included)

In other RDBMS, you may find a different syntax: in Oracle, for example, the current date at midnight can be obtained with the sentence:

```
SELECT TRUNC(SYSDATE) DateValue FROM DUAL;
```

And the logical table would work just the same.

See also

▶ The *Attribute forms – ID and DESC* recipe in *Chapter 3, Schema Objects – Attributes*

3

Schema Objects – Attributes

In this chapter, we will cover:

- ▸ Attribute forms – ID and DESC
- ▸ Using functions in an attribute form
- ▸ Parent-child relationship I
- ▸ Parent-child relationship II
- ▸ Other attribute forms
- ▸ Selecting which forms are displayed
- ▸ Building Data Explorer Hierarchies
- ▸ Creating an attribute only report
- ▸ Parent-child relationship in a report
- ▸ Filters on attributes

Introduction

In every BI project, we find **dimensions** and **facts**. There is an extensive literature about data modeling if you want to look further into this topic; I personally like *The Data Warehouse Toolkit: The Definitive Guide to Dimensional Modeling* by *Ralph Kimball* and *Margy Ross*; a very complete, yet simple-to-read manual.

We learned in the previous chapter that the metadata components that represent the physical structure of the database are called **schema objects**. In this type of objects, we find tables, facts, attributes, hierarchies, and others. We can use schema objects to build more complex elements such as metrics or filters, to name a few.

Every time we create or make a change to a schema object we need to notify MicroStrategy so that it can reload the information from the metadata. This process is called **schema update** (**Schema** | **Update Schema** or press *Ctrl + U*).

In this chapter, we will concentrate on what is generally known as dimension, and—in MicroStrategy vocabulary—is named **attribute**.

It is actually a little more complex than this: when we speak about time or geography dimensions, we're in fact talking about different levels (year, month, day, or country, state, province) that compose a dimension. In this sense, the MicroStrategy term **hierarchy** would be more appropriate; anyway, to make things simple, let's speak about attributes when we refer to the strings attached to our numbers, descriptions that add a context to the facts, in other words, the declarative part of a report, what we use to GROUP BY.

A hierarchy in MicroStrategy is a group of attributes related to each other.

At its very core, MicroStrategy is a powerful SQL statement generator that can produce database-specific and optimized query sentences. It is important to keep this in mind during our journey through the features of this platform. Everything we do with the editors, every setting, and every configuration has the objective of generating a sentence that the RDBMS will execute to return data. It is obvious, but worth reminding, that we are actually talking ANSI SQL to a database via **ODBC** (**Open Database Connectivity**). That's why it is important to have previous experience with this syntax in order to understand what happens behind the scenes.

If you're a SQL rock star, and you're typing at 64 SELECT per second, you may be wondering "Do we need to do all this, just to issue a query to a database?" Well, put it this way: you do not need to, your customers and users do. The main reason behind applications such as this is to relieve the developer from the routine creation of reports by offloading it to end users, so that you can spend your time investigating and creating even more and more beautiful ways to present data.

Attribute forms – ID and DESC

Here comes the attribute. In a star schema, we typically find a dimension table with a code and a description: these two columns are the basic components of every attribute.

Thinking about this table, for example, `DimProduct`: what is the most important thing that we look for in a table? Yes, the primary key. Without primary keys, we're in for trouble. It may sound too old style, but we desperately need a unique way to identify a single instance of an attribute.

I know, nowadays we have a lot of different technologies to represent information, such as NoSQL, unstructured, and XML data among others. But, if we need to analyze how many women's tights were sold last year, we need to know which women's tights we are talking about. Hence, the need for a primary key, name it a code, an ID, or anything else.

Getting ready

Said that, first of all, we identify the unique ID for a single instance of an attribute: in the case of `DimProduct` it is `ProductKey`. If you look at the table structure, you'll see another key (`ProductAlternateKey`), usually referred to as **natural key**. This may lead to dangerous mistakes if there are more records with the same natural key; see `DimEmployee` as an example.

Then we search for a column representing a suitable description or a name. This is what the user will see, for example, `EnglishProductName`.

How to do it...

We are creating our first attribute:

1. Go to the **Schema Objects | Attributes** folder and right-click on the blank part of the right pane. Select **New | Attribute** from the context menu.

2. Three windows will open in rapid succession: you are looking at the Attribute, Forms, and Expressions Editors.

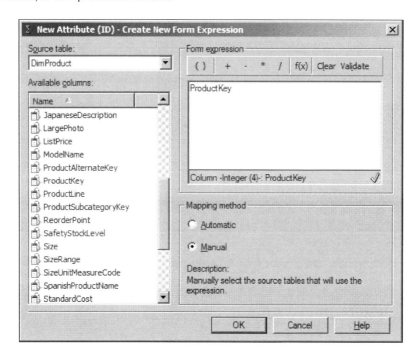

3. Inside the Expression Editor, click on the top-left combobox and select **DimProduct** as **Source table**.

4. From **Available columns** list, drag **ProductKey** to the top right **Form expression** text area, and select the **Manual** radio button below it.

5. Click on the **OK** button and you're in the **Create New Attribute Form** window.

6. In the top right **Source tables** part, click to enable the **DimProduct** table name, it should already appear in boldface. Leave everything else unchanged and click on **OK**.

7. This brings you back to the Attribute Editor: in the **Attribute forms** list you can see that your new attribute has a form with **Form name**: **ID**, **Form category**: **ID**, and **Format type**: **Number**, which is exactly what we just created. This will be the attribute unique identifier.

8. Now click on the **New** button to create another form, the description.

9. In the **Create New Form Expression** window, you will see the **DimProduct** table already selected in the **Source table** combobox. Now drag **EnglishProductName** onto the **Form expression** text area, click on the **Manual** radio button and then on **OK**.

10. In the **Create New Attribute Form** window, select **DimProduct** as source table by checking its box under the **Table name** heading, leave the rest as default, and click on **OK**.

11. Close the Attribute Editor with the top-left button **Save and Close**; when prompted for a name type `Product` and click on **Save**. Great: one more thing, press *Ctrl + U* to update the schema and we're done. Congratulations, you've just created your first attribute.

How it works...

It may be confusing at the beginning: the attributes have forms and the forms are made of expressions.

An attribute form is just a representation, a means for displaying that element. We can have several different forms: **ID** and **DESC** are just two very frequently used. If you think about the Customer attribute we may have other different representations like the e-mail, or the **Social Security Number (SSN)** or the complete name with salutation, and so on. Remember that everything that we design here will eventually come up into a SQL statement. More specifically, here we have defined what appears in the **SELECT** clause and the **FROM** clause:

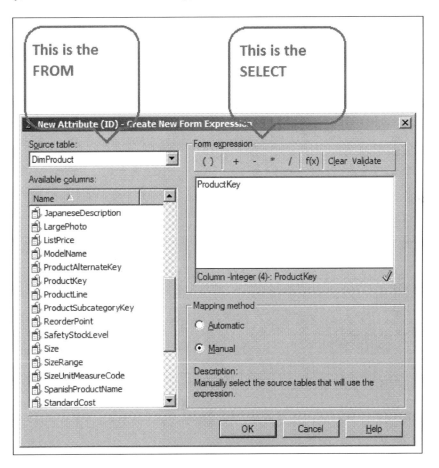

Looking at the screen capture, there is a left part (**FROM**) with a list of available tables and columns, and there's a right part (**SELECT**) where you craft the form expression. You can use column names, constants, as well as functions here. Everything will be converted into:

```
SELECT <Form expression> FROM <Source table>.
```

ID forms are so important not only for their uniqueness, but also because they will be the joining mechanism between tables. That's why we use primary keys, because somewhere (hopefully) there might be a foreign key pointing at it; for example, in the `FactInternetSales` table there is a `ProductKey` column referring to our **Product** attribute.

There's more...

Check the successful outcome of this recipe by going into the **Data Explorer - COOKBOOK** folder and expanding **System Hierarchy**. You will find your brand new **Product** attribute. Double-click on it in the right pane to show a list of products sorted by description. Notice that the ID does not appear by default in the data explorer, and in every report only the description is displayed. More on this later.

You can watch a screencast of this operation at:

▶ `http://at5.us/Ch3V1`

Using functions in an attribute form

When defining an attribute form, we're not limited to column names: as said, we can use constants or choose from a huge list of functions ready to use. These functions are meant for the most common uses: arithmetic, date manipulation, string functions to name a few. Let's see an example with the **Customer** attribute.

Getting ready

We are going to use the `DimCustomer` table for the next recipe. This table has a primary key (`CustomerKey`) and two description fields (`FirstName` and `LastName`).

How to do it...

Follow these steps to create a new attribute:

1. As in the previous recipe, go to the **Attributes** folder and right-click on the right pane.

2. Select **New | Attribute** from the context menu.

3. Create the **ID** form with the **CustomerKey** column of the **DimCustomer** table, set **Mapping method** to **Manual**, and click on **OK**.

4. In the **Create New Attribute Form** window, check only **DimCustomer**, which is bold, and click on **OK**.

5. In the Attribute Editor, click on the **New** button and you're again into the **Create New Form Expression** window.

6. This time, click on the **Insert Function** button which has a small **f(x)** label to bring up the **Select Function** dialog.

7. Open the **Select a category** combobox and choose **String** and then click on **ConcatBlank** in the **Select a function** list. And now click on **Next**.

8. In the **Arguments** dialog, type `FirstName` in **String1** and `LastName` in **String2**, and then click on **Finish**. The **Form expression** text area looks like:
   `ConcatBlank(FirstName, LastName)`.

9. Set **Mapping method** to **Manual** and click on **OK**.

10. In **Source tables**, check **DimCustomer** and click on **OK** and then on **Save and Close**, give it the name of `Customer` when prompted.

11. Remember to update the schema (press *Ctrl + U*).

How it works...

In MicroStrategy Suite, you will find out-of-the-box functions for common transformations; these functions are later translated to their corresponding SQL syntax when running the queries. Different RDBMS may have different way of doing the same function (string concatenation in Oracle is done with the || operator, while SQL Server uses CONCAT or the + operator, and so on). The SQL engine generates the correct syntax according to the dialect of the DBMS type, set in the database connection when creating the database instance configuration (see *Chapter 1, Getting Started with MicroStrategy*).

Mapping method can be automatic or manual. MicroStrategy uses the column name to detect when the same field appears in different tables and automatically uses as source all the tables where that column appears. If the column naming convention is enforced and consistent, this is a very useful and time saving feature. In other cases, when several columns of different tables have the same name but different meaning, the automatic discovery can lead to suboptimal SQL. This is why I always use the manual mapping method, especially in the beginning phase of a project, when I want to force the generated SQL to use a specific table.

There's more...

If you go to the **Data Explorer | System Hierarchy** folder and press *F5*, you will find the two attributes. You can browse customer names by double-clicking on the yellow icon. The `ConcatBlank` function inserted a space between the two string arguments that we set earlier.

You can watch a screencast of this operation at:
> `http://at5.us/Ch3V2`

Parent-child relationship I

Attributes can be related to each other (like in the case of city, province, and country) to form relationships between them. Furthermore, the tables holding attribute data can be normalized, as in the `DimProduct`, `DimProductSubcategory`, and `DimProductCategory` or denormalized as in the `DimGeography` table where we have province and country names repeated in every row. It is important that foreign keys are in place to preserve data integrity and help the RDBMS use the less expensive query path. So, for example, we have in the `DimProductSubcategory` table a foreign key pointing to the primary key in the `DimProductCategory` table.

If you look at the content of the `DimProduct` table, you'll see some records with `NULL` values in the `DimProductSubcategory` column; there are no sales transactions for those products, but this is a very common data quality problem. Missing values in foreign keys is something we usually have to deal with. If those products had sales movements, it would be difficult to aggregate them at the subcategory or category level.

Every developer has his/her silver bullet to solve this, I personally don't like `NULL` values in FK and always try to set them to `-1` (whenever possible) creating a correspondent `-1` value in the parent table with description `n/a`. Why `-1`? Because it is very very very unlikely that another code exists with the same negative value.

I've seen people setting `NULL` values to `9999`, to later discover that the company had more than 10,000 products and the `9999` code was actually allocated; then I saw the same people UPDATE millions of rows to `99999` WHERE `key` = `9999`. To cut the story short, they ended up using an impressive `Z99999` modifying an unspecified quantity of table columns from number to varchar... just in case, you never know.

Getting ready

You need to have completed the previous recipe to continue.

We are creating the `Country`, `StateProvince`, and `City` attributes and relating them with parent-child relationships.

How to do it...

Follow these steps:

1. In the **Attributes** folder, create a new attribute with these forms:
    - ❏ **ID: GeographyKey** from **DimGeography**
    - ❏ **DESC: ConcatBlank** (**City, PostalCode**) from **DimGeography**

2. Save it with the name `City`.

3. In the same folder, create a new attribute:
    - ❏ **ID: StateProvinceCode** from **DimGeography**
    - ❏ **DESC: StateProvinceName** from **DimGeography**

4. In the Attribute Editor, before saving this, click on the **Children** tab on the top-left then click on **Add** and from **Child candidates**, move **City** to the right of the shopping cart and hit **OK**.

5. Now click on **Save and Close** and name it `StateProvince`.

6. Create a new attribute:
    - ❏ **ID: CountryRegionCode** from **DimGeography**
    - ❏ **DESC: EnglishCountryRegionName** from **DimGeography**

7. Before saving, select the **Children** tab and add both **StateProvince** and **City**, hit **OK**, then **Save and Close** and name it `Country`.

8. Update the schema.

How it works...

Since the three attributes come from the same denormalized table we do not need FKs: the data for parent and children will be selected from the same `DimGeography`. Nevertheless, we need to specify which attribute is the parent and which is the child. Sometimes it is not so obvious and we need to do some research to detect the one part in a one-to-many relationship. As a rule of thumb:

▸ **In case of normalized tables**: The table with the primary key is parent, the table with the foreign key is child (no keys? Too bad, see the next point)

▸ **In case of denormalized tables**: An attribute with low cardinality is more likely to be parent, an attribute with high cardinality is probably child.

   When it's not clear at a first look, do some `SELECT COUNT(DISTINCT <column_name>)` on the columns likely to be part of the relationship.

There's more...

If you go to **Data Explorer | System Hierarchy**, you can browse the elements of the three attributes and see if the structure makes sense. Expand **Country**, select one country and expand **StateProvince**, click on one and browse through the elements inside the **City** attribute. Is Paris in France and London in the United Kingdom? Good.

Some cities are repeated, because the granularity is postal code.

You can watch a screencast of this operation at:
► `http://at5.us/Ch3V3`

Exercise 5

Repeat the recipe using the `DimDate` table and create the following attributes:

► `Date`: (ID = `DateKey` and DESC = `FullDateAlternateKey`)
► `Month`: (ID = `CalendarYearMonth` and no DESC)
► `Year`: (ID = `CalendarYear` and no DESC)

The `Month` attribute has `Date` as child, and `Year` has both `Month` and `Date` as children. If you receive a warning message saying that ID for `Month` is `Text`, don't worry, it will work as expected. The curious thing is that the year 2005 begins in July, and the year 2010 only has November (I suppose it is intentional).

Parent-child relationship II

In the previous recipe, we created a three-level dimension with a denormalized table. Let's do it with normalized tables. `Product`, `Product Subcategory`, and `Product Category` all reside in different tables related with referential integrity constraints as clearly described in the database diagram.

Like I said earlier, I always set the mapping method to manual whenever I create a new attribute. That prevents the editor from looking at every column in the database with the same name and add it automatically to the attribute definition. I prefer to have control over which tables are selected and which are not when it comes to generating SQL. You may also have noticed that some tables are bold in the attribute editor and some are not. Bold tables are the primary source for that specific attribute, often referred to as **lookup tables**.

We will begin this time from the top of the dimension, `Product Category`.

Getting ready

You should be able to create attributes by now, and have completed *Exercise 5*.

How to do it...

Follow these steps:

1. Create the **Product Category** attribute and drag **ProductCategoryKey** column as ID from the **DimProductCategory** table, set the **Mapping method** to **Manual**, and hit **OK**.

2. When you are in the **Create New Attribute Form** window, you'll see that there are two tables in the **Source tables** pane on the right (**DimProductCategory** and **DimProductSubcategory**).

3. Check both of them, the bold one should be **DimProductCategory**, if not, use the **Set as Lookup** button to make it bold.

4. Create the DESC form with the **EnglishProductCategoryName** field from **DimProductCategory**.

5. Close the editor and save the attribute as `Product Category`.

6. Now create the `Product Subcategory` attribute, with **ProductSubcategoryKey** as ID, set the **Mapping method** to **Manual**, and check both **DimProduct** and **DimProductSubcategory**, this time the bold one should be the latter.

7. Use **EnglishProductSubcategoryName** as the DESC form (**Manual** mapping).

8. Now before saving the attribute, click on the **Children** tab and add **Product** (the **Product** attribute was created in a previous recipe) then click on the **Parent** tab and add **Product Category**.

9. Click on **Save and Close**, name it `Product Subcategory` and update the schema.

How it works...

The **Product Category** attribute ID appears in two tables: the column **ProductCategoryKey** is PK in the **DimProductCategory** table and FK in the **DimProductSubcategory**. When we set the **DimProductCategory** to bold, we specify that the one with the PK is the lookup, that is, the principal source of information for that attribute, where the description comes from. We then select the second table to tell MicroStrategy that those two columns are the same ID.

Whenever the two tables appear in the same `SELECT`, they will be joined on **ProductCategoryKey**.

Likewise, the **Product Subcategory** and **Product** attributes are related with **ProductSubcategoryKey** being it the PK in **DimProductSubcategory** and the FK in **DimProduct**.

There is hence a cascading relationship that goes from **Product Category** to **Product** passing through **Product Subcategory**, which is the attribute that relates upward with **Product Category** and downward with **Product**.

We need to specify parent/child link only once in either attribute, as the setting will be automatically reflected to the corresponding counterpart.

There's more...

Check the successful completion by browsing the system hierarchy; try to see if the **Product** grouping makes sense.

> You can watch a screencast of this operation at:
> ▸ `http://at5.us/Ch3V5`

Exercise 6

Look at the **DimCustomer** table, the second column is **GeographyKey**:

 ▸ Can you tell if it's a PK, an FK, or else?

 ▸ To which table does it relate to?

 ▸ How should we modify the `City` attribute to handle this relationship?

Other attribute forms

Attributes may have more forms than just an ID or a name. More often than not you'll find long descriptions, SKUs, Social Security Numbers, previous companies' codes still in use, and so on. Or, in the case of a customer, you may have an e-mail address that sometimes you want to use in a report. Those descriptive fields that uniquely refer to an element of an attribute can be used as alternate forms. When creating an alternate form, it is always useful to ask the question: is this a form or a totally different attribute? The customer's birthday, for example, would be a different attribute, since we may later filter or GROUP BY this column; and surely does not uniquely identify a single customer.

Getting ready

You need to have completed the previous recipes to do this one. We are now adding the long description to the `Product` attribute.

How to do it...

We are modifying the `Product` attribute:

1. Go to the **Schema Objects | Attribute** folder. Double-click on the yellow **Product** icon.

2. If you see a message like the one in the following screen capture, it is very important that you click on the second option **Edit: This will lock all schema objects in this project from other users**. Otherwise, you won't be allowed to modify the attribute:

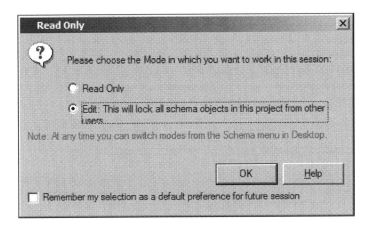

3. When the Attribute Editor opens, click on **New**.

4. In **Create New Form Expression** drag the column **EnglishDescription** to the **Form Expression** text area. Mapping method should be **Manual**. Click on **OK**.

5. Check the **DimProduct** table, and now look at the **Form general information** area down to the left.

6. In the textbox called **Name**, type `LDESC` and close this dialog clicking on the **OK** button. See that in the Attribute Editor now we have three forms.

7. Click on **Save and Close**, update the schema.

How it works...

We can have as many forms as we want in an attribute, as long as they come from the same lookup table. Forms can be text, numbers, dates, or other datatypes. When it comes to displaying forms on a report, DESC will be always displayed by default (if present), and you will have the option to select which other forms are shown by right-clicking on an attribute header.

There's more...

If you selected **Read Only** in step 2 in this recipe, the project schema is now locked. You won't be able to make changes until you unlock it. This is useful in development environments where multiple persons are working on the same metadata and you want to freeze the project.

To unlock it, use the **Schema | Read Only Mode...** menu and uncheck the option.

 You can watch a screencast of this operation at:
► `http://at5.us/Ch3V6`

Exercise 7

Create a new form for the `Customer` attribute. Use the `EmailAddress` field from the `DimCustomer` table. Give the name `EMAIL` and in the **Form format** field select the **Type** as **Email**.

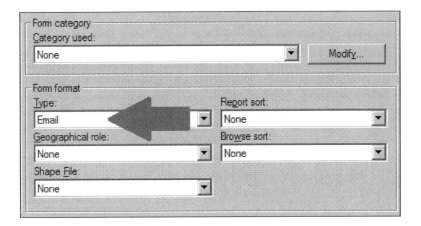

Selecting which forms are displayed

When browsing the attribute elements in **Data Explorer | System Hierarchy**, we noticed that the DESC form is always shown but by default the ID is hidden. To change this behavior and decide how the attribute will appear to the end user, we will modify the settings in the **Display** tab of the Attribute Editor. These settings will affect the way attribute elements are displayed also in dynamic selections and filters which we'll cover in *Chapter 8, Dynamic Selection with Filters and Prompts*.

Getting ready

You need to have completed the previous recipes to continue.

How to do it...

Let's see how to do it:

1. In the **Schema Objects | Attributes** folder, double-click on the **Customer** attribute.

2. Select the **Display** tab, you will find a shopping cart like the one shown in the following screen capture:

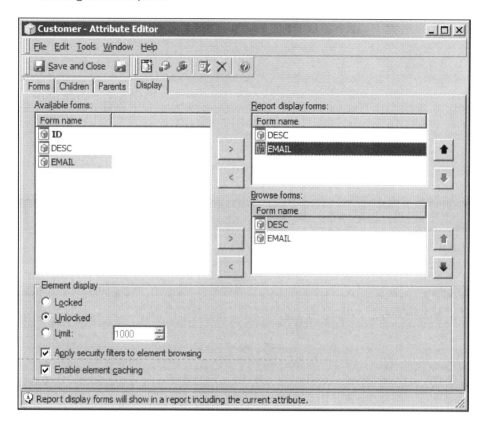

3. In the right part of the cart, select the **EMAIL** form and remove it from both **Report display** and **Browse** by clicking on the small **<** buttons.

4. Click on **Save and Close** and update the schema.

Now if you go to **Data Explorer | System Hierarchy**, you'll notice that the e-mail address is gone. If you still see it, that's because MicroStrategy Desktop keeps a local cache of attribute elements to speed up the application; in this case you need to refresh the elements. Click on the **View** menu and select **Refresh (F5)**.

How it works...

This setting affects the default behavior of the entire project when browsing the attribute. You will still have the possibility to change the display forms on a per report basis.

There's more...

You may want the elements sorted by code, for example, instead of **DESC**.

You can do this from the **Modify Attribute Form** window. Refer to the screen capture:

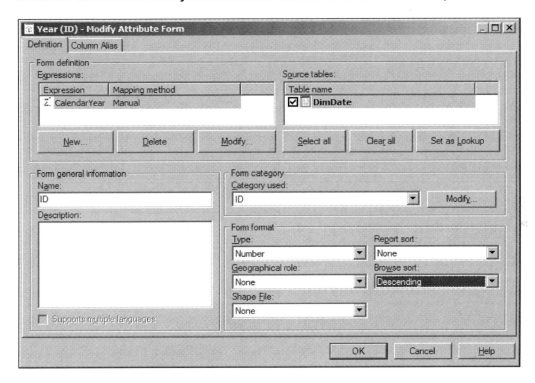

There are two comboboxes down on the right-hand side named **Report sort** and **Browse sort**.

If you change the second one to **Descending** (in the screen capture I am sorting the **Year** attribute), you will see the years' elements sorted backwards. This is especially useful when the users have to select from a dynamic list of years, and you want the most recent to be shown first.

 You can watch a screencast of this operation at:
▸ `http://at5.us/Ch3V7`

Building Data Explorer Hierarchies

In every MicroStrategy project, there is a default system hierarchy that is built automatically based on the information we set into the `Parent/Children` tabs of the Attribute Editor. The default system hierarchy cannot be modified and contains all the attributes in a project.

The hierarchies can be used to drill down and up in reports, for example, from `Year` to `Month` to `Date`; or from `Product Category` to `Product`.

In order to present the attributes in clear and understandable groups to the users, additionally, we can create other hierarchies that we will later use in reports and in dynamic selectors; think of it as a different way to show dimensions to the end user.

Getting ready

You need to have completed the previous recipes to continue.

How to do it...

We are creating the most common hierarchy, the time:

1. Click on the **Schema Objects | Hierarchies** folder. Then open the **Data Explorer** folder.

2. Right-click on the right pane and from the context menu select **New | Hierarchy**.

3. In the shopping cart that appears, choose **Year**, **Month**, and **Date** attributes and move them to the right.

4. By default all the relationship paths are already present in form of arrows from the parent to the child. You can check here if you set the attribute properties correctly.

5. See the green check mark on **Year**? This means this is the highest of the three attributes, therefore MicroStrategy automatically selected it as an entry level.

6. Click on **Save and Close**, a message warns you that this hierarchy will be used for drilling. Click on **OK**.

7. Name it `Time` and click on **Save**.

8. Remember to update the schema and go to the **Data Explorer** folder.

9. Here we can see the **Time** hierarchy, and inside it the entry level: **Year**.

How it works...

We will see that the hierarchy is useful when we create reports and want to give the user the possibility to aggregate or filter by year, by month, or by date without previously knowing which attribute they are going to use.

There's more...

Entry points are the objects from which the navigation begins inside a hierarchy. You have seen, when browsing the **Time** hierarchy that only the **Year** attribute appears at first. To set the **Month** attribute as another entry point, do this:

1. Re-open the **Time** hierarchy by double-clicking on it in **Schema Objects | Hierarchies | Data Explorer**.

2. Click on the **Month** attribute to select it, you will see eight small squares surrounding it.

3. Now right-click on **Month** and in the context menu select **Set as entry point**.

4. Click on **Save and Close**, update the schema.

5. Now go to **Data Explorer | Time** and press *F5* to refresh.

6. The **Month** attribute now appears as an entry point.

It may seem useless now, but please wait until *Chapter 5, Data Display and Manipulation – Reports*.

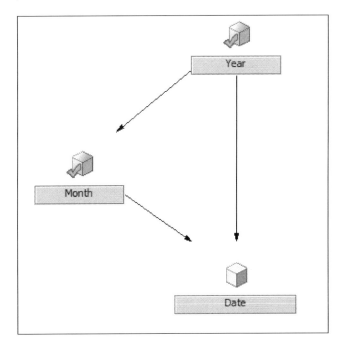

Sometimes—while the project is in progress—we need to provide a quick and easy documentation about the dimensions. I found that doing a print screen of the Hierarchy Editor is very useful and gives a clear idea of how the users can move inside the data.

You can watch a screencast of this operation at:

▸ `http://at5.us/Ch3V8`

Exercise 8

Create the `Products` hierarchy with the following attributes: `Product Category`, `Product Subcategory`, and `Product`.

Exercise 9

Create the `Geography` hierarchy with the following attributes: `Country`, `StateProvince`, `City`, and `Customer`.

Set `Country` and `City` as entry points.

Exercise 10

Go to **Data Explorer | Geography**: how many customers are there in **Frankfurt 91480**? Double-check the names with this query in `sqlcmd`:

```
select LastName from DimCustomer where GeographyKey = 118

go
```

Creating an attribute-only report

You've done a great job until now, and it's time to see some results. I know reports are still two chapters away, and we have a long journey to get there: but here we just want to take a sneak peek at how they work. Remember what we said; that we're just building `SELECT` statements. So it's perfectly legal to create queries that only involve attributes. A very quick one could be the list of countries in our database.

Getting ready

You need to have completed the previous recipes (and exercises) to continue.

How to do it...

Let's do our first report!

1. Look for a folder named **My Personal Objects** and click on it.

2. Double-click on **My Reports**.

3. In the right pane, right-click and choose **New | Report**.

4. In the following dialog box leave **Blank Report** selected and click on **OK**.

5. Here comes the Report Editor. We will have plenty of time to look at this window, but now just concentrate on the left pane that says **My Shortcuts**.

6. Click on the yellow **Attributes** shortcut icon to see the list of available attributes.

7. Right-click on **Country** and select **Add to Rows**. That's it.

8. From the **View** menu, select **Grid View** to run the report. The result is as shown in the following image:

Country
Australia
Canada
Germany
France
United Kingdom
United States

9. Click on **Save and Close** naming the report 01 Countries list.

How it works...

When you add an attribute on the rows of a report, MicroStrategy reads in the metadata where the attribute **ID** and **DESC** come from, and then issues a query to the data warehouse with the proper SELECT statement. Once the result is returned the data is displayed on the screen according to the default report display forms that we specified in the Attribute Editor. The ID is not shown on the grid but it is actually retrieved from the dimension table.

There's more...

Just out of curiosity, inside **My Reports** folder, double-click on the **01 Countries list** icon to execute the report you just saved.

When the grid appears double-click on a country, for example, **France**, what happens?

Now double-click again on **Orleans 45000**, what do you see? Great! You just drilled down the **Geography** hierarchy. No need to create extra reports, MicroStrategy knows its way around dimensions. You can close these two new reports without saving them.

 You can watch a screencast of this operation at:
▶ http://at5.us/Ch3V9

Parent-child relationship in a report

In the previous recipe, we created a very basic report with a list of countries. While we are in a development phase, this type of report is useful to control if the attribute forms have been created correctly. Similarly, to check the parent-child settings, you can create a quick report with two or more attributes involved in the relationships; just to be sure that every son has its father and no family is broken.

Getting ready

You need to have completed the previous recipes to continue.

How to do it...

We are now creating a report on the **Time** dimension:

1. Go to **My Personal Objects | My Reports**, right-click on the right pane and select **New | Report**.
2. Leave **Blank Report** selected and click on **OK**.
3. In **My Shortcuts** pane on the left, click on **Attributes**, and from the list that appears on the right-click on **Year**.
4. Select **Add to Rows**.
5. Do the same with **Month**, you'll see that the two attributes appear as columns in the **Report View** pane.
6. Run the report by selecting the **View | Grid View** menu.
7. You can now click on **Save and Close** and name the report: `02 Calendar`.

How it works...

MicroStrategy reads the metadata to get the information needed to produce the SQL and issues the query. The resulting dataset is then displayed and the `Parent` attribute rows are merged. You only see the `Year` values appearing once in the grid, with the corresponding `Months`, this is the default behavior.

There's more...

Re-run the report and look at the results, isn't it strange? Uh-Oh, year 2005 starts in July. In this particular case, we are using test data and in fact the database only holds dates starting from July 2005. However, in a real-world project, this situation should raise a flag of attention, and we'd better go to the `sqlcmd` console to check the `DimDate` table.

Now scroll to the end of the report. Year 2008 also has fewer months, year 2009 is missing, and year 2010 only has November. Definitely not a very good date dimension: can you imagine what would happen if we had sales in 2009 or 2010? Yes, probably they would disappear from the sales reports due to inner JOIN and this is one of the most common mistakes we can do in BI. Sometimes dimension tables are incomplete, long forgotten, or simply not updated; it helps to check them every now and then.

It happened to a project of mine. Back in 2009, I had a Time table with dates until year 2012: three years is a long life span for a report (I thought), so 2012 would be enough. Wrong! That report survived more than expected and in January 2013 it started returning no rows. With a red face I had to modify the Time table and, since bad habits are hard to break, I inserted dates until 2015. Guess what?

[You can watch a screencast of this operation at:
 ▶ `http://at5.us/Ch3V10`]

Filters on attributes

Attributes can be used not only to label and explain numbers but also to filter results, for example, you may want to report only on sales from one year, or one product category, or items shipped to a specific country. In order to restrict the data that a query returns we use a particular type of object called filter. Filters are then inserted into reports or in metrics to obtain the desired results.

Getting ready

You need to have completed the previous recipes to continue.

How to do it...

1. Open **Public Objects** folder, and click on the **Filters** folder.

2. On the right pane, right-click and select **New | Filter**, leave **Empty Filter** selected and click on **OK**.

3. We're now in the Filter Editor, which is similar to other editors we saw already. Click on the yellow **Attribute** shortcut in **My Shortcuts** panel, you'll see a list of available attributes.

4. Double-click on **Year** and look at the right part of the window, here we have the **Filter definition** area.

5. By default, **Attribute Qualification** is already set to restrict on a list of **Year** elements, we only need to choose which elements we want to use.

6. Click on the button named **Add** to select from a list of years. In the shopping cart, move 2007 and 2008 to the right with the arrow button, and confirm by clicking on **OK**.

7. Click on **OK** again in the **Attribute Qualification** pane, and then click on **Save and Close**.

8. Name the filter Years 2007 and 2008 only, and click on **Save**.

9. Now go to **My Personal Objects | My Reports**.

10. Right-click on the report named **02 Calendar**, and select **Edit** from the context menu.

11. In the Report Editor, click on **Public Object** shortcut in **My Shortcuts** panel, and double-click on **Filters** in the list that appears.

12. You'll see Years 2007 and 2008 only, the filter we just created, right-click on it and select **Add to Report Filter**, now select the **View | Grid View** menu to run the report.

13. Look at the results; verify that now only dates in years 2007 and 2008 appear on the grid.

14. You can close this window without saving the report.

How it works...

When running the report, MicroStrategy adds a WHERE clause to the SQL sentence sent to the data warehouse.

There's more...

MicroStrategy filters are very flexible and allow restricting data based on IDs or any other form defined in the Attribute Editor.

Filters can be applied to attributes as well as metrics. When applied to metrics, they generate a HAVING clause. More on this later.

 You can watch a screencast of this operation at:
  ▸ http://at5.us/Ch3V11

Exercise 11

Create a filter to restrict **Products Categories** to **Bikes** and **Accessories**, save it as
`Categories Bikes and Accessories only`.

Create another filter: `Greater Paris only` to include all 14 elements of `City` that
belong to Paris.

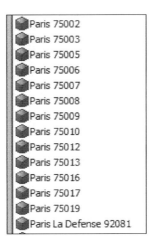

 When selecting the elements, you can type `Paris` in the **Find** box
and click on the button with a little funnel icon.

See also

▶   The *Creating a simple counter fact and metric* recipe in *Chapter 4, Objects – Facts
and Metrics*

4
Objects – Facts and Metrics

In this chapter, we will cover:

- ▶ Creating a simple counter fact and metric
- ▶ Using the SQL view to inspect SELECT statements
- ▶ Understanding the GROUP BY clause
- ▶ Adding more facts
- ▶ Filters on metrics
- ▶ Creating ranking metrics
- ▶ Grouping at a different level (level metrics)
- ▶ Embedding filters inside metrics
- ▶ Using Metric Join Type in reports
- ▶ Creating a previous month metric (transformation)

Introduction

It's time to produce some numbers. In our BI journey, we have walked through the installation, configuration, and creation of a project, and there was not a single number involved. I appreciate your patience reading the first few chapters; now we start looking at what the reports look like and where the results come from. Because, after all, everything we do ends up in a bottom line total.

A Sales Manager once asked me "What is this all about: Business Intelligence?". I politely answered, "It's about taking informed decisions... you know, managing with accurate information, etc.", "Ok, I got the 'business' part," he replied, "but why 'intelligence'? It's just stupid numbers!"

I don't need to remind you that not-so-stupid numbers are the ultimate goal of a BI project (yes, I know, flashing out iPads is also fun), and it is extremely important to know where numbers come from, why they look good or bad.

Chances are that parts of your deliverables will be PowerPointed in a board meeting; and there will be a few grey-headed very important people getting upset looking at the slides. In those moments, you'd better be 110 percent sure that the total is correct, where the numbers came from and—most of all—be able to demonstrate it. We're not responsible for bad numbers, we are responsible for inaccurate ones.

OK now, before we continue, in order to keep things clear and understand the MicroStrategy terms, I need to answer a question: what is the difference between a fact and a metric?

A **fact** is a column in a table and a **metric** is one or more aggregate functions that we apply to that fact. `SalesAmount`, being a column, is a fact; `SUM(SalesAmount)` is a metric. It is actually a little more complicated than this, but in the beginning we stick to this concept:

- **Fact** – a column (or expression, or function ...) from a table
- **Metric** – an aggregate function of a fact at a certain level

A metric always has a level: when we want to measure numbers like sales for example, we usually consider them as a total per year, per region, per customer, or any other dimension. To put it another way, the list of attributes in a report is called the **Report Level**. A grid with the product, month, and number of sold items has a Report Level of products and month. If I change the month with year and add customer, I have a Report Level of product, year, and customer. Metrics are computed by default at the Report Level (which is represented, in the metric formula, by {~}); however, we'll see later, specific metrics can be calculated at a level that is different from the default.

Moreover, we can have several metrics based on the same fact with different aggregation functions: `MAX(SalesAmount)`, `AVG(SalesAmount)`, and so on. Facts are schema objects, while metrics are application (public) objects; that is, schema must be updated after we create or change a fact, but it's not necessary to do so after modifications in metrics.

In the following recipes we will create both facts and metrics, and see their effect on reports.

One more thing: we cannot use a fact directly in a report; we always need to wrap the fact into a metric in order to display it on a grid or a graph. Sounds weird? Well, think that we are issuing a SELECT query with a GROUP BY clause, so every field that is not in the GROUP BY should be aggregated someway. It will be easier to see as we read on.

Creating a simple counter fact and metric

Before we play with sales figures, we need to know some basic information: how many records are we talking about? How many rows should I expect to be returned from a fact table?

Getting ready

I think it's useful to create a shortcut on the Windows desktop to the sqlcmd utility, so that we can easily open the command-line SQL interface to verify the correctness of the statements generated by MicroStrategy.

This is the one liner that I use (should be written on a single line):

```
C:\Windows\System32\cmd.exe /c sqlcmd -S (localdb)\v11.0 -d
AdventureWorksDW2008R2
```

So, whenever I click on the shortcut I jump directly into the data warehouse.

Once you get in please run this:

```
select count(1) from FactInternetSales
go
```

This will show the real number of rows contained in the fact table (FactInternetSales) that we are going to use. And this:

```
select sum(SalesAmount) from FactInternetSales
go
```

This will return the total sales of all-time on the Internet channel. It's important to note down these numbers, 60398 and 29358677.2207 respectively, as we will use them as a confirmation that everything is going well.

How to do it...

Open the desktop application and create the counter fact:

1. Click on the **Schema Objects | Facts** folder. Right-click on the right pane and select **New | Fact**.

2. You are presented with the Fact Editor, which is very similar but simpler than the Attribute Editor. We select **FactInternetSales** from the **Source table** dropdown on the left and see all the columns in that table.

3. This time instead of choosing a field we simply type `1` into the **Fact Expression** textbox. This **1** will be our first fact.

4. Set **Mapping method** to **Manual** and click on **OK**.

5. Check **FactInternetSales** in the **Source tables** list.

6. Click on **Save and Close**.

7. Name it `One from FactInternetSales` and click on **Save**.

8. Now go to **Public Objects | Metrics** folder; right-click on the right pane and select **New | Metric**.

9. Leave **Empty Metric** selected and click on **OK**.

10. You're now inside the Metric Editor. We have an **Object Browser** part on the left and the metric definition on the right. In **Object Browser** there is only one fact: **One from FactInternetSales**, which we just created. Click-and-drag it to the text area where it says **Enter your formula here**.

11. Now in the text area select the function `Sum` and change it to `Count`, so that the resulting formula is:

    `Count([One from FactInternetSales]) {~}`

12. Click on **Save and Close** and name it `Count One from FactInternetSales`.

13. Update the schema.

14. Go to **My Personal Objects | My Reports**. Create a new report by right-clicking on the right pane and selecting **New | Report** from the context menu.

15. Leave **Blank Report** selected and click on **OK**.

16. When the Report Editor opens, go to the left **My Shortcut** pane and click on **Public Objects**.

17. The **Object Browser** list will display a series of folders: double-click on **Metrics**.

18. Double-click on **Count One from FactInternetSales**, the **Report View** area will show the header of the metric in the grid.

19. Run the report with the **View | Grid View** menu.

20. After few moments the report will show the result.

21. If it matches the number of rows we measured at the beginning, then we're ok, else go to step 1.

22. Click on **Save and Close** and name it 03 FactInternetSales row Count.

How it works...

In our first example the fact is a constant: the number 1. This way we are telling MicroStrategy to SELECT 1 from the FactInternetSales table. Because the table has 60398 rows we would retrieve 60398 times the number 1; but we said that we cannot put a fact directly into a report, we need to create a metric to aggregate that number to a meaningful total.

So, we create a metric using the fact and the aggregate function Count(), in order to get a total number of rows from the FactInternetSales table. This is a very simple query, useful to verify the size of the table, and to familiarize with the way the SQL syntax is generated.

There's more...

In this particular case, the aggregate functions Sum() and Count() would have returned the same result:

```
select count(1) from FactInternetSales
```

would be the same as:

```
select sum(1) from FactInternetSales
```

I personally prefer using Count() because it is conceptually more appropriate.

You can watch a screencast of this operation at:
▶ http://at5.us/Ch4V1

Exercise 12

Now do the same with a real fact. Pick the column **SalesAmount** and create the fact named SalesAmount from FactInternetSales first, then build a metric with the SalesAmount from FactInternetSales fact aggregated using the function Sum(). Name the metric Sum SalesAmount from FactInternetSales.

Exercise 13

Did you remember to update the schema?

In a new report, drag the metric you just created and view the result. Is it what you expected? Don't worry about the decimals, we'll deal with them later.

Save the report as 04 FactInternetSales Total SalesAmount.

Using SQL View to inspect SELECT statements

A developer's best friend: **SQL View** is a way to look at the statements that MicroStrategy sends to the RDBMS. This window is probably the most useful debugging tool that we have at our disposal.

During the development phase or for customer support, from this view it is easier to troubleshoot a report that takes forever, returns no rows, or just fails with no evident reason. But it is even more useful to understand how the SQL generator interprets the objects that we build day after day. I call it my personal peep show.

Getting ready

You need to have completed the previous recipes and exercises to continue.

How to do it...

1. If not already there, go to **My Personal Objects** | **My Reports** folder.

2. Double-click on **03 FactInternetSales row Count** to run the report.

3. When the result appears select the **View** | **SQL View** menu.

4. Look at the window, there is a lot of useful information here (number of rows/columns returned, query execution time, and so on). And, near the end there is a section called SQL Statements.

5. This is the list of queries that the MicroStrategy Engine runs on the database server. See the Pass0 statement (select count(1) WJXBFS1 from FactInternetSales a11).

6. You can copy this statement and run it into sqlcmd and it will return the same dataset as the report.

7. Switch back to the grid with the menu **View** | **Grid View** and click on **Save and Close**.

How it works...

Based on the information stored into the metadata the query is issued to the ODBC driver and executed in the data warehouse. The returning rows are then processed and displayed on a grid. You can see that the sentence is exactly the same as we did at the beginning of the chapter to count the rows in the fact table.

There's more...

You cannot change the query in the SQL view. Unfortunately, it is read-only. So, if the SQL is not what you expected to be, you need to modify the schema objects used to build this report.

The SQL view is not always this simple. Going on in the project you will find more and more content in here, until it becomes almost unreadable to human. Very complex reports have several passes of SQL and use temporary tables to store intermediate results before displaying it to the user. It will become harder to follow, yet this is the best place to look for errors when things go wrong.

 You can watch a screencast of this operation at:
▸ `http://at5.us/Ch4V2`

Exercise 14

Create a new blank report. Drag to the **Report View** area the two metrics we created in previous recipes. Click on **View | Grid View** and check the results. Now go to **SQL View**: what do you expect to see in the SQL statement Pass0?

Save the report as `05 Two Metrics from FactInternetSales`.

Understanding the GROUP BY clause

Aggregate data is what reports are made of; speaking ANSI SQL, this means GROUP BY. MicroStrategy applies GROUP BY to all the attributes present on a report grid. Well, this is not completely correct, but we begin with this simple concept:

Every attribute on a grid is reflected in the GROUP BY clause of the resulting SELECT statement.

Hence, we have:

▸ Metrics that represent the aggregation (sum, count, and so on) of facts

▸ Attributes BY which we GROUP the data

I hope this is clear enough, because this concepts will return every now and then with metrics. In this recipe, anyway, we'll see an example of how it works.

Getting ready

We are using now the `SalesAmount` metric and the `Product` attribute. Before going on we need to establish a connection between the fact table and the attribute table, so that MicroStrategy knows how to `JOIN` them.

FactInternetSales		DimProduct	
	SalesOrderNumber	**PK**	**ProductKey**
	SalesOrderLineNumber		
		U1	ProductAlternateKey
FK2,I5	**ProductKey**	**FK1,I1**	ProductSubCategoryKey
FK3,I4	**OrderDateKey**		WeightUnitMeasureCode
FK4,I3	**DueDateKey**		SizeUnitMeasureCode
FK5,I7	**ShipDateKey**		**EnglishProductName**
FK1,I2	**CustomerKey**		**SpanishProductName**
FK7	PromotionKey		**FrenchProductName**

The connection is represented by the FK (`ProductKey`) in `FactInternetSales`. In other words, the **ID** form of **Product** is present in both the fact and the dimension tables, so we need to specify that those two columns are the same **ID** in order to `JOIN` them in the SQL statements.

How to do it...

First, we modify the **Product** attribute then we create a new report:

1. Go to **Schema Objects | Attributes** and right-click on **Product**. From the context menu select **Edit**.

2. You're in the Attribute Editor and the **ID** form is already selected, click on the **Modify** button.

3. In the modify **Attribute Forms** dialog, on the right there is a panel with **Source tables** where we have selected **DimProduct** and set it as lookup. Now click to select **FactInternetSales** too, like in the following screen capture, and click on **OK**:

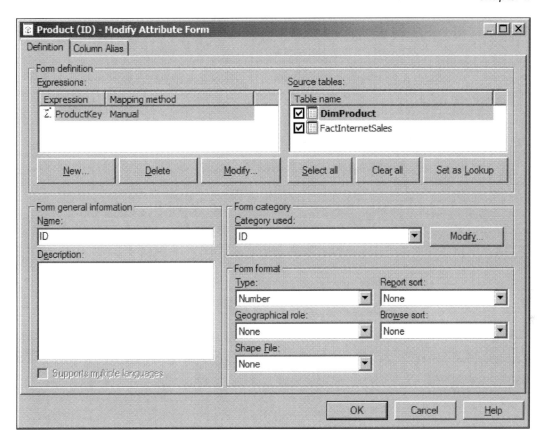

4. Back in the Attribute Editor, click on **Save and Close**.

5. Now go to the folder **Schema Objects | Tables** and right-click on **FactInternetSales**, selecting **Edit** from the context menu.

6. You're in the Table Editor: see in the **Logical View** tab, that the **Product** attribute is present together with the two facts we created previously.

7. Below the list of objects there is a checkbox that says **The key specified is the true key for the warehouse table**; be sure to uncheck this because **ProductKey** is not the PK in this table.

8. Click on **Save and Close**, and update the schema.

9. Now go to **My Personal Objects | My Reports** folder, right-click on the right pane and select **New | Report** from the context menu.

10. Leave default **Blank Report** selected and click on **OK**.

11. Here we are in the Report Editor. First, click on the **Attributes** icon in **My Shortcut** panel then double-click on the **Product** icon in the list that appears: note that the **Product** attribute is added to the grid.

12. Now click on the **Public Objects** icon in **My Shortcut** panel and in the list that appears double-click on **Metrics** to see the list of metrics that we have in the project

13. Double-click on the metric named **Sum SalesAmount from FactInternetSales**, the metric is added to the grid.

14. From the **View** menu select **Grid View**, and the report shows the results.

15. You see the **DESC** and **LDESC** forms of the **Product** attribute and if you scroll to the right there is the column of **Sum SalesAmount from FactInternetSales** at the **Product** level.

16. We do not need the **LDESC** form in this report so we remove it. Scroll to the beginning of the grid until you see the header of the **Product** attribute. Right-click on the cell containing the **Product** header and from the context menu select **Attribute Forms**.

17. You see that there are three **Attribute Forms** here: **ID**, **DESC**, and **LDESC**. Uncheck **LDESC** and leave only **DESC** checked.

18. The **LDESC** form has disappeared and we have a **SalesAmount** report grouped by **Product**.

19. Now select the menu **View | SQL View** to see SQL sentence. There is a `GROUP BY` clause with the `Product` PK, the fact `SalesAmount` is aggregated with the `Sum()` function and grouped by **Product**.

20. Go back to **Grid View** with **View | Grid View** and click on **Save and Close**.

21. Name the report `06 SalesAmount by Product`.

How it works...

In this case we put a single attribute and a single metric on the report. The metric is calculated at the level of the single attribute: `sum(SalesAmount) from FactInternetSales group by ProductKey`. Easy to guess, if we put more than one attribute on the grid the `GROUP BY` clause would contain more columns.

There's more...

Refer to *Chapter 3, Schema Objects – Attributes*, for details about how attribute forms are displayed in reports.

You can watch a screencast of this operation at:
  ▶ `http://at5.us/Ch4V3`

Exercise 15

Following the steps in this recipe create a new report with `SalesAmount` by customer.

Remember to modify the **Customer** attribute in order to include the `CustomerKey` column from the `FactInternetSales` table (and update the schema). The first few rows of the report should look like this image:

Customer	Metrics	Sum SalesAmount from FactInternetSales
Jon Yang		8,249
Eugene Huang		6,384
Ruben Torres		8,114
Christy Zhu		8,139
Elizabeth Johnson		8,196
Julio Ruiz		8,121
Janet Alvarez		8,119

Save the report as `07 SalesAmount By Customer`.

Adding more facts

Now we want to complicate things a little more so we need more data: `OrderQuantity`, `TotalProductCost`, `SalesAmount`, `TaxAmt`, and `Freight` from `FactResellerSales`. It is another fact table that we did not include in previous recipes, so we are adding it now.

Getting ready

From the **Schema** menu, open the **Warehouse Catalog** window and add the **FactResellerSales** table from the left list to the right **Table being used in the project** list. Then click on **Save and Close**.

How to do it...

1. Go to **Schema Objects | Facts** and create a new fact.

2. In the **Create New Fact Expression** dialog, select **FactResellerSales** from the **Source table** dropdown.

3. Drag **OrderQuantity** from the **Available columns** list to the **Fact expression** text area.

4. Very important: set **Mapping method** to **Manual** and click on **OK**.

5. In the Fact Editor, check **FactResellerSales** in the **Source tables** list.

6. Click on **Save and Close** and name it `OrderQuantity from FactResellerSales`.

7. Repeat steps 1 to 6 and create similar facts with the following columns:

    ❑ `TotalProductCost`

    ❑ `SalesAmount`

    ❑ `TaxAmt`

    ❑ `Freight`

8. Name every fact with the column name + `from FactResellerSales`.

9. Create one last new fact, select **FactResellerSales** as table, but this time in the **Fact expression** type:

    `SalesAmount + TaxAmt + Freight`

10. Set **Mapping method** to **Manual** and click on **OK**.

11. Save it as `TotalPaid from FactResellerSales`.

12. Update the schema.

How it works...

We can include calculations inside facts, for example we add the values of three columns to compute how much the customer paid for a specific product, including taxes and shipping.

There's more...

You can also use functions with columns, like `Round2(DiscountAmount, 4)` to return a specified number of digits after the decimal separator.

Exercise 16

Create a fact named `ProductMargin from FactResellerSales` using this formula:

    `SalesAmount  -  TotalProductCost`

And now update the schema.

Exercise 17

Create the following metrics:

- Sum OrderQuantity from FactResellerSales
- Sum TotalProductCost from FactResellerSales
- Sum SalesAmount from FactResellerSales
- Sum TaxAmt from FactResellerSales
- Sum Freight from FactResellerSales
- Sum TotalPaid from FactResellerSales
- Sum ProductMargin from FactResellerSales

Since metrics are not schema objects there is no need to update the schema.

Exercise 18

Create a report with all the metrics you just created, go to **SQL View** and verify the SQL sentence. It should look like:

```
select  sum(a11.OrderQuantity)  WJXBFS1,
  sum(a11.TotalProductCost)  WJXBFS2,
  sum(a11.SalesAmount)  WJXBFS3,
  sum(a11.TaxAmt)  WJXBFS4,
  sum(a11.Freight)  WJXBFS5,
  sum(((a11.SalesAmount + a11.TaxAmt) + a11.Freight))  WJXBFS6,
  sum(((a11.SalesAmount - a11.TotalProductCost))  WJXBFS7
from  FactResellerSales  a11
```

And the numbers should look like:

Metrics	
Sum OrderQuantity from FactResellerSales	214,378
Sum TotalProductCost from FactResellerSales	79,980,114
Sum SalesAmount from FactResellerSales	80,450,597
Sum TaxAmt from FactResellerSales	6,436,048
Sum Freight from FactResellerSales	2,011,266
Sum TotalPaid from FactResellerSales	88,897,911
Sum ProductMargin from FactResellerSales	470,483

Hint: right-click on the header cell named **Metrics**, select **Move | To Rows** to pivot.

Save this report as `08 Multiple Metrics from FactResellerSales.`

 You can watch a screencast of this operation at:
  ▸ `http://at5.us/Ch4V4`

Filters on metrics

In *Chapter 3, Schema Objects – Attributes*, we learned how to build filters on attributes to restrict the data returned from the data warehouse using a list of elements. Similarly, we can create filters using values of metrics. The difference—as said—is how the SQL sentence will be generated when applying the filter: attribute filters appear in the `WHERE` clause, while metric filters appear in the `HAVING` clause. For those of you SQL superstars, I do not need to explain that `WHERE` restricts before aggregation, while `HAVING` restricts (of course...) after aggregation.

Getting ready

In the previous recipe we added a new fact table. Before we go on, we should specify the `Product` FK so that MicroStrategy can `JOIN` the `FactResellerSales` table with the `Product` dimensions. We see from the database ER diagram that `FactResellerSales` has a `ProductKey` column that points to the `DimProduct` table.

So, open the **Product** attribute (double-click) and modify the **ID** form to include **FactResellerSales** as a source table (as in the following screen capture):

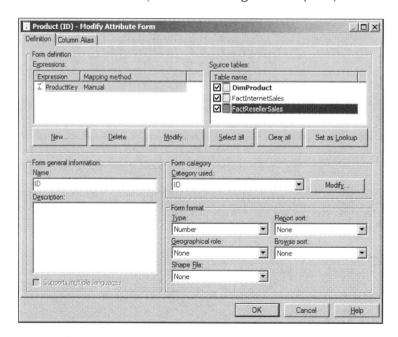

Save the attribute and then go to **Schema Objects | Tables** and open the **FactResellerSales** table and uncheck **The key specified is the true key for the warehouse table**. Then click on **Save and Close** and update the schema.

To introduce this scenario, we first create a basic report with **Sum ProductMargin from FactResellerSales** grouped by **Product Category**. No need to save it.

Product Category	Metrics	Sum ProductMargin from FactResellerSales
Bikes		(990,700)
Components		1,032,966
Clothing		232,423
Accessories		195,793

Uh-oh: we're losing money on **Bikes**..., this won't please the board. This is a typical case where we need to be sure of the numbers and be able to give an explanation to the Product Manager whose temperature is rising.

How to do it...

We decide to create another report showing only the products that have negative profit margin. First, we need a filter on **Sum ProductMargin from FactResellerSales**:

1. We begin by opening the **Product** attribute to remove the **LDESC** form from the default display, go to **Schema Objects | Attributes**, double-click on **Product** and click on the **Display** tab. Remove **LDESC** from **Report display forms**. Then click on **Save and Close**.

2. Open the folder **Public Objects | Filters** and right-click on the right pane. Select **New | Filter** from the context menu. Leave **Empty Filter** selected and click on **OK**.

3. In the Filter Editor, click on **Public Objects** shortcut in **My shortcut** panel, and double-click on the **Metrics** folder from the list that appears.

4. You will see a list of metrics; double-click on **Sum ProductMargin from FactResellerSales**.

5. The **Filter definition** area is automatically populated with metric qualification. See the **Parameters** group: **Operator** is set by default to **Exactly**. Since we want to see the products with negative profit, we need to select **Less than** in the **Operator** combobox and type 0 (zero) in the **Value** textbox.

6. That's it, click on **OK** and then on **Save and Close**. Name the filter ProductMargin less than zero.

7. Update the schema (we modified the **Product** attribute).

8. Go to **My Personal objects | My Reports**, create a new blank report with the **Product** attribute on rows and **Sum ProductMargin from FactResellerSales** on columns, and then click on the **Public Objects** shortcut, double-click on **Filters**, and right-click on the **ProductMargin less than zero** filter.

9. From the context menu, select **Add to Report Filter** and switch to **Grid View** to see the results.

10. Here's the list of the 121 products losing money, better do something about it; save the report as 09 Non profitable Products.

How it works...

If you look at the SQL view, you will notice the HAVING sum((all.SalesAmount - all. TotalProductCost)) < 0.0 clause. This is the part introduced by the filter on the metric. During the SQL generation process, the filters on attributes and metrics are appended to the SELECT statement sent to the data warehouse.

There's more...

If you right-click on the **Sum ProductMargin from FactResellerSales** header and select **Sort rows by this column | Ascending**, you will get an ordered list starting with the worst product **Touring-1000 Yellow, 60**.

 You can watch a screencast of this operation at:
- http://at5.us/Ch4V5

Creating ranking metrics

Now we know **Touring-1000 Yellow** is to blame; but there are also other underperforming products (so to speak). The bikes Product Manager and the Sales Manager are very curious to know the 10 less profitable products in our shop, in order to review the catalog, and come up with a creative way to cover losses. You are tasked with the "10 most money-losing products of all time" report. How would you do it? Well, yes, sort them and print just the first 10 lines could be an easy fix; but there's a more elegant solution. Use the **Rank** function.

Getting ready

My opinion is that in BI there is not only one "single" solution to reporting requests. Everyone has his/her preferences, we can get to the same results from different path and, as long as the numbers are true, there is no wrong or right way of doing things. There may be different performance issues and different levels of complexity, but the message is: if you can provide the correct number one way or the other it's OK. Do as you feel more comfortable. In this recipe I will show one way to do this, surely it's not the only one, but it gives me the opportunity to show metrics of metrics (nested metrics).

How to do it...

1. Go to **Public Objects | Metrics** and create a new empty one.

2. When the Metric Editor appears, look at the big text area on the right named **Definition**, click on the little button with the **f(x)** label. This will bring up a list of functions.

3. Open the **Select a category** dropdown and click on **Rank and NTile**. From the **Select a function** list, choose **Rank** and click on **Next**.

4. In the **Arguments** window, click on ellipses (**...**) next to **ValueList**. In the dialog that opens, double-click on **Public Objects**, then **Metrics**, then **Sum ProductMargin from FactResellerSales**, and back to the **Arguments** windows click on **Finish**, the definition should look like this screen capture:

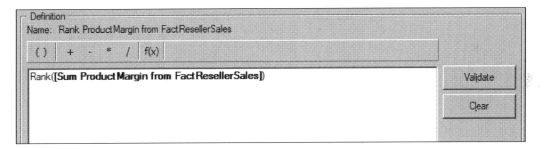

5. Click on **Validate** to check it; if no error appears, click on **Save and Close**.

6. Name the metric Rank ProductMargin from FactResellerSales.

7. Now go to **Public Objects | Filters**, and create a new empty filter.

8. In the Filter Editor, select the **Public Objects** shortcut, open the **Metrics** folder, and double-click on the one we just created.

9. This time we want to filter just the first (top) 10 values of the metric: so modify the **Operator** option to **Less Than or equal to** and set **Value** to 10, click on **OK**.

10. Click on **Save and Close** the filter and name it 10 worst ProductMargins.

11. In **My Personal Objects | My Reports** folder, create a new blank report.

12. Add the **Product** attribute, the **Rank ProductMargin from FactResellerSales** metric, and then add the **Sum ProductMargin from FactResellerSales** metric too.

13. Click on **Public Objects** shortcut, enter the **Filter** folder and right-click on the **10 worst ProductMargins** filter, from the context menu select **Add to Report Filter**. Go to **Grid View**, and sort on the first metric column.

14. Now we have only the 10 less-profitable products and how much money we lost on them, sadly for the PM they're all bikes.

15. Save the report as 10 Less profitable Products.

How it works...

Here we have a Sum metric nested into a Rank metric. The sum of profit margin is first calculated grouping by **Product**, then ranked from bottom to top (negative numbers first). The filter on the Rank metric restricts to the first 10 values of **Rank**.

There's more...

The Rank function assigns numbers from the minimum value going up to the maximum, since we are in the negative profit range the biggest loser is first. If we wanted to rank positive numbers from big to small, like in top 10 selling products, we should have created a metric and edited the rank parameters in the Metric Editor.

Try it yourself:

1. Open the **Rank ProductMargin from FactResellerSales** metric by double-clicking on it.

2. Click on **File | Save As**, and save it with it a different name like Rank ProductMargin from FactResellerSales DESC.

3. In the newly saved metric, highlight with the mouse the formula **Rank([Sum ProductMargin from FactResellerSales])**, and while it is highlighted right-click on it.

4. From the menu that appears, select **Rank parameters**.

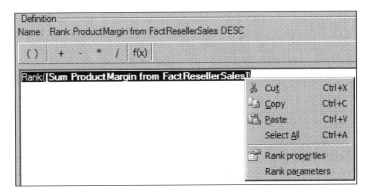

5. This will open a dialog box with three parameters, set the first one **ASC** to `false`, click on **OK** and then on **Save and Close**.

Exercise 19

Create a report with the top five profitable products (as shown in the following image):

Product	Metrics	Rank ProductMargin from FactResellerSales DESC	Sum ProductMargin from FactResellerSales
Mountain-200 Black, 38		1	146,318
Mountain-200 Black, 38		2	136,026
Mountain-200 Black, 42		3	133,379
Mountain-200 Silver, 42		4	116,205
Mountain-200 Silver, 38		5	115,896

 You can watch a screencast of this operation at:
▶ `http://at5.us/Ch4V6`

Grouping at a different level (level metrics)

In every report we did until now, the numbers were always grouped by the attributes in the grid (Report Level). This means that a GROUP BY clause was added at the end of every SELECT including all **ID** forms of those attributes. In other words, the granularity of the report is always the smallest possible with the columns in the grid. Take a report with year, month, and date: the granularity will be at date level. This is the default behavior of metrics, and it is somehow limiting: what if I want to see in the same grid the monthly sales and the yearly sales? Here comes the level metric that allows us to decide the level of aggregation of a number. Sounds interesting, and surely it takes a little getting used to, but they give a great flexibility and together with nested metrics allow the developer to satisfy many reporting needs.

 Before we go on, a slight detour with dates. We have different dates in the fact tables: OrderDate, ShipDate, and DueDate; but we only have a single dimension table DimDate. This poses a classic riddle to the BI developer: how to handle dimension roles. It is not in the scope of this book the discussion about the best modeling solution, you may find a lot of literature and opinions about this. Nevertheless, with MicroStrategy tools, the general wisdom is to duplicate dimension tables with aliases and treat them as separate attributes. For this recipe anyway, we will only focus on OrderDate and forget for a while about the other dates.

Getting ready

We need to specify the FK pointing from the fact table to the dimension table. The FK in this case is the column OrderDateKey. Since the column name is different from the corresponding PK, we need to set it explicitly in the Attribute Editor.

How to do it...

1. Double-click on the **Date** attribute to edit.

2. With the **ID** form selected, click on **Modify**.

3. In the **Modify Attribute Form** window, below the **Expressions** list click on **New**, and in the **Create New Form Expression** dialog select **FactResellerSales** from the **Source table** combobox.

4. Drag the column **OrderDateKey** to the **Form expression** text area, set **Mapping method** to **Manual** and click on **OK**.

5. Now with the **OrderDateKey** expression selected on the left, click on **FactResellerSales** in the **Source table** list and click on **OK**.

6. Click on **Save and Close**, update the schema, and create a report with the **Sum SalesAmount from FactResellerSales** metric and the **Year** attribute. Note down the numbers.

Metrics	Sum SalesAmount from FactResellerSales
Year	
2005	8,065,435
2006	24,144,430
2007	32,202,669
2008	16,038,063

7. Now click on **View | Design View** to modify this report and include the **Month** attribute.

8. See that the numbers are now grouped by **Year** and **Month**:

Year	Month	Metrics	Sum SalesAmount from FactResellerSales
	2005/07		489,329
	2005/08		1,538,408
2005	2005/09		1,165,897
	2005/10		844,721
	2005/11		2,324,136
	2005/12		1,702,945
	2006/01		713,117
	2006/02		1,900,789
	2006/03		1,455,280
	2006/04		882,900
	2006/05		2,269,117
2006	2006/06		1,001,804
	2006/07		2,393,690
	2006/08		3,601,191
	2006/09		2,885,359
	2006/10		1,802,154
	2006/11		3,053,816
	2006/12		2,185,213

9. If we want to have on the same grid another column with the yearly figure, we need to create a level metric. Save this report as `11 SalesAmount by Month`.

10. Go to the **Metrics** folder, right-click on **Sum SalesAmount from FactResellerSales** metric and select **Edit** from the menu.

11. In the Metric Editor, look at the top-right pane and click on **Level (Dimensionality) = ReportLevel**.

12. See that the lower-right part displays a **Level (Dimensionality)** grid with one **Report Level** row.

13. From the left list of attributes, drag **Year** onto the second row of this grid. The upper-right part now says **Level (Dimensionality) = ReportLevel, Year**.

14. Click on **File | Save As** and give this metric a new name: Sum SalesAmount from FactResellerSales (Year Level). Close the editor window.

15. Go back to **My Reports** and right-click on **11 SalesAmount by Month**, then click on **Edit**.

16. In the Report Editor, go to **Public Objects | Metrics** and add the newly created metric to the report by right-clicking on it and choosing **Add to Columns**.

17. Open the **View** menu and select **Grid View**. See the second metric now displays the total aggregated by year.

18. Save the report as 12 SalesAmount by Month and Year.

How it works...

There are two metrics on this report; they both aggregate the SalesAmount column from the FactResellerSales table using the Sum function. The first one (standard metric) is grouping on the smallest level of detail on the grid (Report Level), in this case **Month**: you can see in the SQL view there is a first SELECT statement with a GROUP BY a12. CalendarYearMonth.

The second one (level metric) aggregates at the year level because we set the **Year** attribute in the dimensionality. You can see in the SQL view there is a second SELECT statement with a GROUP BY a12.CalendarYear clause.

There is also another noteworthy component in this report: temporary tables. As the SQL statements begin to complicate, MicroStrategy does an extensive use of temporary tables. You may want to discuss this with your DBA, because you will need CREATE TABLE rights on the data warehouse. Temporary tables are deleted after the successful execution of the reports, see the DROP TABLE command towards the end of the SQL view.

There's more...

We can create level metrics with any attribute we want, for example, a metric at the **Product Category** level or at the **City** level.

As with other metrics we can nest level metrics:

1. Create a new blank metric.

2. In the Metric Editor, go to **Public Objects | Metrics** and from the list double-click on **Sum SalesAmount from FactResellerSales**. Now click on the division (/) operator button or type / in the **Definition** text area.

3. Double-click on **Sum SalesAmount from FactResellerSales (Year Level)**. The definition should look like this:

    ```
    ([Sum SalesAmount from FactResellerSales] / [Sum SalesAmount from
    FactResellerSales (Year Level)])
    ```

4. Click on **Tools | Formatting | Values...** to bring up the **Format Cells** dialog box.

5. Select **Percent** from the **Category** list and click on **OK**. Click on **Save and Close** and name it `Percentage of the Year SalesAmount from FactResellerSales.`

6. Add this new metric to the **12 SalesAmount by Month and Year** report, we now have the total monthly amount, the total yearly amount, and the percentage that every month represents in the year.

 You can watch a screencast of this operation at:
   ▶ `http://at5.us/Ch4V7`

Exercise 20

Create the report `13 Internet SalesAmount by Country and State`:

Country	StateProvince	Metrics	Sum SalesAmount from FactInternetSales	Sum SalesAmount from FactInternetSales (Country Level)	Percentage of the Country SalesAmount from FactInternetSales
Australia	New South Wales		3,934,486	9,061,001	43%
	Queensland		1,988,415	9,061,001	22%
	South Australia		618,256	9,061,001	7%
	Tasmania		239,938	9,061,001	3%
	Victoria		2,279,906	9,061,001	25%
Canada	Alberta		22,468	1,977,845	1%
	British Columbia		1,955,340	1,977,845	99%
	Ontario		37	1,977,845	0%
Germany	Brandenburg		57,919	2,894,312	2%
	Bayern		399,967	2,894,312	14%
	Hessen		662,103	2,894,312	23%
	Hamburg		479,126	2,894,312	17%
	Nordrhein-Westfalen		566,114	2,894,312	20%
	Saarland		729,083	2,894,312	25%

Only the first lines of result data are displayed in the image.

Embedding filters inside metrics

Filters can be used in reports to restrict the result of the entire grid, or can be embedded into a metric to restrict only one particular number. For example, when you want to compare sales during holiday season against the whole year or the margin of one category of product as compared to another category.

If you put a holiday season filter on the report, all the metrics values would be restricted by the WHERE clause; whereas if you put the filter inside one single metric, only those specific values would be filtered, while the rest of the numbers won't be affected.

Getting ready

We need to add a new dimension table and create the **Promotion** attribute. From the **Warehouse Catalog** window, add the table **DimPromotion**, click on **Save and Close**, and create a new attribute with these columns:

- ▶ **ID**: The **PromotionKey** column in the tables **DimPromotion** (lookup) and **FactResellerSales**
- ▶ **DESC**: The **EnglishPromotionName** column in the table **DimPromotion** (lookup)

Save the attribute as Promotion and update the schema.

How to do it...

Next we create a filter:

1. Go to **Public Objects | Filters** and create a new empty filter.
2. In the Filter Editor, from **Attributes** double-click on **Promotion**, when the **Attribute Qualification** panel appears, click on the **Add** button next to **Element List**.
3. In the shopping cart move **Touring-1000 Promotion** to the right and click on **OK**.
4. Click on **OK** again and on **Save and Close**. Name the filter Touring-1000 Promotion only.
5. Now go to the **Metrics** folder and double-click on **Sum SalesAmount from FactResellerSales** to open the Metric Editor.
6. In the upper-right pane, click on a line that says **Condition = (nothing)**.
7. The editor automatically shows the available filters, double-click on **Touring-1000 Promotion**, see that it gets added to the right **Selected condition** pane.
8. Click on **File | Save As** and give a different name: Sum SalesAmount from FactResellerSales (Touring-1000 Promotion). Save and close the editor window.

9. In **My Reports** folder, create a new blank report. From the **Public Objects | Metric** folder, double-click on **Sum SalesAmount from FactResellerSales** and **Sum SalesAmount from FactResellerSales (Touring-1000 Promotion)**, adding the two metrics on the grid.

10. Go to **Grid View** and look at the result: the first metric is the total `SalesAmount`, while the second is filtered and showing only the `SalesAmount` during **Touring-1000 Promotion**.

11. Close the report and save it as `14 Reseller SalesAmount during Touring-1000 Promotion`.

How it works...

If you look at the SQL view, you'll notice two `SELECT` statements, both retrieve `sum(a11.SalesAmount)`, the first with no restriction, and the second with a `WHERE a11.PromotionKey in (14)`. The two numbers are then displayed on the grid. There is no `GROUP BY` clause because we do not have any attribute on the report.

There's more...

The last `SELECT` statement is a `CROSS JOIN` between the two temporary tables. It's OK; they both have one row so the result is correct.

Exercise 21

Add the **Year** attribute to this last report, to have the `SalesAmount` aggregated by year: what happens to the numbers? Can you spot the error?

 You can watch a screencast of this operation at:
  ▶ `http://at5.us/Ch4V8`

Using Metric Join Type in reports

We left the previous recipe with a doubt: where have all the numbers gone? We added the **Year** attribute to the report and the overall reseller sales dropped from 80 million to 32 million. No mystery, it's the standard way of joining metrics. The metrics on a grid are `INNER` joined. What does that mean? And most important, who told MicroStrategy to do so? That means that we have a first metric with values for 2005, 2006, 2007, and 2008, then we have a second metric—filtered on a promotion—that only has data for the year 2007, because that promotion was limited in time during 2007. During the creation of the grid the two metrics are joined on the **Year** attribute, resulting in a single-row report. Let's see how to avoid this inaccurate and dangerous result.

Getting ready

Re-open the **14 Reseller SalesAmount during Touring-1000 Promotion** report, and save it with a new name, for example, `15 Reseller SalesAmount during Touring-1000 Promotion (OUTER)`.

How to do it...

From the **Grid View** of this report:

1. Click on the **Data** menu, and select **Report Data Options**.

2. In the **Report Data Options** dialog, click on **Calculations | Metric Join Type** in the **Categories** list.

3. On the right in the grid that appears open the **Join Type** combobox and select **Outer** for both metrics.

4. Click on **OK** and then **Yes** to re-execute the report.

5. Now the grid shows the correct numbers for `SalesAmount`.

How it works...

By default the numbers are shown on a grid when there is data for all the metrics involved in the report. To override this, we need to set the metric **Join Type** option as **Outer**.

There's more...

There are cases when the metrics should always be OUTER joined, like in this scenario. There is a way to specify the default join behavior on a metric-by-metric basis. Try it yourself:

1. Go to **Public Objects | Metrics** and edit **Sum SalesAmount from FactResellerSales (Touring-1000 Promotion)**.

2. In the Metric Editor, click on the **Tools | Metric Join Type** menu.

3. Uncheck **Use default inherited value**, click on **Outer** and then on **OK**.

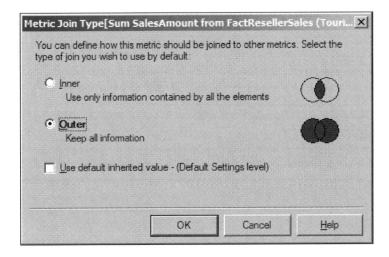

4. Click on **Save and Close**. Now this metric will always be OUTER joined.

More Info

There is a way to set the default value to **Outer** for all the metrics of a project. See Technical Note: *TN5700-7XX-1338* on MicroStrategy support site for more info.

 You can watch a screencast of this operation at:
▸ `http://at5.us/Ch4V9`

Creating a previous month metric (transformation)

Transformations are schema objects, and a very powerful tool that MicroStrategy offers to modify the results of a metric, think about the classic "this month versus previous month" report. But it's not only that. Normally, when the SQL statement is generated, the fact table is joined to the dimension tables using the **ID** forms of the attributes on the grid.

The transformation allows altering the join path between fact and dimension by introducing an extra step. This extra step could be a helper table, or could be a calculation. Think about the `SalesAmount` in the `FactResellerSales` table: when we join the fact to the `DimDate` table on the `OrderDateKey`, we get the amount of sales for that particular day. By introducing a helper table we can alter the date so that we get the same number but with a different date, for example one month earlier.

We will see an example in a moment.

Getting ready

We need to create a helper table to calculate the previous month for every month in the `DimDate` table. Bring up the `sqlcmd` window and type this command (find it in the companion code file):

```
select distinct CalendarYearMonth, CONVERT(VARCHAR(7), DATEADD(month,
-1, FullDAteAlternateKey), 111) PreviousCalendarYearMonth into
DimDateMonthTransform from DimDate
```

```
go
```

This statement creates a new table called `DimDateMonthTransform` with two columns: `CalendarYearMonth` and `PreviousCalendarYearMonth`.

How to do it...

Now we add the new table to the project schema and create the transformation:

1. Go to the **Schema | Warehouse Catalog** menu.

2. Select **DimDateMonthTransform** on the left and add it to the **Tables being used in the project** list, and then click on **Save and Close**.

3. Go to **Schema Objects | Attributes**, double-click on **Month**. Answer yes if prompted to edit.

4. In the Attribute Editor, with the **ID** form selected click on **Modify**.

5. In the **Modify Attribute Form** window check the **DimDateMonthTransform** table in the **Source tables** list.

6. Click on **OK** and then on **OK** again on the warning that appears. Then click on **Save and Close**.

7. Go to **Schema Objects | Transformations**, on the right pane right-click and from the context menu select **New | Transformation**.

8. When the **Select a Member Attribute** dialog appears click on **Month** and hit the **Open** button.

9. Now you're looking at the **Define a new member attribute expression** window. Select **DimDateMonthTransform** from the **Table** drop-down list, and drag the **PreviousCalendarYearMonth** column from the **Available columns** to **Member Attribute expression**, click on **OK**.

10. Click on **Save and Close** and name it `Previous Month`. Update the schema.

11. Now go to **Public Objects | Metrics** and double-click on **Sum SalesAmount from FactResellerSales** to open it.

12. In the upper-right panel there is a line that says **Transformation = (nothing)**, click on it and the lower pane will show a grid named **Transformation**.

13. From the left list drag the **Previous Month** transformation onto the first line of the grid, see that the line above now says **Transformation = [Previous Month]**.

14. From the **File | Save As** menu give it another name like: `Sum SalesAmount from FactResellerSales (Previous Month)` and click on **Save**.

15. Close the editor window.

16. In **My Personal Objects | My Reports**, create a blank new one.

17. Put the **Month** attribute and the two metrics **Sum SalesAmount from FactResellerSales** and **Sum SalesAmount from FactResellerSales (Previous month)** on the **Report View: Local Template** section.

18. Open **View | Grid View** to run the report and see the result. August 2005 has 1,538,408 and 489,329 in the **Previous Month** column.

19. In order to see July 2005 you need to set the metrics as outer joined, from the **Data | Report Data Options | Metric Join Type** menu (see the previous recipe).

20. Once you have the metrics OUTER joined, you can see that the **SalesAmount** for July 2005 was in fact 489,329. Save the report as `16 FactResellerSales SalesAmount Previous Month`.

Congratulations, you have completed this chapter!

How it works...

If you look at the SQL view, you will see that the first column is selected joining **FactResellerSales** to **DimDate** directly on **(a11.OrderDateKey = a12.DateKey)** and grouping on **CalendarYearMonth**. While the second metric is selected joining **FactResellerSales** on **(a11.OrderDateKey = a12.DateKey)** to **DimDate** first and next to **DimDateMonthTransform** on **(a12.CalendarYearMonth = a13.PreviousCalendarYearMonth)**; the number is then aggregated grouping on **CalendarYearMonth** that comes from the helper table, returning in fact the following **CalendarYearMonth**.

When the two datasets are merged on the grid based on the value of the month, the first column shows the current month, while the second column is shifted one row forward.

There's more...

The interesting thing is that you can cascade transformations. If you add an extra **Previous month** transformation to the metric, you get the result of two months ago, and so on. Isn't this exciting? (Not really...)

Creating a **Previous Year** transformation with the **Year** attribute it is even easier. Since year is just a number we don't need a helper table, we simply specify that the transformation is `(Year -1)`.

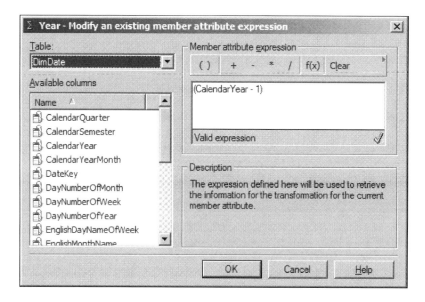

Try it yourself:

1. Create a new transformation based on the **Year** attribute.

2. In the **Member attribute expression** area, type `CalendarYear - 1`.

3. Save the transformation as `Last Year` and create a new **SalesAmount from FactResellerSales (Previous Year)** metric with this transformation, using the original **SalesAmount from FactResellerSales**.

4. In a new report, put the **Year** attribute and the two metrics: **SalesAmount from FactResellerSales** and **SalesAmount from FactResellerSales (Last Year)**.

Exercise 22

Do you see the numbers for year 2005 and 2009? If not, can you tell why and correct?

> You can watch a screencast of this operation at:
> ▸ `http://at5.us/Ch4V10`

See also

▸ The *Going deeper into data with drill down* recipe in *Chapter 5, Data display and manipulation – Reports*

5
Data Display and Manipulation – Reports

In this chapter, we will cover:

▶ Going deeper into data with drill down

▶ Manipulating grids – Pivot and page-by

▶ Dynamically adding and removing objects in reports

▶ The bottom line – customizing subtotals

▶ Avoiding missteps – NULL values in facts

▶ Sorting data in grids

▶ Emphasizing numbers with conditional formatting

▶ Printing and exporting reports

▶ Restricting results with view filters

Introduction

In the previous chapter, we learned how to create different facts and metrics: if you endured the exercises until now, you won the title of "The Fact and the Furious" (as a colleague of mine likes to say...); so we can go on and have a deeper look at how to modify reports and enrich the data.

Before we continue, I'd like to make a little digression; we said already that our job is all about numbers, and we are ultimately responsible for the accuracy and completeness of the results. To reinforce that, I'd say that we don't sell numbers; we sell confidence. We must be trustworthy; otherwise, our best looking dashboard would be useless.

In order to achieve this, it is vital that we always present the totals as they are, without makeup and without euphemisms. Occasionally, in the course of a project, someone may enter your office and ask you to sweeten the pill; after all, a 40 percent loss is just a little more than 20 percent and, compared to last year's data, it could also appear as a growth.

In this case please raise your hands and say: "I'm sorry, I can't do that." Don't be afraid to lose your job. If the company is doing -40%, you will lose it anyway; credibility is our most valuable asset.

Back to the business; let's explore the many ways you can display and manipulate reports.

Going deeper into data with drill down

In BI, when we analyze numbers at a deeper level or at a higher level, we speak about drilling. Going deeper is referred to as drill down and vice versa is called drill up. Sometimes, you may also find the term drill across, which refers to a change in the point of view by moving the perspective to a different dimension (or hierarchy).

MicroStrategy uses hierarchies to drill into data. In *Chapter 3, Schema Objects – Attributes*, we learned how to create a hierarchy from several related attributes: these are called **user hierarchies**. In addition to those, there is a default **system hierarchy** that is created automatically with all the attributes in a project.

So, for example, using the time hierarchy we created before, users can drill down from year to month and month to date. It is a very useful feature and users generally like it; as always, a little training can be useful to not get lost in the map.

Getting ready

You need to have completed the previous chapters to continue.

How to do it...

Let's start by creating a new report with the **Product Category** attribute and the **Sum SalesAmount from FactResellerSales** metric.

Once you have the report in **Grid View**, follow these steps to drill down:

1. Position the cursor on the **Product Category** header; you'll see it changing shape to a cross-arrow pointer.

2. Right-click and select **Drill** from the context menu that appears, then select **Down** from the nested **Drill** menu, now click on **Product Subcategory**.

3. A new report is created automatically with the same metric and the **Product Subcategory** attribute.

4. Now repeat the steps by right-clicking on the **Product Subcategory** header, **Drill |
   Down | Product**.

5. Another report opens with the **Metric** and the **Product** attribute.

6. Close the two new reports without saving them and go back to the original one with
   Product Category.

7. Now click on the category element named **Components**, see that the entire row
   is selected.

8. Right-click on **Components** and, from the context menu, drill down to **Product
   Subcategory**.

9. This new report now shows fewer rows than before: only the subcategories belonging
   to **Components** are displayed.

10. Now right-click on **Handlebars** and drill down to **Product**.

11. Only those products that belong to handlebars subcategory are displayed.

12. Close the two new reports without saving them.

13. In the original **Product Category** report, select **Bikes**.

14. From the **Data** menu, click on **Drill** and the **Drill** dialog box appears.

15. Unfold **Down** in the **Drilling options** tree, and click on **Product Subcategory**.

16. In the **Keep parent** combobox, select **Yes** and hit **OK**.

17. In the new report that appears, both **Product Category** and **Product Subcategory**
    are shown. Select **Mountain Bikes**.

18. From the **Data | Drill** menu, select **Down** to **Product** and set **Keep parent** combobox
    to **Yes**.

19. In the resulting report, there are now three attributes. You can close all those reports
    without saving them.

How it works...

When drilling, it is very important which element is selected: if we drill from an attribute
header, we drill to a new complete report, whereas, if we drill from a specific element of the
attribute (row), we are silently applying a filter on that element so that only children of the
selected row will be displayed.

By enabling the **Keep parent** feature, the new report will maintain the original drilled-from
attribute plus the drilled-to one.

Similarly, you can drill up from a lower-level attribute to its parent. Be careful: the filters are
kept from one report to the other when moving up and down repeatedly and you may end up
with inconsistent numbers.

There's more...

Try the drill across:

1. From the same report with the **Product Category** attribute and the **Sum SalesAmount from FactResellerSales** metric, select the **Bikes** row and right-click on it.

2. From the context menu, select **Drill | Other directions | Time | Year**, as shown in the following screen capture:

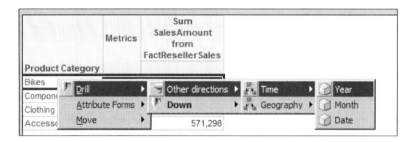

3. You will get a new report with the sales amount by year filtered by the **Bikes** category:

More Info

Your users will love this feature, and some will abuse it. Be sure to explain to them how the parent row filter works or they will drill their way into a spider web of conditions and eventually get tangled in their own exploring routes.

You can watch a screencast of this operation at:
  ▶ `http://at5.us/Ch5V1`

Manipulating grids – Pivot and page-by

A little time ago someone posted a question on a MicroStrategy forum; it was something along the lines of: "Do you think that Excel is the ultimate BI analysis tool?".

The topic did not get a lot of attention, but the question was really legitimate and caught my eye. No matter how fast, interactive, user-friendly, eye-candy, and flash-powered your report is, there will always be a manager asking you to e-mail it in an Excel sheet. We cannot win this battle, I have assumed this, and resigned to the workbook vision of the world.

But, what does a user do with a report when he/she finally gets to squeeze it into a spreadsheet?

Nine times out of ten: a Pivot table!

Getting ready

In this recipe, we will learn how we can use rows, columns, and pages to give our report different shapes. Before going on, we need to add the **OrderDateKey** FK in the **FactInternetSales** table to the **Date** attribute (see the screen capture and update the schema):

Next, create a report containing the following objects:

- ▶ The **Year** attribute
- ▶ The **Product Category** attribute
- ▶ The **Country** attribute
- ▶ The **Sum SalesAmount from FactInternetSales** metric

How to do it...

Now we start to pivot the data:

1. Hover the cursor on the **Year** header, when it changes to a cross-arrow, right-click and, from the context menu, select **Move | To Page-by**.
2. MicroStrategy creates a button with the **Year** attribute that shows 2005.
3. Click on the **Year: 2005** button and select **2007**, the grid now shows 18 rows.
4. Hover on the **Country** header and right-click on it, from the menu select **Move | To Columns**.
5. The countries now appear as columns and the grid shows three rows.
6. Go to **View | Toolbar | Move** to enable the Pivot buttons.
7. On the new toolbar that appears, click on the first button **Swap Rows and Columns**; the grid now shows six rows and the position of the attributes is inverted.
8. Save the report as `17 Internet Sales by Category, Country and Year`.

How it works...

Once the data is retrieved from the database, we can move rows and columns and change their order and position; no additional SQL is generated because these manipulations are handled by the Intelligence Server. The page-by feature is useful in case of very long reports to quickly slice data on one or more attributes. Try the different options yourself by moving columns and rows with the toolbar buttons or by dragging the headers.

There's more...

It is possible to page by metrics also. If you have more than one, you can move them to the page-by section, as shown in the following screenshot:

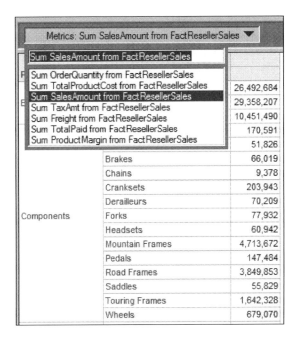

This adds even more flexibility to the grid. Excel users will be delighted...

 You can watch a screencast of this operation at:

> ► `http://at5.us/Ch5V2`

Dynamically adding and removing objects in reports

One of my favorite features of reports in MicroStrategy is called **dynamic aggregation**. As per the product manual, this feature allows you to change the level of report aggregation without having to re-execute the SQL query against the data warehouse. It is part of the product component called **OLAP Services** for which you need an additional license. Thankfully, in the free reporting suite, it comes at no charge.

Getting ready

In this recipe, we will move objects in and out of a very long report grid and see the results. Before going on, we need to modify a default MicroStrategy rule that limits the result set to 32,000 rows.

How to do it...

Follow these steps:

1. Right-click on the name of the project (it should be **COOKBOOK** if you've followed all the chapters) and select **Project Configuration** from the context menu.

2. In the left **Categories** tree list open **Governing Rules | Default | Result sets** and find on the right pane a textbox named **All other reports**, which is usually set to **32000**.

3. Modify this number to 64000 and click on **OK**.

4. Now create a new report with the following objects:

    ❏ The **Sum SalesAmount from FactInternetSales** metric

    ❏ The **Country** attribute

    ❏ The **City** attribute

    ❏ The **Customer** attribute

    ❏ The **Product Category** attribute

    ❏ The **Product Subcategory** attribute

5. Go to **View | Grid View** to run the report, after a while the result will show 44,734 rows.

6. Hover on the **Customer** header and, when the cursor changes to a cross-arrow, click-and-drag the **Customer** attribute to the left part of the screen into the area named **Report objects**.

7. The grid will update immediately and display 4,343 rows. Notice that the metric values are recalculated in accordance to the new grouping, but no SQL is executed.

8. Now click on the **Product Subcategory** header and drag this attribute onto the **Report objects** area, only 947 rows are shown.

9. Similarly, drag to remove the **Product Category** attribute.

10. On the **Report objects** pane, right-click on the **Product Category** and select **Add to Columns** from the context menu; the attribute is added to the grid and the metric is recalculated.

11. In the same way, add the **Product Subcategory** to the columns and drag the **City** attribute to remove it from the grid.

12. Save the report as 18 Dynamic Aggregation by Country and Product.

How it works...

OLAP Services is a component of the Intelligence Server and performs calculations in memory rather than on the RDBMS; hence saving time and network bandwidth. The part responsible for this is called **Analytical Engine**. The results are displayed quickly on the client machine, and—as long as all the needed attributes are present in the **Report objects** list—there is no need to perform any further SELECT statements.

There's more...

When you right-click on an attribute header on the grid, you have two similar options: **Remove from Grid** and **Remove from Report**. See the following screen capture:

Try it yourself: with the **Remove from Grid** option, the effect is the same as dragging it to the **Report objects** list—you're not really removing the attribute and the results are recalculated on the fly. With the second option, **Remove from Report**, you are actually creating a new SQL sentence and running a new query on the data warehouse.

More Info

Other features of OLAP Services include **derived metrics**, **derived elements**, **view filters**, and **In-Memory cubes**. We will see some of them in the next recipes; please refer to the OLAPServicesGuide.pdf in the product documentation for more details.

 You can watch a screencast of this operation at:
  ▶ http://at5.us/Ch5V3

The bottom line – customizing subtotals

It all eventually boils down to a bottom line. With MicroStrategy, you have the option to add several totals and subtotals and have fairly detailed control over them. In this recipe, we'll see how to add grant totals, subtotals, and custom totals.

Getting ready

Say that you have a report like the one in the image:

Product Category	Country	Metrics	Sum SalesAmount from FactInternetSales
Bikes	Australia		8,852,050
	Canada		1,821,302
	Germany		2,808,514
	France		2,553,576
	United Kingdom		3,282,843
	United States		8,999,860
Clothing	Australia		70,260
	Canada		53,165
	Germany		23,565
	France		27,035
	United Kingdom		32,240
	United States		133,508
Accessories	Australia		138,691
	Canada		103,378
	Germany		62,233
	France		63,407
	United Kingdom		76,630
	United States		256,422

You can use the **18 Dynamic Aggregation by Country and Product** report we created in the previous recipe and modify it. If you want to simply add a total on the last line, you'd select the **Data | Grand Totals** menu or press *F11*; if you want to add subtotals by **Product Category**, read on.

How to do it...

We want to add a subtotal at the end of **Bikes**, **Clothing**, and **Accessories**, which is like saying we want a total of all the countries where we sold bikes, all the countries where we sold clothing, and so on.

1. Click on the **Data | Subtotals** menu to bring up the **Subtotal** dialog box:

2. With **Total** selected, click on **Advanced**.

3. In the lower part there is a group named **Applied levels** with the first option **By position** selected. Check the second option: **Across level**, and in the list that appears check the **Country** box (remember we want the total of the countries belonging to bikes).

4. Click on **OK** and then on **OK** again. Now you have the subtotals grouping the **Country** attribute at the end of every category, and no total at the bottom.

5. To add both the subtotals and the grand total, click on the **Data | Subtotals** menu.

6. Click on the **Advanced** button and check the **Product Category** box. Then click on **OK** and then on **OK**.

How it works...

Totals can be added by position (rows, columns, and page) or by level. If you add them by position, they aggregate the entire report and display only one number. If you want a total to display only a partial aggregation, you can add them by level. When totaling by level, you check the box next to the attribute "at the end of which" you want the number to appear. If you check the **Country** attribute the subtotal will appear at the end of the countries belonging to the attribute on the left, in this case, **Product Category**. At first, this may be misleading: but after a couple of reports all the totals will fall into place.

There's more...

Some people like to see **Bikes Total**, **Clothing Total**, and so on; this is very useful in case of long reports where you cannot see the element of the attribute on the left. To do this, we must create what is called a custom subtotal:

1. From the **Data** menu, select **Subtotals**; with the **Total** line selected, click on the **Advanced** button.

2. Uncheck the **Country** attribute and click on **OK** to confirm. Now click again on **Advanced** and hit the **New** button.

3. In the **Custom Subtotal Properties** window, go to the first textbox, remove `New Custom Subtotal` and write `#1 Total`.

4. Hit **OK** and now click on the line that reads **#1 Total** (it has a different icon) to select it.

5. When the **Applied levels** group appears, click on the **Across level** radio button and check the **Country** box.

6. Click on **OK** and then on **OK** again.

7. See that the subtotals now have the name of the category element they belong to.

More Info

There is another very useful setting in the **Subtotals** window. If you click on the **Display Options** tab, you will be able to change the position of the bottom line and set it to be the top line; in case you prefer to see the subtotals at the beginning of each group instead of the end. See the following screen capture:

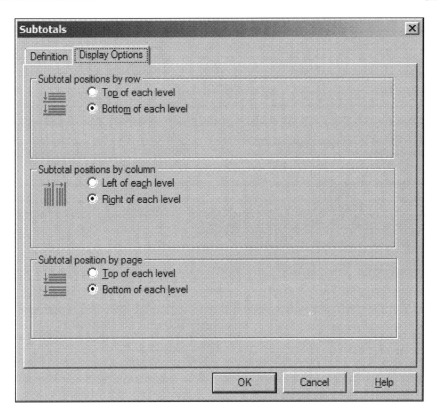

You can watch screencasts of this operation at:

▸ `http://at5.us/Ch5V4`
▸ `http://at5.us/Ch5V5`

Avoiding missteps – NULL values in facts

We learned that with MicroStrategy, it is very easy to create reports that please the Sales Managers who may say "show me the products we have sold on the Internet". But what about the products we did not sell, those we need to remove from the catalog or try to bundle with something else? To find them we first need to learn how to manage the NULL values. In SQL it would be just an OUTER JOIN between the DimProduct and fact table; how to do this in a report?

Getting ready

Create a report with only the **Product** attribute and run it. How many products do we have? Now add the **Sum SalesAmount from FactInternetSales** metric and run it again. How many rows are displayed?

So, we know that we sold 158 out of 606 products in our selection. We need to display the 448 rows of the `DimProduct` table where the value of the metric is `NULL` (actually there is no row in the fact table for those products).

How to do it...

This is done by changing a setting in **Report Data Options**:

1. Open the **Data** menu and select **Report Data Options**.
2. In the window that appears, select **Attribute Join Type** in the **Categories** list and uncheck the **Use defaults** box.
3. A series of radio buttons is now enabled, select the last one which says **Preserve lookup table elements joined to final pass result table based on template attributes with filter.**.
4. Click on **OK** to confirm and answer **Yes** when prompted to re-execute the report.
5. Now the report shows the full 606-product list.
6. Save and close the report, give it the name `19 Products Sales on Internet`.

How it works...

Look at the SQL view to spot the difference. In the first case, with the default setting, the `SELECT` query is:

```
from   FactInternetSales   a11
  join   DimProduct   a12
    on   (a11.ProductKey = a12.ProductKey)
group by   a11.ProductKey
```

In the second case, with the "Preserve lookup table..." setting the query is done in two steps; first step selects the sum of sales amount into a temporary table and the second looks like:

```
from   DimProduct   a11
  left outer join   ##TVP3OQJ22OL000   pa12
    on   (a11.ProductKey = pa12.ProductKey)
```

The `OUTER JOIN` with the dimension table is performed only in the second SQL statement.

There's more...

If you try to add the **Product Subcategory** to this report, you will have a disappointing surprise. Some products disappear from the radar. This is because in the database those products do not have a subcategory, in other words: the FK column `ProductSubcategoryKey` is set to NULL. This is something we should be aware of when dealing with normalized dimension tables. There is the possibility that if the integrity constraints are not enforced, we may lose some elements.

Different data warehouse designers may have different solutions to this problem; my personal philosophy is zero tolerance with NULL in dimension tables. During the ETL phase, I always set the empty FK values to -1 and then add a dummy row to the parent dimension table with -1 as the key and "not available" as description.

Let me stress that this is my personal way of dealing with it, and I found this solution acceptable in most of the projects involving MicroStrategy; nonetheless, another BI professional may have a different approach.

Try this:

1. Modify the **19 Products Sales on Internet** report to include **Product Subcategory** and run it, note that the number of rows is **397**.

2. In a command prompt window, open the `sqlcmd` utility and type the following instructions while using the `AdventureWorksDW2008R2` database (find the command in the companion code file):

```
SET IDENTITY_INSERT DimProductCategory ON


insert into DimProductCategory (ProductCategoryKey,
ProductCategoryAlternateKey, EnglishProductCategoryName,
SpanishProductCategoryName, FrenchProductCategoryName) values (-1,
-1, 'not available', 'no disponible', 'sans objet')
go


SET IDENTITY_INSERT DimProductCategory OFF


SET IDENTITY_INSERT DimProductSubcategory ON


insert into DimProductSubcategory (ProductSubcategoryKey,
ProductSubcategoryAlternateKey, EnglishProductSubcategoryName,
SpanishProductSubcategoryName, FrenchProductSubcategoryName,
ProductCategoryKey) values (-1, -1, 'not available', 'no
disponible', 'sans objet', -1)
go
```

```
update DimProduct set ProductSubcategoryKey = -1 where
ProductSubcategoryKey is null

go
```

3. Run the report again with the **Data | Reexecute Report** menu, this time the row count is **606** and the products without subcategory appear next to the not available element.

With the previous INSERT and UPDATE statements, we created dummy -1 rows in the category and subcategory tables, and set all the NULL foreign keys in the product table to -1.

> You can watch screencasts of this operation at:
>   ▶ http://at5.us/Ch5V6
>   ▶ http://at5.us/Ch5V6a

How to sort data in grids

In a report grid we can sort rows, columns, and page-by elements. To sort on a single column, simply right-click on the header and select **Sort | Ascending** or **Descending** from the context menu that appears. If you want more complex sorting, you can use the **Advanced Sorting** window.

Getting ready

Prepare a new report with the following objects:

  ▶ The **Country** attribute on page-by
  ▶ The **Product Category** attribute on rows
  ▶ The **City** attribute on rows
  ▶ The **Sum SalesAmount from FactInternetSales** metric on columns

Run the report; by default, the cities are ordered alphabetically.

How to do it...

We want to sort the cities in reverse order based on the sales amount inside each category:

1. Go to the **Data | Advanced Sorting** menu.

2. In the **Sorting** window, the **Rows** tab is displayed by default, click on the **Add** button. A new line is added automatically with the leftmost attribute that appears in the grid, in this case **Product Category** and the sort order is set to **Ascending** (you may have to enlarge the columns a little to see the field contents). Leave this row as it is.

3. Click again on the **Add** button to create another line. This time in the column **Sort By**, change the default **City** value to **Sum SalesAmount from FactInternetSales**, and in the column **Order** set the value to **Descending**.

4. Click on **OK** to confirm.

5. Note that the categories are now sorted alphabetically and inside each category the cities are in descending order of sales amount.

6. Save the report as 20 Cities sorted by SalesAmount.

How it works...

The sorting is done by the Analytical Engine on the Intelligence Server, not on the database. Switching to **SQL View**, you can see that the SELECT statement doesn't change (no ORDER BY clause is created).

There's more...

Use the **Sorting** window to order columns or page-by elements also. In this last report, for example, France appears after Germany when looking at the drop-down list. To correct this:

1. Open **Data | Advanced Sorting**.

2. Click on the **Pages** tab.

3. Click on the **Add** button to insert a new line, leave the defaults and hit **OK**.

    Now France appears before Germany.

4. Save and close this alphabetically (and politically) correct report.

 You can watch a screencast of this operation at:
> http://at5.us/Ch5V7

Sorting NULLs

If you try to sort the **19 Products Sales on Internet** report (from the previous recipe) in descending order of sales amount, you'll notice that the nulls are displayed before any other value: sometimes this is not what we'd expect.

In MicroStrategy, null values come first by default; to change that while you're in **Grid View**:

1. Go to **Data** | **VLDB Properties** and expand the **Analytical Engine** folder in the left tree.

2. Click on the **Display Null On Top** option and uncheck the **Use default inherited value** box.

3. Select the first radio button **Display NULL values in bottom while sorting**, as shown in the following screenshot:

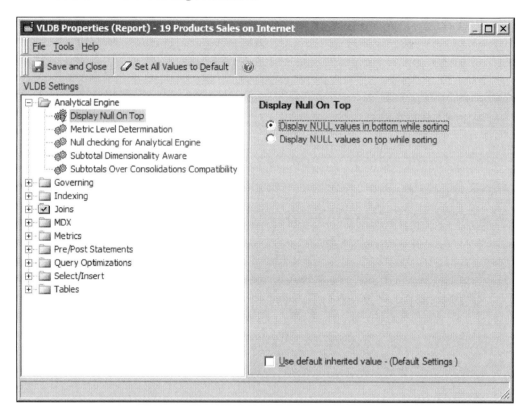

4. Click on **Save and Close**; the report will be re-executed and the NULL values sent to the bottom of the grid.

Emphasizing numbers with conditional formatting

Another useful feature that many analysis tools offer is the ability to color values depending on a condition. In MicroStrategy, these conditions are called **thresholds**.

Getting ready

In this recipe, we will color some cells in the **20 Cities sorted by SalesAmount** report based on the metric value.

How to do it...

Double-click on the report to run it:

1. Click on the **Data | Thresholds...** menu.

2. In the **Thresholds** window, click on the text **New Threshold** and change the name to Less than 4000.

3. Hover the mouse on the **Click here to start a new qualification** link and click on it; the text changes to **Field Operator Value**.

4. Select **Field** and choose the **Sum SalesAmount from FactInternetSales** metric.

5. From the **Operator** list, choose **Less than** and under **Value | Type a value**, enter 4000 and then click on the white text area on the right, where it says **1234.12** to bring up the **Format Cells** dialog.

6. Here, you can apply different colors to different parts of the cell; for example, click on the **Background** tab, open the **Background style** drop-down list and select **Solid**.

7. Then choose a **Fill color** from the palette (for example, **Gold**) and click on the **Font** tab.

8. Here, change the **Color** combobox to red and the **Bold** value to **Yes**, then confirm by clicking on **OK**.

9. Hit **OK** again and the values below 4,000 are now highlighted.

10. We can add as many conditions as we want. Let's make another for the values under 10,000. Click on **Data | Thresholds...** and then on the **New...** button, which looks like a small traffic light in the toolbar.

11. A new condition is added; now rename it `Less than 10000`.

12. Create the condition with the **Sum SalesAmount from FactInternetSales** metric, **Less than**, and type a value of **10000**.

13. In the **Format Cells** dialog, set **Background style** to **Solid** and **Fill color** to **Light Yellow** and in the **Font** tab set **Color** to **Brown** and **Bold** to **Yes**; confirm with **OK** and **OK** again.

14. Now the values between 10,000 and 4,000 arc highlightcd differently.

How it works...

The order of the threshold conditions is important. They are applied starting from the bottom to the top; so that the top rule overrides the bottom one. Try it yourself: in the **Thresholds** window there are arrow buttons in the toolbar to move the conditions up and down the list. See the effect on the report when you change the order of the conditions.

There's more...

Not only can we change the formatting but also replace the value by typing a text or inserting a small image. Think about the green up arrow and the red down arrow in many stock exchange reports. When you click on the **Format** label, a small listbox appears where you can select how to modify the metric value, as shown in the following screenshot:

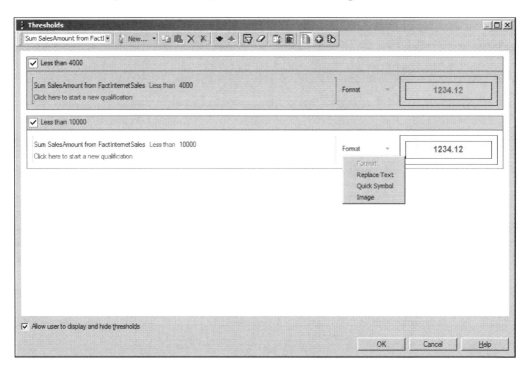

Try to select **Replace Text** and write `underperforming` in the text area on the right.

 You can watch a screencast of this operation at:
▶ `http://at5.us/Ch5V8`

Printing and exporting reports

There are many ways to deliver a report; one of them is the PDF format. The main advantage of PDF is that it can be easily distributed, printed, and most of all cannot be tampered with...

MicroStrategy allows you to export the grid in several other formats including but not limited to Microsoft Word and... yes, Excel.

Getting ready

In order to complete this recipe you need to have Adobe Reader installed on the machine.

How to do it...

Open the **20 Cities sorted by SalesAmount** report, if it's not already open, and follow these steps:

1. Go to **Data | Export To** and select **PDF File** from the nested menu.
2. If you have Adobe Reader installed, you'll see the ready-to-print PDF document; otherwise, the file will be saved in your `%temp%` folder. Notice that the original colors are maintained.
3. Close or minimize Adobe Reader and go to the **Data | Export To** menu; this time select **HTML File**.
4. The report will be opened with your default browser, this time in HTML format.
5. Minimize or close the Internet browser and go to **Data | Export To**. You may select **Text File** and the Notepad would show a tab delimited version of the data.
6. Or you can prefer **Export To | MS Excel** and—if the application is installed—have a look at the data with your favorite spreadsheet software.
7. If you want to print the report, go to the **File | Print** menu.

How it works...

MicroStrategy internally stores report data as XML. It then renders the output to fit the desired format.

There's more...

If you don't want to see the title and description, or the filter details in the exported file, you can open the **Data | Export Options** menu:

1. In the **Export Options** window, select the application that you are using to export, for example, **HTML File**.

2. Click on the **Appearance** tab and in the **Exported fields** list check or uncheck which details you want to appear in the output, see the screen capture:

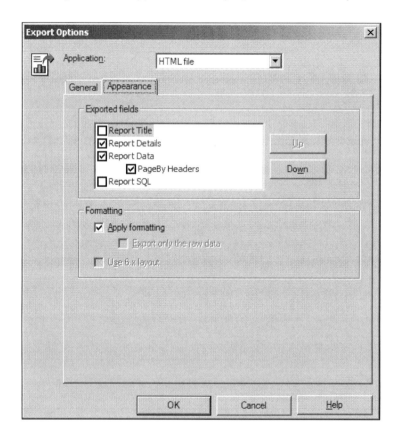

 You can watch a screencast of this operation at:
  ▶ http://at5.us/Ch5V9

Restricting results with view filters

Like dynamic aggregation, view filters are part of MicroStrategy OLAP Services; they are used to reduce the amount of data displayed on the grid without having to re-execute the query on the data warehouse. This means that the filtering is executed in the Intelligence Server memory and it is faster than filtering on the RDBMS side.

When dealing with a large volume of data it may sometimes be tempting to retrieve a full dataset in the first place and then play with view filters on the client side. Please see the Intelligent Cube feature on the OLAP Services guide in this case. In *Chapter 12, In-Memory Cubes and Visual Insight*, we'll see some examples.

Report filters differ from view filters in the fact that they apply a WHERE clause to the SELECT statement and re-execute the report every time a filtering condition is changed. View filters do not.

Getting ready

You should have already created the report **19 Products Sales on Internet**, if not, please go back to the *Avoiding missteps – NULL values in facts* recipe and do it. In that report we wanted to list the products that we did not sell on the Internet; in fact we listed all of them. Now we will complete our analysis by applying a view filter on it.

How to do it...

Run the report and follow these steps:

1. The **View filter** pane should appear right above the grid of the report; if you don't see it, you can activate it from the **View | View Filter** menu.

2. Click on **New** in the gray area, now there are three blue links saying **Field Operator Value**.

3. Use the **Field** link to select the **Sum SalesAmount from FactInternetSales** metric.

4. From the **Operator** link, select **Is Null** and then click on **Apply** in the gray area.

5. The filter is applied and only those products with null sales appear on the grid (total row number should be **448**).

6. Now in order to reverse the filter and display only those products with sales, we need to click on the **Is Null** red link and change it to **Is not Null**.

7. Remember to click on **Apply** every time you modify the condition.

How it works...

The view filter condition is similar to a threshold, and can be used to restrict data based on attributes or metrics. You may also add more than one condition and create very complex view filters by joining them with operators: AND, OR, and more.

There's more...

If you check the box **Auto-Apply changes**, there will be no need to click on the **Apply** button every time the condition is modified. This comes handy in case of quick tests and small datasets, so that you see the immediate effect on results.

Exercise 23

Modify the view filter so that only products with no sales or with sales under 5,000 are shown.

> [You can watch a screencast of this operation at:
> ▶ http://at5.us/Ch5V10]

See also

> ▶ The *Displaying both grid and graph in the same view* recipe in *Chapter 6, Data Analysis and Visualization – Graphs*

6

Data Analysis and Visualization – Graphs

In this chapter, we will cover:

- ▶ Displaying both grid and graph in the same view
- ▶ Drag-and-drop objects using drop zones
- ▶ Beautify your chart
- ▶ Display multiple metrics with dual axis charts
- ▶ Conditional formatting with thresholds

Introduction

Charts have an importance equal, if not major, than reports. They are the first impression of our entire work: an appealing and clearly understandable image can engage the user and transmit a concept much faster than a grid. So, it is very important that, besides having done our homework and verified all the numbers, we create a simple yet effective graphical way of transmitting the information and getting the attention of the reader.

Creating graphs is not easy, at least for me, and sometimes it takes more time than the underlying report itself. But satisfaction is worth the effort: we will see how to modify some of the most common properties and settings in order to paint attractive masterpieces of data imagery.

This chapter is intended as an overview. Of course it's not possible to touch every single type of graph, and I recommend you to read *Chapter 9* of the *Advanced Reporting guide* in the product documentation, for more details.

Another thing I'd like to mention before we continue is that the graphic generation engine inside MicroStrategy is, in fact, an external library licensed from **Three D Graphics, Inc**.

Displaying both grid and graph in the same view

When looking at a report grid you have the option to switch to **Graph View** by clicking on the **View | Graph View** menu.

If you save the report while in **Graph View**, it will be saved as a graph.

Getting ready

We'll start with an easy one; create a report of **Sum SalesAmount from FactResellerSales** by **Country**. Since in the FactResellerSales table we don't have a Country FK, we need to create a Reseller attribute that links the fact table to the Country dimension. At this point, you should already know how to do it. Remember to select the correct columns for the ID and set the Reseller attribute as a child of Country.

How to do it...

Once you have the report on grid view, save it as 21 Reseller Sales by Country, then:

1. From the **View** menu, click on **Graph View**.

2. When the **Graph Type** selection window appears, leave the default **Vertical Bar:Clustered** selected and click on **OK**.

3. From the **File** menu, select **Save As** and give it the name 21 Reseller Sales by Country Graph.

4. Now click on the **View** menu and choose **Grid and Graph View** to see both the tabular data and the vertical bars.

5. From the **View** menu, enable **Toolbar | Move** and then click on the **Swap Rows and Columns** button; you can click on it multiple times and see the difference between having attributes on rows or in columns.

How it works...

When creating graphs we speak about categories and series; as a rule of thumb remember that categories correspond to the rows of the report and are pictured on the X axis, while series correspond to the columns of the grid and are pictured on the Y axis. Depending on the type of graph, you may need more than one attribute or more than one metric. See the manual for the requirements of each different graph.

If the graph is not showing what you expected, sometimes it is necessary to pivot the data, and here the **Grid Graph View** and the button on the move toolbar come in very handy. See what I mean in the following image:

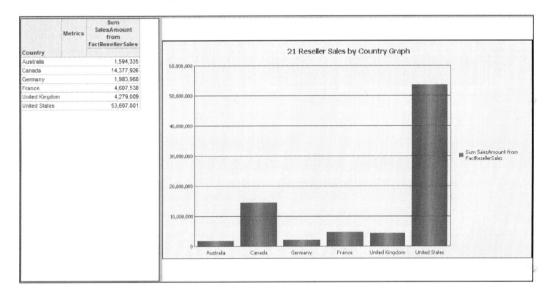

There's more...

By default MicroStrategy sets the colors by series, which means, in our case, when the Country attribute is on the rows and there's only one metric, the bars are all blue. There is a setting to invert this behavior and have the bars colored by category:

1. Click on **Graph | Graph Options** menu to bring up the **Preferences** window.

2. In the left **Properties Category** tree, select the **Vertical Bar Options | Display**, (see the following screen capture):

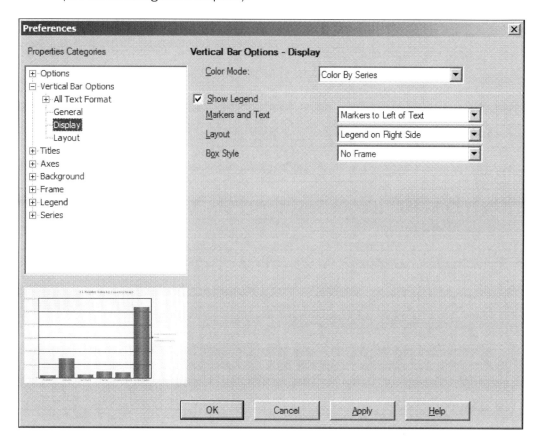

3. Modify the value of the **Color Mode** dropdown from **Color by Series** to **Color by Categories**.

4. Click on **Apply**, now the bars have different colors based on the value of the **Country** attribute.

More Info

When switching the **Color Mode** to categories, please note that the **Legend** does not reflect the change and it's now misleading; you may want to remove it. In the same **Property Category** as the **Color Mode** there is a checkbox labeled **Show Legend**, deselect it and click on **OK**.

 You can watch a screencast of this operation at:

> ► `http://at5.us/Ch6V1`

Drag-and-drop objects using drop zones

We said that the categories correspond to the rows of a report and the series to the columns. While in **Grid Graph** mode, it is easy to pivot the objects, yet the real estate for the graph is somewhat limited, especially in the case of very large reports.

Meet the drop zones: they are a valuable tool when it comes to position the attributes in their place. The previous chart had one attribute and one metric. The next one will complicate things a little by adding a time dimension.

Getting ready

We need a report with **Sum SalesAmount from FactInternetSales** grouped by **Product Category** and by **Month**. You can put the attributes on rows and the metrics on columns; we'll adjust them in a moment.

How to do it...

Here's how to use the drop zones:

1. Run the report in **Grid View**, then click on **View | Graph View** menu.

2. When the **Graph Type** window appears, click on **Line** in the left listbox, the **Vertical** tab is automatically selected. Now choose the first type (**Vertical Line:Absolute**) and click on **OK**.

3. The image that appears is not very useful, is it? We'd better move the **Product Category** to series in order to have each category in a different color.

4. Look for a button in the toolbar whose tool tip says **Show Drop Zones**, it looks like the one in the following icon:

5. When you click on it, you'll see three areas appear on the sides of the graph. They show the objects that are pictured on the chart and allow you to move them from one zone to the other.

6. Pick **Product Category** with the mouse and drag it from the **Categories** zone to the **Series** zone, dropping it below the **Metrics** box.

7. Now the image changes and there are three lines one for each **Product Category**, the **Legend** reflects the change and the image starts looking like something useful, yet there is space for improvement.

8. The legend is very confusing with the name of the metric and the product category; so we click on the **Data | Report Data Options** menu.

9. In the **Report Data Options** window we select **Display | Alias** from the tree on the left.

10. There is a grid named **Object Alias Settings** with two columns: **Object** and **Alias**. In the row corresponding to **Sum SalesAmount from FactInternetSales**, we click in the **Alias** column and type a blank space.

11. The blank space is practically invisible so when we click on **OK** and re-execute the report, the **Legend** will display only the product category names.

12. In order to tell the user which metric we are looking at, we modify the graph title. Right-click on the title, it may be something like **New Report (n)** and from the context menu that appears select **Titles...**.

13. In the **Preferences** window, modify the **Title** textbox from `{&REPORTNAME}` to `Sales Amount from Internet`.

14. Now it looks better and we can save it as `22 Internet Sales by Product Category and Month`.

How it works...

Drop zones are a useful tool to help fine tune the aspect of a graph. When it comes to charts I personally have a theory: only the information that is needed and the least possible information. We don't want the user to stare at a **Miró** masterpiece (`http://www.todocuadros.com/tienda/pinturas-abstractas/fantasia-miro`) and call us for support.

There's more...

The data markers, while useful, are sometimes too crowded for my taste. That is why I tend to remove when they're not badly needed, or at least to reduce their size:

1. From the **Graph | Graph Options** menu, expand **Series** on the left tree: here you have **Bikes**, **Clothing**, and **Accessories**. We can enable or disable data markers independently for each product category.

2. Click on **Bikes** and on the right uncheck a box labeled **Show Markers on Line**.

3. Click on **Clothing**, leave **Show Markers on Line** checked but decrease the **Marker Size** to `20`.

4. Click on **Accessories**, leave the default values and change **Marker Shape** to `Circle`.

5. When you confirm with **OK**, the graph will be updated accordingly.

You can watch screencasts of this operation at:

▸ `http://at5.us/Ch6V2`

▸ `http://at5.us/Ch6V3`

Beautify your chart

In the previous recipe we created a vertical line graph, simple but effective. There is still something that we can do to smooth edges, improve the readability, and make it more pleasant for the eye.

Getting ready

We run the **22 Internet Sales by Product Category and Month** graph, and save it as `23 Bikes Internet Sales by Month`. Next, we apply a view filter to the graph. We learned in the previous chapter how view filters work; we can add one to this dataset so that only the bikes are displayed. If you don't see the **View Filter** area click on the **View | View Filter** menu, and create a new one with the condition `Product Category In List {Bikes}`.

How to do it...

And now we start the aesthetic process:

1. First thing the background; click inside the graph on an empty area, close to the border so that the edge changes from continuous line to dashes. Once you have the background selected you can right-click and choose **Format Background...** from the context menu.

2. In the **Preferences** window, change the **Color** dropdown to **White** and click on **Apply**.

3. In the left **Properties Categories** tree, select **Frame** and change the **Color** selector to **White** and click on the **Apply** button.

4. Now go to the top of the **Properties Categories** tree and select **Options**.

5. Towards the end of the right pane there is a checkbox labeled **Enable curved lines**, check it and click on **Apply**. Now confirm with **OK**.

6. On the top left of the frame right-click on the first value of Y, should be **2,000,000** and select **Format Y1 Axis Label**. When the **Preferences** window appears, click on **Number Formatting** on the left tree; now set the **Category** listbox to `Fixed`, **Decimal places** to `zero`, uncheck **Use Thousand separator**, and choose the value `Thousands` in the combobox labeled **Abbreviation**.

7. Click on **Apply** and notice that the number now shows 2000K. Without leaving the **Preferences** window, go to **Axes | Category | Grids and Scales** in the left tree.

8. Enable both **Show Major** and **Show Minor**, leaving the defaults **Regular Grid** and **Inner Ticks** respectively; enable **Use Manual Number of Categories** and set **Between Gridlines** to 2. **Apply**.

9. In the left tree move to **Major Gridlines**, set the **Color** to `Grey-50%`, **Apply** and do the same for **Minor Gridlines**. Click on **Apply** and then on **OK**.

10. The X axis labels sometimes get too close to each other and look cluttered, especially in large datasets. We can add space between them by showing just one every three or four values, to give more breath to the horizon. Do this by clicking on the **Set Layout to Manual** button on the toolbar, like the one shown in this icon:

11. Now right-click on one X axis value and select **Grid and Scales** from the context menu. In **Axes | Category | Axis Labels**, click on the radio button labeled **Use Manual number of Categories** and set **Between Labels** number to 3 (or 4 or 5 depending on the size of your screen).

12. The legend is now useless since we only have one series of data; hide it clicking on the **Show Legends** button on the toolbar. You can modify the title to read **Bikes Sales Amount from Internet Sales**.

13. And lastly—since we're touching the title—we can click on it and drag it inside the graph area. You can position it where you like, resize, or modify the background box color, as you please. It looks better now, doesn't it:

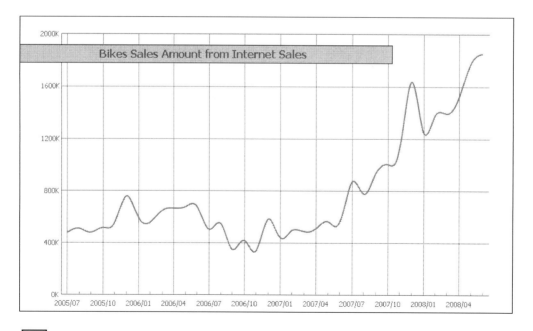

How it works...

There are plenty of options in the **Graph Preferences** window, and it is easy to get lost. Look in the help (*F1* key) of the application for some clues, or just try changing a value and see the effect on the chart. As they say, some days of trial and error can save you minutes of reading the manual.

There's more...

If you'd like to read more, there is a very good article about graphs at `http://www.microstrategyblog.com/2013/02/how-i-like-my-microstrategy-graphs/`.

I totally subscribe what the author says.

 You can watch a screencast of this operation at:
  ▶ `http://at5.us/Ch6V4`

Display multiple metrics with dual axis charts

There are cases when I need to display two metrics on one single graph; the matter gets complicated if the two have very different values, such as an absolute number and a percentage, or—generally speaking—when the values of one metric fall in a range different from the values of the other. We have seen that most of the times the numbers are displayed as series on the Y axis; so we have a minimum number and a maximum number on the left vertical margin of the graph (Y1). If the second metric has minimum and maximum values that do not fall into the first metric range, we can create a second Y axis and have the new minimum and maximum values displayed on the right margin of the chart (Y2). Let's see it with a practical example. We want to picture the sales amount from the resellers and the real product margin that each category of products has scored. We know from the previous chapters that we lost money on `Bikes`...

Getting ready

Create a new report with the following objects:

  ▶ The **Product Category** attribute on rows
  ▶ The **Sum SalesAmount from FactResellerSales metric** on columns
  ▶ The **Sum ProductMargin from FactResellerSales metric** on columns

When you run it in the grid view you'll see that the numbers are different from each other: the first column ranges from 521K to 66M while the other has a negative minimum value.

How to do it...

In **Grid View**, select **View | Graph View** menu:

1. From the **Graph Type** window, choose the default **Vertical Bar:Clustered** and click on **OK**.

2. The resulting graph is not very meaningful; the losses on bikes are barely visible. So, we go to the **Graph | Graph Type** menu.

3. In the **Graph Type** window, we scroll down the **Vertical** tab and select the next-to-last one **Vertical Bar:DualAxis Absolute**.

4. In this case we have a double grid: horizontal blue lines correspond to numbers on the right and the black to the numbers on the left. Now it is easier to spot the losses but still difficult to read, so we bring up the **Graph Type** window once again.

5. This time, we select the last **Vertical** type labeled **Vertical Bar:Bipolar Absolute**.

6. The two metrics are now pictured one above the other, with the horizontal lines clearly pointing to the left and right axis labels.

How it works...

In MicroStrategy, the first metric is the one that is used to generate the left Y labels; in our example from 0 to 70M. The second column is then scaled to fit into this range. Clearly, smaller numbers are likely to disappear. So we use a dual axis graph, with Y1 labels on the left and Y2 labels on the right, and the two sets of columns proportional to their own scales. In this particular chart, there is an added complication: the negative `Bikes` value. We need space below zero to create the `Product Margin` columns, so we choose another type of dual axis graph, where we have two zero baselines, generating actually two separate bar charts one above the other.

There's more...

Try this:

1. Go to **Graph | Graph Options** menu and select **Vertical Bar options | Dual Y Options** from the left tree.

2. There is a shopping cart with a button in the middle labeled **<>**, click on it and then **Apply**.

3. See that the order of the metrics is inverted; now **Product Margin** has more importance and drives the left labels.

4. Now move the **Split Position** slider to `30` and click on **Apply**.

5. See now the upper bars have more vertical space than the lower ones.

By playing with these two settings you can give more visibility to one metric and try to draw attention to the most important numbers; see the following image:

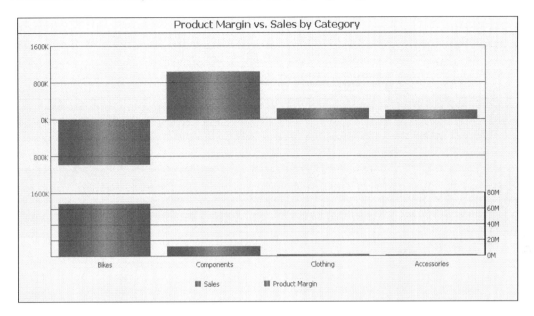

 You can watch a screencast of this operation at:

> `http://at5.us/Ch6V5`

Conditional formatting with thresholds

Data in graphs can be sorted the same way as we sort a grid (with the **Data | Advanced Sorting** menu). Take the previous recipe as an example: if you sort the data by **Product Category**, you will see the **Accessories** bar in the first place on the left.

We can also apply conditional formatting to the color of the series by using thresholds.

Getting ready

You should have completed the previous recipe to continue.

How to do it...

Let's see an example; say that you want the negative values of **Product Margin** to shout out loud in your chart:

1. Run the **24 Product Margin vs. Sales Amount by Category** report.

2. Once the chart appears, click on menu **Data | Thresholds**.

3. In the **Thresholds** window the **Sales** metric is selected by default and an empty condition is created. We need to remove this one before going on, so click on the small button labeled **Delete** on the toolbar, the one that has an **X** icon like the this:

4. Answer **Yes** to the message asking you if you want to delete the threshold **New Threshold** and open the drop-down list at the top-left corner of the window.

5. Select **Product Margin** and then click on the semaphore **New...** button next to it, a new blank condition is created.

6. Click on **New Threshold** to rename it and type `Negative Margin`.

7. Then using the **Click here to start a new qualification** link, set the condition to:

    ❑ **Field**: **Product Margin**

    ❑ **Operator**: **Less Than**

    ❑ **Value**: Type a value and enter `0`

8. Now click on the white **1234.12** textbox on the right to bring up the **Format Cells** dialog.

9. On the **Background** tab open **Background style** and select **Solid**.

10. In **Fill color** choose black and confirm with **OK**.

11. You are back to the **Thresholds** windows, look at the toolbar and click on the third button from the right, the one that resembles a ruler (the tool tip on the button says **Apply the thresholds on metric values only**) similar to the this icon:

12. When you click on it, the button on the left (tool tip: **Enable threshold on Graph**) changes to enabled. Now click on this one that looks like a small graph to activate the conditional formatting on the chart:

13. Close this window by clicking on the **OK** button, now the negative **Profit Margin** for **Bikes** is black.

    If you like simple and plain graphs with no 3D rendering you can switch off the rounded effect this way.

14. From the **Graph** menu, go to **Graph Options**.

15. Select **Options | General** on the left.

16. Towards the end of the window see a checkbox labeled **Apply rounded effects to all series**, click to unselect it and press **OK**.

    The image is now flat 2D. Now let's change the bar colors to make it "funkier".

17. There is a button in the toolbar as shown in the following icon, its tool tip says **Color Palettes**:

18. If you click on the button, nothing happens (ouch!); you should instead click on the extra-small downward arrow on the right of the button. From the list that appears, click on **Metro**.

Ain't it funky now?

How it works...

To change the color of a series conditionally, remember to set the threshold on the correct metric. Only the background color setting is used.

There's more...

You can create very good pictures with a little patience, taking advantage of the transparency settings:

1. Right-click on a bar and select **Format Bar Riser...**.

2. Set the **Transparency** slider to something lower than 100, like 50 or so.

3. Click on the **Bevel** button and select **Sphere** from the **Bevel Type** dropdown.

4. Set **Light Angle** to 90, click on **OK** and then on **OK** again.

5. Similar settings exist for the background and the frame of the chart.

 You can watch a screencast of this operation at:
   ▶ http://at5.us/Ch6V6

Exercise 24

With some time and practice you can create tasty pieces of art like this one:

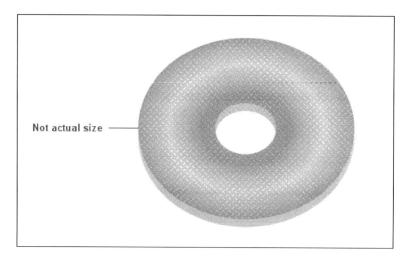

Not actual size

See also

▶ The *Setting up MicroStrategy Web* recipe in *Chapter 7, Analysis on the Web – Documents and Dashboards*

7

Analysis on the Web – Documents and Dashboards

In this chapter, we will cover:

- ▸ Setting up MicroStrategy Web
- ▸ Creating your first "Hello World" document
- ▸ Adding data to a document – the dataset
- ▸ Modifying the grouping in a document
- ▸ Stepping up to dashboards
- ▸ Using the editable mode to fine-tune the design
- ▸ Adding interactivity with panels and selectors
- ▸ Embedding images, HTML, links
- ▸ Switching to the Adobe Flash mode

Introduction

We are halfway through our journey in MicroStrategy Suite. During the preceding chapters we learned the basics of creating projects, reports, and graphs. It's time to step up and see the results of our work on the Web; after all, the vast majority of our users are consuming data via some sort of Internet browser.

MicroStrategy has a web interface, which is quite powerful and allows the user to explore the data in many different ways; unlike the Desktop application that has a fairly traditional look (very "VisualBasish"), the web interface is changing with every major release of the product. More features are added and the trend is to mimic the modern data discovery tools nowadays on the market.

While this is perfectly understandable, I would prefer to consider MicroStrategy as a complete enterprise-oriented BI suite, not just another Flash-based colorful Pivot table. But that's my personal point of view.

As I am writing, the Version 9.3.1 is generally available, with some important changes that please the non-IT user by steering the focus onto the **Visual Insight** part of the system, which we'll cover in *Chapter 12, In-Memory Cubes and Visual Insight*.

During the course of this book—anyway—I'll continue using the Version 9.3.0 to be consistent with what we have learned until now.

When I started writing the skeleton of the book, Version 9.3.0 was brand new; so apparently I am writing at a slower speed than they code, I blame the word processor for this.

Setting up MicroStrategy Web

The **Web Universal** (as it is called) has no particular requirements, other than IIS or a J2EE application server. Remember from the setup that there are actually two types of web interfaces, one is .NET based for the Windows world, and the other one is a set of Java servlets that run pretty well in most of the Java Containers (I personally use Tomcat, but it can run on WebLogic, WebSphere, JBoss, you name it).

Getting ready

Since we are using Windows as an operating system, we'll rely on IIS. One thing worth noting is that you need to be logged into the operating system using `Administrator` and the administrator's password must be set (that is, no blank password). Configuring an Internet Information Server is beyond the scope of the book, but if you followed the instructions in *Chapter 1, Getting Started with MicroStrategy*, I'm confident there is nothing more to do.

As a further measure, if you're superstitious like I am, you can disable the **Internet Explorer Enhanced Security Configuration** for the administrators, as we can see in the following screen capture:

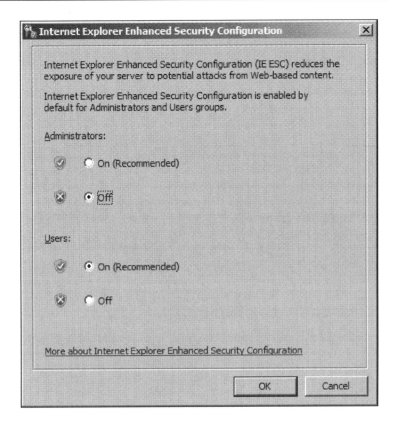

Refer to the operating system manual for details.

I don't think it has anything to do with the IIS but you never know; by the way we're in a test machine, of course we wouldn't do it in a production environment, would we?

How to do it...

Follow these steps to configure the connection between MicroStrategy Web and the Intelligence Server:

1. Log on to the operating system using Administrator (with password).

2. From the **Start | All programs** menu, go to **MicroStrategy | Web** and select the icon named **Web Administrator**.

3. This will open **Internet Explorer** and direct you to the admin page on localhost.

4. When prompted, type Administrator as **User name** and the corresponding password. These are the Windows operating system credentials not MicroStrategy ones. Check **Remember my password** (if you want) and click on **OK**.

5. If you see a **Microsoft Phishing Filter** window, just choose the most dangerous **Turn off automatic Phishing filter** and click on **OK**.

6. If you see an **Information Bar** message, check **Don't show this message again** and click on **Close**.

7. If you see a yellow bar on top of the Internet Explorer window saying that **Intranet setting are now turned off by default**, click on it and select **Enable Intranet Setting** and confirm that **Intranet settings use a less secure level** by clicking on **Yes**. As a result, we now have a pretty insecure machine: as said earlier, this is a learning environment, not a production one.

8. In this admin page, we need to input the name of the Intelligence Server that we configured in *Chapter 1, Getting Started with MicroStrategy*. If you did those recipes following all the steps, this is the same name of the physical machine (hostname).

9. To find the machine name, we use a command prompt window: go to **Start | Run**, type cmd and hit **OK**.

10. In the black window that appears, type hostname.

11. Copy the output to the clipboard and paste it into the **Add a server manually** textbox inside Internet Explorer, then click on **Add...**.

12. When the **Server properties | Connection Properties** show up, click on the radio button **Automatically connect to Intelligence Server when Web Server or Intelligence Server is restarted**.

13. Click on **Save**. That's it! You're back to the **Connected Servers** list and a new server name displays the machine you have just connected. You can close Internet Explorer.

How it works...

This procedure is needed only the first time we configure a machine. If we checked the **Automatically connect...** option, MicroStrategy will keep the Web Server and the Intelligence Server in contact and reconnect them if needed. This operation must be done with the operating system administrator user due to restrictions on the Web Admin page.

Now the Web tier is able to connect to the Intelligence Server, which in turn reads the metadata that holds information about all the projects available in the platform.

There's more...

Check the successful outcome of the operation by opening the MicroStrategy Web:

1. From the **Start | All programs** menu, go to **MicroStrategy | Web** and select the icon named **Web**.

2. This time, Internet Explorer opens the main Web Interface page, and this can take a while, because IIS has to compile a series of .NET resources.

3. When completed, the page shows the projects present in the metadata, in our case only one: **COOKBOOK**.

 You can watch a screencast of this operation at:
  ▸ http://at5.us/Ch7V1
  ▸ http://at5.us/Ch7V2

More Info

You can log off from the administrator account and continue with your standard user.

Creating your first "Hello World" document

MicroStrategy documents can be considered as HTML pages; they're very complex at times, but still they belong to the Web world. We will see that it is also possible to use HTML tags in them. In a document we can represent various objects, and use data from different reports and graphs.

With the Desktop application we were limited to one grid or graph at a time; with MicroStrategy Web there is no such limitation and we have the possibility to put several datasets on a single page plus images, shapes, links, and HTML code.

Documents have different visualization modes: as with reports, we create and modify objects in **Design View**, while the users will consume the data in **Interactive View**. In fact, there are more types of views, but for the moment let's remember those two: Design and Interactive.

Getting ready

Enough said, let's get our hands dirty and create a very simple document. You need to have all the schema objects and all reports from the previous chapters to continue.

How to do it...

Start the Web Interface:

1. From the **Start | All Programs** menu, go to **MicroStrategy | Web** and select the icon named **Web**.

2. If prompted for a username and a password, type the operating system account that you used to log in. Optionally check **Remember my password** and click on **OK**.

3. If you see an **Information Bar** message, check **Don't show this message again** and click on **Close**.

4. If you see a yellow bar on top of the Internet Explorer window saying that **Intranet setting are now turned off by default**, click on it and select **Enable Intranet Setting** and confirm that **Intranet settings use a less secure level** by clicking on **Yes**.

5. You are now looking at the **WELCOME MicroStrategy 9** page, click on the **COOKBOOK** project icon to go to the login page.

6. Type Administrator in the **User name** textbox and the metadata password. These are the MicroStrategy credentials not the operating system ones and press the **Login** button.

7. You are now in the **Home page** of the **COOKBOOK** project. Notice that there are several folders similar to the Desktop application: **My Reports**, **Shared Reports**, and so on.

8. Scroll down a bit and click on the **Create Document** icon, see the following image, and you will be redirected to the **Create Document** page:

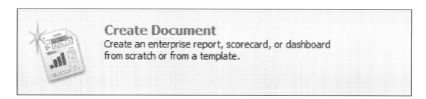

9. Here we have several templates. Scroll down to the section named **Document Templates** and click on **Blank Document**, as shown in this image:

10. We're in the Document Editor: there is a **Dataset Objects** pane on the left and the **Layout** area on the right. See that the **Layout** is divided into sections: **Page Header**, **Document Header**, **Detail Header**, and so on. (refer to the *How it works...* section for details).

11. Click on the **Detail Header** gray title to select the section. Look at the **Insert** menu, see that there's a very small arrow shaped icon next to it? Click on the arrow to open the menu and choose the first option labeled **Text**:

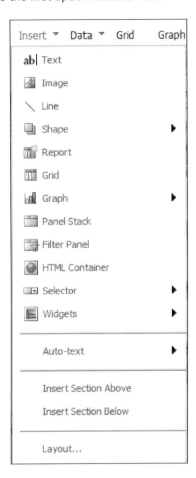

12. The cursor changes its shape to a cross. Now click on the white empty part of the **Detail Header** section and drag the mouse to design a rectangle.

13. When you release the mouse button, the focus is inside the textbox and you can type `Hello World` in it.

14. Now click on the small arrow icon next to the **Format** menu and select **Properties and Formatting....** This will bring up a dialog like the one in the following screen capture, where you can modify several textbox settings:

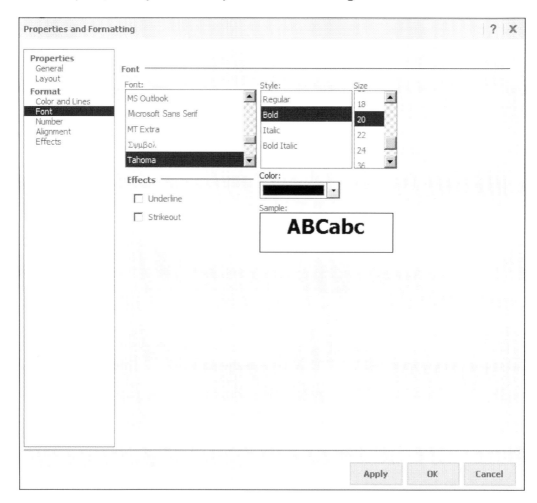

15. Look on the left and click on **Format | Font** in the left list. On the right pane, set the **Size** to **20** and the **Style** to **Bold**.

16. Click on **OK** to confirm and you'll see the newly created textbox with a bigger font.

17. Now look at the toolbar and click on the interactive mode button (tool tip: **Interactive Mode**). It's right next to the design mode button, which is now depressed.

18. The document is executed and you will be shown the result: a blank page with the **Hello World** text, not extremely useful, but it's a start.

19. From here click on the first button on the toolbar named **Save As...** and name the document `25 Hello World Document`. Click on **OK**.

20. When prompted select **Run newly saved document** and you'll be back to the **Hello World** page.

How it works...

MicroStrategy documents have several different sections and it is important to understand how they work:

- **Page Header**: appears at the beginning of every page; use it to write page numbers or the name of the company.

- **Document Header**: appears only once at the beginning of the document. If there is more than one page, the page header is repeated but the document header is not; use it to write the name of the document, a description, or an address.

- **Detail Header**: appears only once right before the details; use it to display column headers or aggregated values.

- **Detail**: appears as many times as there are rows in the underlying dataset; for example, if you have a report of 10 rows, the detail section is repeated 10 times; use it to display single values.

- **Detail Footer**: same as the detail header but after all the detail rows; use it for the bottom line totals.

- **Document Footer**: same as the document header but at the end; use it to write additional information such as data source, disclaimers, or KPI descriptions.

- **Page Footer**: similar to the page header; use it for copyright notices or any other small piece of information at the end of each page.

There's more...

The documents section can be enabled or disabled. If you do not need all of them, as often happens, you can prevent the section from displaying. While in the design mode, open the **Tools | Sections** menu. Here, you can check and uncheck as needed. See the following screen capture:

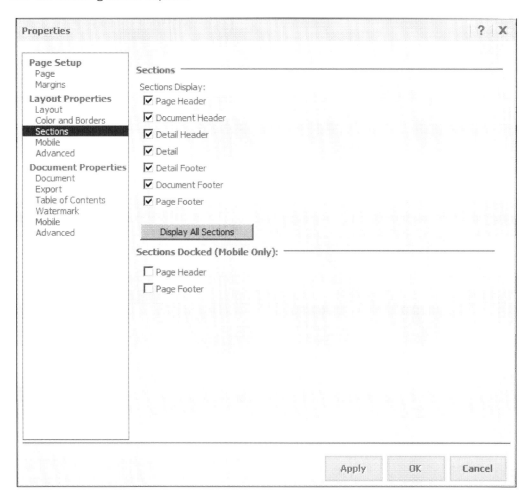

Please note that at least one section must be present, otherwise you'll get an error.

Try this: uncheck all sections but **Detail Header**. You still have your **Hello World** text and nothing else.

You can watch a screencast of this operation at:
> ▶ `http://at5.us/Ch7V3`

By default, when running the document, sections will be hidden if empty (that is, they have nothing to display), even if they are enabled in the **Tools | Sections** dialog. To override this behavior, in design mode right-click on a section header, open the **Properties and Formatting...** dialog, go to **Properties | Layout** and uncheck the **Hide if Empty** option.

Adding data to a document – the dataset

In our "Hello World" document we used a string constant to greet our users. While some of them may find this polite, it is bluntly useless; now it is time to give some more information, and we will add a report to the document to display real numbers.

When creating documents we speak about **datasets**; a report is a dataset, a graph is also a dataset, and we said that a document can be based on more than one dataset.

Before going further, I would like to clarify a point and give my own point of view: the document datasets do not have to be pre-existing reports. We can build them specifically for the sole purpose of document creation. And it is perfectly acceptable: let me explain.

There is something that happens every now and then in MicroStrategy projects. First, we create reports (many of them, with different levels of aggregation and filters); then we try to fit as much information as possible into a document. In the case of small sets of data this is usually not a problem, but with millions of rows, the result can be suboptimal performance. By suboptimal I mean that your users would not receive data in a "Go grab a cup of coffee" timeframe.

Putting many datasets into the same document causes extra work to the Intelligence Server, because it has to join every single one using common attributes and produce a resulting ultimate mega dataset (called **virtual dataset**). If there are no attributes in common between two or more reports, the ultimate mega dataset would contain a Cartesian product, which we want to avoid.

Speaking about the Cartesian product, I always remember a scene from the 1984 movie Ghostbusters:

Dr. Spengler: "There's something very important I forgot to tell you."

Dr. Venkman: "What?"

Dr. Spengler: "Don't cross the streams."

Dr. Venkman: "Why?"

Dr. Spengler: "It would be bad. [...] Try to imagine all life as you know it stopping instantaneously and every molecule in your body exploding at the speed of light."

Dr. Stantz: "Total protonic reversal."

Dr. Venkman: "Right. That's bad. Okay. All right. Important safety tip."

So, in order to avoid the total protonic reversal in our document, we may consider creating a single dataset with only the columns that we will effectively use, not more not less, Dr. Spengler docuit.

Getting ready

We start by creating an ad hoc report for the next document. This report has `Product Category`, `Product Subcategory`, and `Sum SalesAmount` from `FactInternetSales`. Save the report as `26 InternetSales by Product and Subcategory`.

How to do it...

Once you have the report created (no totals needed) you can follow these steps:

1. If you're still on the **Hello World** document, click on the red star MicroStrategy logo on the top-left corner of your browser. See the following icon:

2. From the menu that appears select **Home** to return to the main project page.

3. Now click on **Create Document** and next, choose the **Blank Document** template.

4. We have a blank layout with an empty dataset. In the empty area on the left, click on the **Please click on the button to add a dataset** icon, see the following screen capture:

5. When the **Select Dataset** window appears, open the first combobox that shows **Shared Reports** and select **My Reports**. The **Available** list below shows all the reports in the directory. Scroll down and pick the number 26.

6. Click on **OK** and the **Dataset Objects** pane is populated with the attributes and metrics present in the report.

7. Drag the **Sum SalesAmount from FactInternetSales** metric from **Dataset Objects** to the **Detail Header** section; notice that the edge of the section is highlighted in yellow when you hover onto it. Drop the metric close to the right border of the layout.

8. Now that the textbox containing the metric is selected (there are six small squares around its border), click on the word **Format** in the menu, so that the formatting toolbar displays the buttons to modify the font and the size of the text. Click on the **Bold** button.

9. Click on the small arrow icon next to the **Insert** menu and select **Text**, the cursor changes to a cross. Click-and-drag to draw a rectangular textbox on the left of the metric you just added and type `Total`. Make it **Bold** too.

10. We created two textboxes in the **Detail Header**; now go to the **Dataset Objects** pane and drag the **Sum SalesAmount from FactInternetSales** metric, this time drop it into the **Detail** section right under its header counterpart close to the right edge.

11. Click on the **Interactive Mode** button to run the document. See the result and save it as `27 InternetSales by Product and Subcategory`, then click on **Run newly saved document**.

How it works...

If you scroll through the results, you'll see that there are 17 rows plus the total. The report granularity is at subcategory level, this means that the **Detail** section is repeated for each row of the dataset and the **Detail Header** only appears once. Just as expected.

Another behavior is worth noting: the row in the **Detail Header** shows a grand total. This is how metrics work: if placed in the detail section, they show a single row value; put them in a header and you'll get an aggregate. This is very important to remember.

There's more...

You can edit documents in both the Web and the Desktop application. I am used to doing it in Web because I can see immediately how it looks like; but if you feel more comfortable you can create and modify the documents just as well with the Windows client. Try it yourself:

1. Open MicroStrategy Desktop, go to **My Reports** and right-click on **27 InternetSales by Product and Subcategory**.

2. Click on **Edit**. See that the Document Editor is very similar to the Web Interface.

3. Now click on **View | HTML** to run the document. The result is identical.

4. Close without saving.

You can watch a screencast of this operation at:

▸ `http://at5.us/Ch7V4`

Modifying the grouping in a document

Our second document has data but it's not ready for prime time yet. There are metrics but no attributes in it. So, let's go on and add some.

Getting ready

You need to have completed the previous recipe to continue.

How to do it...

We start from where we left the previous document:

1. Click on the **Design** icon in the toolbar to return to design mode.

2. In the **Dataset Objects** pane, click on the **Product Subcategory** attribute, drag it into the **Detail** section, and position it just below the **Total** textbox.

3. Click on the **Interactive Mode** icon to run the document.

4. Much better, we see the description of each subcategory and the corresponding amount; note that the **Total** is still showing 29M.

5. Click on **Design** and go back to design mode. This time, we add the category but instead of dragging it onto the layout we create a group. Right-click on the **Category** attribute and from the context menu select **Add to Grouping**.

6. The **Product Category** is added to the **GROUPING** pane above the layout and there are now two more sections: **Product Category Header** and **Product Category Footer**.

7. Pick the **Product Category** attribute and drag it onto the **Product Category Header**, dropping it close to the left border.

8. Now run the document in interactive mode and see the result. We have a paging control at the top of the document where we can select the **Product Category**, and most important, the **Total** is different. Can you tell why?

9. Click on the **Product Category** paging combobox and select **Clothing**, the document is updated and the **Total** changes, do the same for **Accessories**, what do you expect?

10. One last time select **(All)** from the combobox to see the entire dataset in one single view.

11. Save the document as it is, overwrite the existing one, and click on **Run newly saved document**.

How it works...

The grouping pane works like the page-by in reports, but with an added feature. You have more sections in the document where you can put attributes and/or metrics; always remember that depending on their location the metrics are aggregated and grouped at different levels, hence displaying different totals.

There's more...

You can add as many groupings as you want, each attribute on the **Grouping** pane will add its own **<Attribute Name> Header/Footer** sections to the layout. The nesting of groups is driven by the position; right-most attributes are nested inside left-most attributes.

Exercise 25

Where should we put the metric now in order to have a grand 29M total?

 You can watch a screencast of this operation at:

  ▶ `http://at5.us/Ch7V4a`

Stepping up to dashboards

We learned how to create documents: these are useful for PDF publications, for example, or personalized invoices or any kind of printed communication. Actually, what customers want nowadays, is something more interactive: meet the dashboard.

Dashboards are in fact documents with all sections disabled but the **Detail Header**, and are intended for the Web or mobile usage instead of print. They add the ability to interact with, filter, or slice data using selectors and links to other documents; therefore, they can be considered as an "information cockpit" for managers and decision makers.

Still, they'll never substitute Excel in the heart of your users—just joking, I am myself an Excel user, and proud of it.

Designing dashboards is not trivial; I personally consider it the most challenging task in the whole BI project (if we exclude documentation, of course). More often than not, I spend more time creating useful and eye-catching panels, than in the whole schema objects creation. This is partly because data analysis is a moving target of ever changing specs and requirements, and to a certain extent we should get used to that. Let's not forget we get paid for coding.

Getting ready

We need to create another report with:

- ▶ **Year**
- ▶ **Product Category**
- ▶ **Product Subcategory**
- ▶ **Country**
- ▶ **Sum SalesAmount from FactInternetSales**

The position of objects inside the report grid is not relevant.

How to do it...

If you're not in the home page of the **COOKBOOK** project, click on the red star icon menu and select **Home**:

1. Go to **Create Document** and from the list of templates choose **Blank Dashboard**.

2. The dashboard template is a document with a single big gray panel that corresponds to the **Detail Header**, we will design objects inside this area.

3. First, pick a report as dataset by clicking on the **add a Dataset** icon and selecting number 28 from **My Reports** folder. The list of objects is populated with attributes and the metric.

4. Click on the small arrow icon next to the **Insert** menu and from the list that appears choose **Grid**. Now that the cursor is cross shaped, click-and-drag to create a small rectangular area of about 2 by 2 inches close to the left border.

5. When the mouse button is released, you can see a grid with four placeholders. In the **Dataset Objects** pane, click on the **Product Category** attribute and drag it onto the placeholder that says **Drop objects here to add rows**. A yellow border highlights the left margin of the grid. Release the button and **Product Category** now displays as a row header.

6. Now pick the metric and drag it onto the **Drop Metrics here to add data** placeholder. Now **Sum SalesAmount from FactInternetSales** occupies the column.

7. Repeat steps 4 to 6 to create another grid object of about 2 by 2 inches on the right of the first grid. Use the **Year** attribute on rows and the metric.

8. We now have two grids on our panel. Let's create another one below those two. You may need to use the scroll bars on your browser window to focus on the lower part of the gray area.

9. Similarly, go to **Insert | Grid** and draw a rectangle 2 inches tall and about 4 inches wide, so that it spans the entire space below the other two grids.

10. In this last grid, drop the **Country** attribute and the metric.

11. Click on **Interactive Mode** to run the dashboard and look at the result.

12. We have three grids with different attributes and different totals. However, they all read data from the same dataset. The numbers are aggregated according to the attributes present in each one. Colors and sizes of the grids can be improved and fine-tuned, I agree, but now we have a working panel with three perspectives of our data. Good job!

13. Click on **Save As...** and name it 29 InternetSales Dashboard, then hit **Run newly saved document**.

How it works...

We can add as many grids (and graphs) as the space on a dashboard allows. The metrics values in the document's grids are always calculated on the fly by the Intelligence Server, based on the elements on the rows and columns. Grids on a dashboard share the same behavior and features as grids in reports, so you can move and pivot the objects, add thresholds, change the format of the numbers and a lot more... you can even maximize or minimize a single grid with the small buttons on the title bar. Feel free to play a little with all the menu options and the format settings available.

Click on the magnifying glass in the top-left of a grid title bar, what happens?

There's more...

From a grid in a document we can drill and analyze data including attributes that are not in the original dataset, such as Month or Product. This is a very powerful and potentially dangerous capability of the Web Interface. Remember, when you wander through the data, you can go back on your footsteps using the Web Interface buttons **Back** and **Forward**, see the following image:

It is better to use MicroStrategy Web buttons rather than the browser back and forth feature, because the Web Interface keeps track of the reports that you run and makes a rational use of the Intelligence Server cache, resulting in less burden for the network and a smoother experience for the user.

 You can watch a screencast of this operation at:
  ▶ http://at5.us/Ch7V5

Using the editable mode to fine-tune the design

Switching from design to interactive mode takes time, and during the development phase it can be frustrating to change the view so many times. The editable mode is a fantastic resource for fine-tuning the layout of a document. It also helps configuring the data interaction between one object and the others. Editable mode allows the designer to work in a "What You See Is What You Get" environment, so that every applied change is immediately visible on the screen, with no need to switch back to design mode. You will use the design mode only if you need to add or remove datasets or new objects to the layout.

Getting ready

We are going to modify the previous recipe dashboard resizing and modifying some settings of the grids. You need to have completed the **29 InternetSales Dashboard**.

How to do it...

We run the dashboard as usual, and next:

1. From the interactive view, click on the **Save As...** button, rename it 30 InternetSales Dashboard, and click on **Run newly saved document**.

2. Now go to the toolbar and click on the **Editable Mode** button (see the following icon) next to the **Interactive Mode** button:

3. The view doesn't change a lot but the functionality of this screen allows you to select individual elements on the layout and apply settings.

4. Hover the mouse cursor on the title of the top-left grid (the one with the Product Category attribute), and notice that a couple of small buttons appear sitting above the upper edge. The first one looks like a cross arrow: it's the handle, click and hold it to move the grid by dragging it around the area of the document.

5. It takes a little time to get used to it; if you just click and release, the object will be selected and you can tell it by the eight little white squares around its border.

6. So, with some clicking and dragging of the two top grids, switch their positions so that the **Year** attribute grid is now on the left and the **Product Category** grid is on the right.

7. Now try to resize the left grid to 1 inch tall by 5 inches wide, clicking and dragging on the small white squares.

8. When you're done right-click on the **Year** header to bring up a context menu for the attribute and open **Move | To Columns** to pivot the report.

9. Now click on the **Sum SalesAmount from FactInternetSales** header to bring up the metric context menu and select **Rename/Edit...**.

10. In the dialog box that appears, change the second textbox **Name** to `InternetSales` and click on **OK**.

11. The grid looks better now. Hover on its title bar and when the cross-arrow appears, right-click on it to bring up the context menu for the entire grid.

12. Depending on the size of the screen you may need to scroll down a bit, search the **Properties and Formatting...** option and click on it.

13. In the **Properties | General** pane, uncheck **Show Title Bar** and move on to **Properties | Grid**. Here, click on the **Remove extra column** checkbox and next hit **OK**. The title and the metric cell have disappeared.

14. Resize as appropriate, resize the right grid also to about 1 inch tall by 3.5 inches wide.

15. Move and resize the third grid so that it occupies almost all the rest of the remaining space. Click on the top-left grid (with the **Year** attribute) to select it.

16. Now go to the toolbar on the top of the Web Interface and click on the last button (see the following icon) to restore **Normal Screen Mode** and show the menu:

17. On the menu, click on **Grid** and see part of the toolbar changing. Open a dropdown that says **Accounting**: this is the AutoStyle selector. Apply the second style named **Agent** then move on to the second grid and set its style to **Business Green** (it's my favorite: since I'm working in a hospital at the moment... it really gives an "ER" touch).

18. Now click on the third big grid to select it, right-click on the cross-arrow icon and choose **View mode | Graph View**.

19. The grid changes to a bar chart. I think we're done for now. Save the work, replacing the existing document, and click on **Run newly saved document**. Now that looks like a dashboard! Not bad, the best is yet to come:

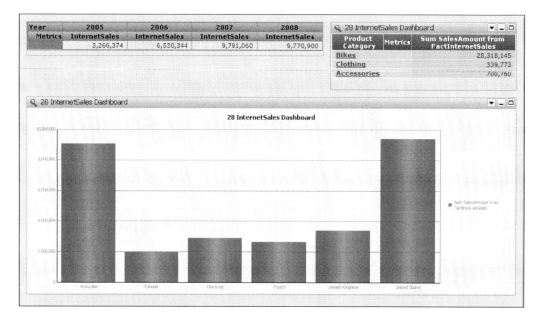

How it works...

The editable mode is very handy as it allows you to speed up the long process of having everything straight in place and with the right colors. From here, you have access to the context menu of all objects and the whole menu and toolbar (when you restore the normal screen mode). Of course, it looks scary at the beginning, for the sheer quantity of options and settings. But no problem, you'll rapidly narrow down the 15 or 20 most used options. Feel free to play around with them and see the result on the screen. Save with a different name often, you won't regret it.

There's more...

In most Internet browsers the *F11* key activates the full-screen mode. I often find this feature useful during design to have even more space available.

 You can watch a screencast of this operation at:
  ▸ `http://at5.us/Ch7V6`

Adding interactivity with panels and selectors

Now that we know how to design a dashboard, we need to learn how to make it interactive, so that our users can slice data and view it from different perspectives. Selectors are one of the most, if not the most, useful features on a dashboard and can really make a difference in your BI project. They may seem tricky at the first bite, yet your customers will appreciate the effort and ask for more.

A panel is a group of controls (textboxes, lists, buttons, grids, and more) that act together responding to the user's input. Think of a panel as a layer, or—in HTML terms—as a <DIV> tag. They can be nested like containers; as a general rule remember this: the outer panel drives the inner panel, in other words, the inner panel inherits the filtering conditions of the outer panel. The big empty gray area where you put objects is, in fact, the mother of all panels, a container for the entire dashboard, let's call it the root. Once you have this in mind, you're already halfway through the title of "Dashboard Landlord".

Getting ready

We will reuse the dataset of the preceding recipe but with an added attribute: Product. So, open the Desktop application and modify the **28 InternetSales Dashboard** report.

How to do it...

Once you have the report ready, open the Web Interface:

1. From the **Home** page of the project, click on **Create Document | Blank Dashboard**, and add the report 28 as dataset.

2. Now click anywhere in the gray area (the root panel). Next, right-click on the **Product Category** attribute and from the context menu select **Add Element Selector**.

3. The element selector has a cross-arrow handle, click-and-drag it inside the gray area until you see the yellow border around the root panel. Release the selector.

4. Click again inside the root panel and from the **Insert** menu choose **Panel Stack**.

5. With the cross-cursor, draw a rectangular area to the right of the selector, big enough to have other elements inside it. This will create an inner panel; select it and when it has the eight white squares around its border, right-click on the **Product Subcategory** attribute and click on **Add Element Selector**.

6. Drag the newly created selector inside the inner panel. Drop it when you see the yellow line surrounding the border.

7. Again select the inner panel and insert another panel stack into it. I call this a Matrioska panel.

8. With the innermost panel selected, click on the green plus icon just below the panel title bar, labeled **Add Content**.

9. From the drop-down menu, click on **Grid**, and complete this grid with the **Product** attribute and the metric.

10. In summary: we have the root panel with the **Category** selector, the middle panel with the **Subcategory** selector and the inner panel with the **Product** attribute in grid, as shown in this screen capture:

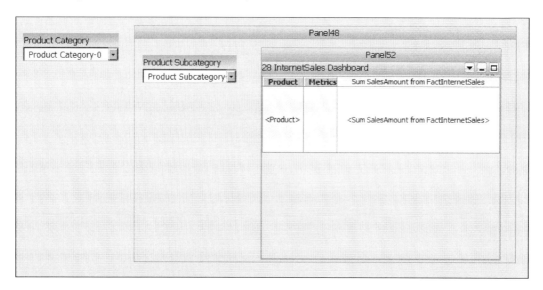

11. Click on **Save As...** and name it 31 Panels and Selectors. Then click on **Run newly saved document**, and play a little with the selectors to see the effect on the innermost grid.

How it works...

The panels are nested and have a parent-child dependency. So, when you select a category, the middle and the inner panels are affected; when you select a subcategory, only the inner panel changes. In this case the three attributes belong to the same hierarchy, but it would work just as well with Year for example.

When changing values inside selectors, you may find that the grid displays no data and an error appears: **No data returned for this view. This might be because the applied filter excludes all data**.

In this case:

1. Switch to **Editable Mode**. Select the **Product Subcategory** selector, right-click on it and open the **Properties and Formatting...** window.

2. Go to **Properties | Selector**, uncheck **Apply selections as a filter** and check **Automatically update when there is no data for the current selection**.

3. Confirm with **OK**. Notice that when you switch the category, by default the first subcategory is automatically selected.

4. When you save the document, the current status of the selectors is used as default; so, next time you open the dashboard, you will see the same selection.

> Please refer to the online MicroStrategy help at `http://www2.microstrategy.com/producthelp/9.3/WebUser/WebHelp/Lang_1033/Applying_selections_as_filters_or_slices.htm` for more details about filtering and slicing.

There's more...

You are not limited to dropdowns. Right-click on a selector, open the **Properties and Formatting | Properties | Layout** settings and choose from a series of controls, see screen capture:

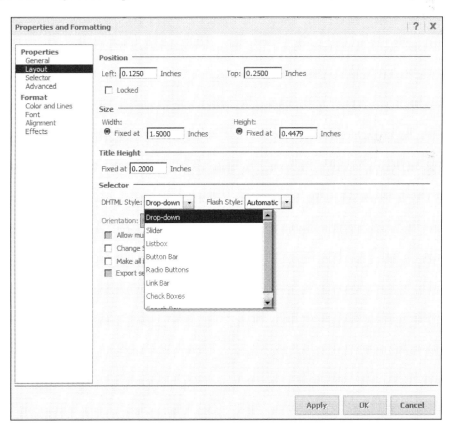

You can watch a screencast of this operation at:
  ▸ `http://at5.us/Ch7V6a`

Embedding images, HTML, and links

There are many components that we can add to our dashboards to make them more attractive and useful. Images or backgrounds are one of them. Often customers ask to add a company logo to the documents or a link to the corporate portal. We can also embed HTML code (or JavaScript) inside a dashboard, a very good feature that we can leverage to accomplish things that couldn't be done otherwise. Security-concerned people may raise an eyebrow: it indeed poses a security issue, please check your company policies regarding this matter.

Getting ready

We are creating a brand new dashboard, so no special requirements.

How to do it...

Create a new document (**Blank Dashboard** template) and:

1. Click on the green plus icon inside the gray area and from the drop-down menu select **Image** and wait a couple of seconds.

2. The **Properties and Formatting** window appears with the **Image Source** textbox. Type a URL to an image, for example: `http://images1.wikia.nocookie.net/__cb20130504095628/gtawiki/images/thumb/8/8a/Optional_Background.jpg/1024px-Optional_Background.jpg`, and the preview will show it:

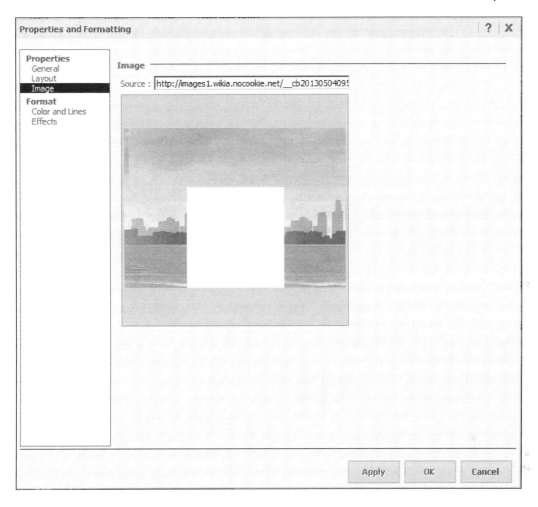

Properties and Formatting

? X

Properties
General
Layout
Image
Format
Color and Lines
Effects

Image

Source : http://images1.wikia.nocookie.net/__cb2013050409{

Apply   OK   Cancel

3. When you click on **OK**, the image appears in the document. Now that the image is selected click on it and drag it outside the gray area. Notice that the yellow border is highlighting the outer part of the document. Drop the image.

4. While the image is still selected right-click on it and choose **Order** | **Send to Back**, so that the gray area is now visible over the image.

5. Select the root panel and right-click on it, go to **Properties and Formatting | Format | Color and Lines**.

6. Under **Fill**, open the **Color** control and click on **No Fill**; under **Borders** check **All** and specify **Thick** white color. Hit **OK**.

7. Add a dataset and choose the number 28 in **My Reports**, then add a grid inside the root panel with the **Product** attribute and the metric.

8. Run the document and see the result. The grid should be visible on the image background:

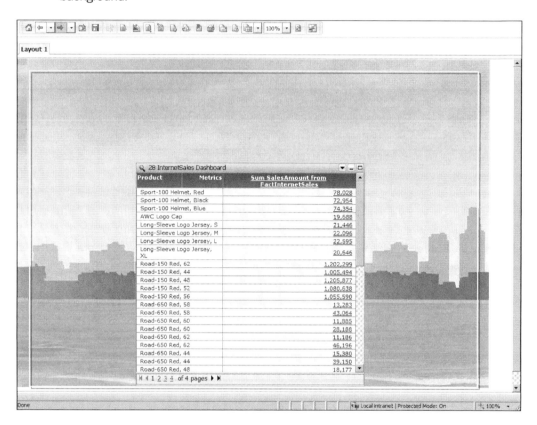

9. Save it as 32 Background and run the newly saved document.

10. Go back to design mode. Now select the root panel and from the **Insert** menu click on **HTML Container**. Draw a little rectangle and release the mouse button. Inside the HTML container type this (the code should go on a single line):

```
<button type="button" onclick="alert('hi hi hi hi hi!');">Tickle</button>
```

11. While the HTML container is still selected right-click and go to **Properties and Formatting | Format | Color and Lines**. Set **Color** to **No Fill** and **Borders** to **None**.

12. Run in **Interactive Mode** and click on the **Tickle** button, do you see the message box? Click on **OK** and save the document overwriting the existing one. Click on **Run newly saved document**.

13. Switch to **Editable Mode**. Right-click on the metric header and select **Edit links...**.

14. In the **Links** dialog box locate a textbox labeled **Run this report or document**. Click on the **Select Target** button with ellipses icon and navigate to **My Personal Objects | My Reports** to find the **31 Panels and Selectors** dashboard (you may need to go to the second page to find it if there are many).

15. Click on **OK** and then on **OK** again. Save, overwrite, and run again.

16. Now the metric values are underlined, if you click on one of them, you will be redirected to the document 31. To go back, use the green **Back** arrow on the toolbar.

How it works...

The objects that we used in this recipe do not necessarily contain data but they do help you enrich the functionality and the appearance of your documents. You can use custom HTML and JavaScript, and with links you can enable the users to explore different documents and reports. It's easy to imagine that with these tools the possibilities are almost endless. With good HTML skills on your side you can rock and roll!

There's more...

I imagine some of you trying to insert CSS styles in the HTML container. There are some limitations: consider that you are writing inside the `<BODY>` of the page, but you cannot access the `<HEAD>` section. To do that, we would need to use the SDK and modify some system files, which is a little beyond the scope of this book. But yes, it is possible. Check the `https://www.facebook.com/MicroStrategyHacks` page to read some interesting tricks and insights about this technique.

You can watch screencasts of this operation at:
- `http://at5.us/Ch7V7`
- `http://at5.us/Ch7V8`

Switching to Adobe Flash mode

Beside the **Interactive** and **Editable** modes you can display a dashboard in **Flash** mode. No modification is necessary to the documents: you only need to have the Adobe Flash player installed. Flash visualization is usually slower in the loading phase (due to the size of the SWF components and XML data needed to bootstrap the dashboard), especially if the document contains a lot of data, but offers a whole set of widgets to enrich the user's experience.

Getting ready

Most probably the Flash player is already installed in your PC; if not, go to `http://www.adobe.com/go/getflash/` and download the appropriate installer for your browser and operating system.

How to do it...

Create a new document based on the **Blank Dashboard** template:

1. Add to the **Dataset Objects** the **28 InternetSales Dashboard** report.
2. From the **Insert** menu, go to **Widgets | Flash** and click on **Data Cloud**.
3. Draw a rectangle on the top-left part of the root panel.
4. You will see the same placeholders as when you create a grid: drop the **Product Category** on rows and the metric as data. It looks exactly as a grid.
5. Now move to the right part of the dashboard and add a standard grid with the **Product** attribute and the metric.
6. Click on the toolbar button that's right next to **Interactive Mode**, with a small **F** on the icon (tool tip: **Flash Mode**).
7. The left widget displays a series of product subcategories with different sizes, the bigger the font the higher the sales amount. We can now set this widget as a selector so that when we pick a subcategory in the left, the right grid is filtered accordingly. Go back to the design mode.
8. Right-click on the **Product Subcategory** header on the left grid, click on **Use as Selector** and run it again in **Flash Mode**.
9. See that you can click on a subcategory and drive the right grid, cool! With *Ctrl* + click you can multi-select, multi-cool!

How it works...

MicroStrategy creates a SWF file in the background and runs it inside the browser, see the following image:

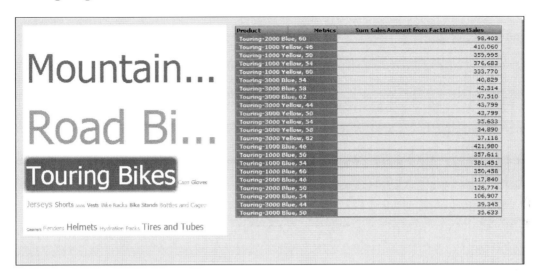

Few widgets can work in DHTML also, please refer to the documentation: *Dashboards and Widgets Creation Guide* for details on the requirements and the capabilities of each object.

There's more...

You can set the default visualization for a dashboard, so that the users don't have to switch between Interactive and Flash when they open the document. When in design mode, from the **Tools | Document Properties** menu, look for a setting labeled **Run by Default as**.

 You can watch a screencast of this operation at:
  ▸ http://at5.us/Ch7V9

See also

  ▸ The *Restricting rows – compare an attribute to another attribute* recipe in *Chapter 8, Dynamic Selection with Filters and Prompts*

8
Dynamic Selection with Filters and Prompts

In this chapter, we will cover:

- ▶ Restricting rows – compare an attribute to another attribute
- ▶ Restricting rows – evaluate on moving dates
- ▶ Changing the level of a metric filter
- ▶ Adding interactivity to filters using prompts
- ▶ Using prompts as object selectors

Introduction

Filters and prompts are two types of objects used to restrict the result dataset; we already learned how to create filters, we also created conditional metrics (metrics with a filter embedded). In this chapter, we'll focus on advanced filtering techniques and on how to get input from the users.

Prompts are, in my opinion, underestimated objects. When used in reports or documents they can save a lot of work on the development side. We will see in this chapter how to leverage them in filters and reports. We'll also try the **dynamic dates** feature to create moving date ranges.

Restricting rows – compare an attribute to another attribute

Most of the time, we filter attributes based on values, be it an element or a list of elements, always belonging to the same attribute (Year = 2007; Product in list....). There are cases when we want to look at two separate attributes to see if they match or not. The classic example being the order date and the ship date (order date = ship date), to control if our warehouse is preparing the orders during the same day they are processed. That example is way too common, so we'll complicate the things a bit. Our Sales Manager wants to know which orders from the resellers were originated by employees outside the sales territory where they belong (???). In other words, who are those employees who sell in a sales territory where they should not.

The `FactResellerSales` table has a column `SalesTerritoryKey`, and the `Employee` table also has `SalesTerritoryKey`, so we will create two attributes: one `Reseller SalesTerritory` and the other `Employee SalesTerritory` then use an attribute to attribute qualification to search for the cross-sellers. In the ER diagram of AdventureWorks DW there is an inconsistency (it happens sometimes, doesn't it) and `EmployeeKey` is not listed in the `FactResellerSales` table, but—in fact—is there, and you can prove it with the SQL command line or from the **Warehouse Catalog** window inside MicroStrategy Desktop. So, we will join the `FactResellerSales` table and the `DimEmployee` table on that column.

Getting ready

We need to create the `Employee`, `Reseller SalesTerritory`, and `Employee SalesTerritory` attributes. To do this more tables are needed: the `DimEmployee` table and two `DimSalesTerritory` tables (one for the `Reseller SalesTerritory` attribute and one for the `Employee SalesTerritory` attribute).

How to do it...

From the Desktop application, open the **Warehouse Catalog** window:

1. Add the **DimEmployee** table. If you completed the exercises in *Chapter 2, The First Steps in a MicroStrategy Project*, there should already be a **DimSalesTerritory** table in the schema, otherwise add this one too. Click on **Save and Close**.

2. Go to the **Schema Objects | Tables** folder and right-click on the **DimSalesTerritory** table. From the context menu, select **Create Table Alias**. This will add a second copy of **DimSalesTerritory**.

3. Rename the two tables, `DimSalesTerritory (Employee)` and `DimSalesTerritory (Reseller)` respectively. Refresh the schema.

4. Now go to the **Attributes** folder and create a new attribute with these columns:

    ❑ **ID**: **EmployeeKey** from **DimEmployee** (lookup) and from **FactResellerSales**

    ❑ **DESC**: **ConcatBlank(FirstName, LastName)** from **DimEmployee**

5. Save the attribute as `Employee`.

6. Create a new attribute like the one in the following screen capture:

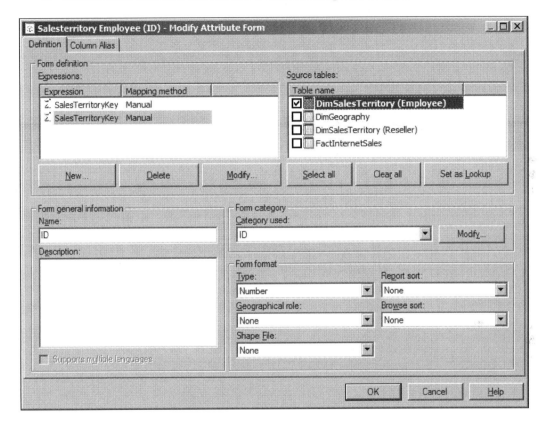

    ❑ **ID**: **SalesTerritoryKey** from **DimSalesTerritory (Employee)** as lookup and from **DimEmployee**

    ❑ **DESC**: **SalesTerritoryRegion** from **DimSalesTerritory (Employee)**

7. Add the **Employee** attribute as **Children** and save it as `Salesterritory Employee`.

8. Create a new attribute like the one shown in the following screen capture:

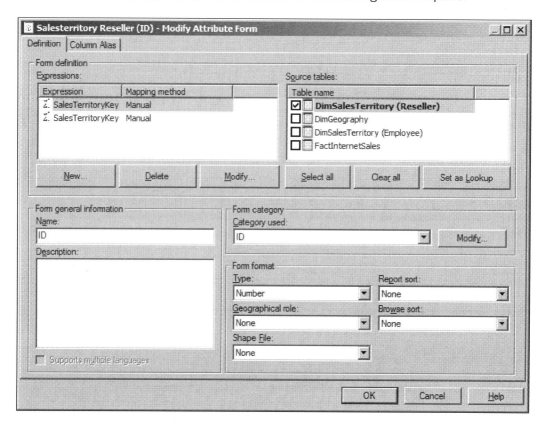

- ❑ **ID**: **SalesTerritoryKey** from **DimSalesTerritory (Reseller)** as lookup and **FactResellerSales**

- ❑ **DESC**: **SalesTerritoryRegion** from **DimSalesTerritory (Reseller)**

9. This one has no children, save it as `Salesterritory Reseller`. Update the schema.

10. Go to **My Reports** and create a blank one, drag the **Sum SalesAmount from FactResellerSales** metric to **Columns** and the **Employee** attribute to **Rows**.

11. Now click on the **SalesTerritory Employee** attribute and drop it into the report filter, the **Attribute Qualification** pane appears.

12. Select **Qualify on**: `ID`, change the **Operator** to `Different From`. And below **Operator**, open the dropdown that says **Value** and click on **Custom**.

13. Now click on the **Salesterritory Reseller** attribute and drag it onto the empty textbox on the right of **Custom**.

14. The textbox now shows **[Salesterritory Reseller]@ID**.

15. Click on **OK** to close the **Attribute Qualification** pane and run the report.

16. Look at the result; these are the employees who cross their borders. Now switch to SQL view.

17. Look at the WHERE clause and you'll see something like: **a12.SalesTerritoryKey <> a11.SalesTerritoryKey**.

18. Go back to **Grid View** and save the report as 34 Cross selling Employees.

How it works...

This type of filter is rarely used but very useful. Note, that in this recipe, we had to create table aliases for the DimSalesTerritory table in order to build two independent attributes. This technique is used to deal with "role dimensions", which means the same physical table plays two or more roles in the data warehouse. Typically, time or geography tables serve multiple attributes: think about Customer City, Store City, Call Center City. The table alias creates a "shadow" table, forcing MicroStrategy to believe that those are conceptually different lookups. Another option would be to create views on the DBMS side. Both SQL views and table alias are acceptable solutions; less so if you duplicate the real table, as you may be introducing errors in the long run and causing more workload on the ETL or maintenance team.

There's more...

Pay special attention, when creating attributes for role dimensions, to the tables that you select for the ID form. One of the most common errors in this case is mixing the source tables; and "when the SQL gets tough, the tough gets nervous". I mean, with complex reports, it is really complicated to read the SELECT statements in SQL view and spot the error. Always use the manual mapping method or MicroStrategy will check all the tables for you and probably generate an incorrect SQL no matter what you say.

Exercise 26

Why do we use the metric in this kind of report? Wouldn't it be easier to just drop the Employee attribute? Try to remove the metric from the report 34 and see what happens: can you tell why? Tip: look at the SQL view.

 You can watch a screencast of this operation at:
> http://at5.us/Ch8V1

Restricting rows – evaluate on moving dates

Dates are at the core of every BI project and possibly the most used filter conditions in reports. The debate about how to deal with date dimensions is as old as the data warehouse business. I personally am a "surrogate key orthodox" in the sense that I would put surrogate keys on everything that moves. Being a reasonable person I also understand that too much is too much. In small databases with modern SSD drives, the point of creating SK for the date dimension has probably less sense. And—yes, I agree—the calendar isn't likely to change in the lifespan of our BI projects... so the Ides of March will always be the same date.

Hence, the debate goes on, having primary keys as integers or as date datatypes. It really matters depending on the software you use to do the reports. And, I should add, on how you feel more comfortable, based on previous projects and the possibility to re-use the creation scripts.

When reusing scripts from previous projects I always remember one episode. I was a junior BI developer and one of my colleagues sent me a ZIP file with a lot of SQL to create the date dimension tables. I run them carelessly and it felt very good: no errors, all lookup tables ready in a snap. Unfortunately, as I came to realize months later, for no apparent reason the tables were missing the 6th of June. Easy to guess, all the projects that were created with those scripts suffered from the same glitch. Since that episode, I've been creating the date dimension tables with recursive SQL, you bet.

Getting ready

A note before going on: the database we're using has data between 2005 and 2008, just keep that in mind when creating date filters.

We want to analyze the exchange rate of the British Pound over time.

From the ER diagram we can see that the `DimCurrency` table and the `DimDate` table are related many-to-many through `FactCurrencyRate` (sometimes this type of the intermediate table is referred to as "Helper Table").

So, in order to complete the following recipe we need more tables and the corresponding `Currency` attribute; furthermore, we need to modify the `Date` attribute to include a form of type date.

So, bring up the **Warehouse Catalog** window to add **DimCurrency** and **FactCurrencyRate** in the tables used by the project. Click on **Save and Close**.

How to do it...

Follow these steps:

1. Go to the **Attributes** folder, right-click on **Date**, and select **Edit**.

2. Modify the ID form and include **FactCurrencyRate** as source sable. Then click on **OK**.

3. In the **Date - Attribute Editor** window, click on **New...** and drag **FullDateAlternateKey** onto the **Form expression** text area, click on **Manual** and then on **OK**.

4. Check **DimDate** in the **Source tables** list, and then hit the **Modify...** button in the **Form category** group.

5. In the **Form Categories** dialog, write DATETYPE in the **Form category name** box and click on **Add**; next select the **DATETYPE** you just created from the **Form category list** and click on **OK**.

6. In the **Form general information** group, write DateType in the **Name** textbox and confirm with **OK**. Then click on **Save and Close**.

7. Create a new attribute using these columns:

    ❏ **ID**: **CurrencyKey** from **DimCurrency** (lookup) and **FactCurrencySales**

    ❏ **DESC**: **Currency Name** from **DimCurrency** (lookup)

    ❏ **Children**: **Date**

8. In the **Children** tab, open the **Relationship type** combobox and choose Many to Many.

9. Click on **Save and Close** and name it Currency.

10. Go to the **Facts** folder, create a new fact with the **EndOfDayRate** column from the **FactCurrencyRate** table, and set the **Mapping method** as **Manual**. Click on **Save and Close**, name it Exchange rate from FactCurrencyRate.

11. Go to **Public Objects | Metrics**, create a new metric with the fact we just created modifying the aggregate function to Min, so that the resulting formula is: **Min([Exchange rate from FactCurrencyRate]) {~}**.

12. From the **Tools | Formatting** menu, select **Values...** and in the **Format Cells** dialog go to the **Number** tab.

13. Uncheck **Use Thousands separator**, increase **Decimal places** to 3, click on **OK**.

14. Click on **Save and Close** and name it Minimum Exchange Rate. Update the schema.

15. Go to **My Reports** and create a blank report. Add **Minimum Exchange Rate** to the columns add the **Currency** and **Date** attributes to the rows.

16. Now drag the **Currency** attribute to the report filter, click on the **Add...** button and select **United Kingdom Pound**. Click on **OK** and then on **OK** again.

17. Run the report and look at the result.

18. Right-click on the **Date** header, select **Attribute Forms** from the menu and uncheck **DESC**. We have values from 2005 until 2008.

19. Click on **File | Save As** and name this report `35 All time GBP Exchange Rates`. Do not close the report.

20. Switch to **Design View** and drag the **Date** attribute onto the report filter. In the **Attribute Qualification** pane, open the **Qualify on** dropdown and choose **DateType**.

21. Two small square buttons appear on the right. Click on the one that looks like a calendar (**Date Editor**).

22. The window that pops up is the **Date and Time Editor**, this allows us to specify **Static** or **Dynamic** date values based on the system current date.

23. Click on **Dynamic Date**. In **Choose a view point date**, on the right side select **Minus 72 months**. It is now May 2013 for me, so I subtract 72 months to hit year 2007; chances are that for you it's a different day, so calculate the number of months to subtract, so that you will land somewhere in time between 2005 and 2008, as shown in the following screen capture:

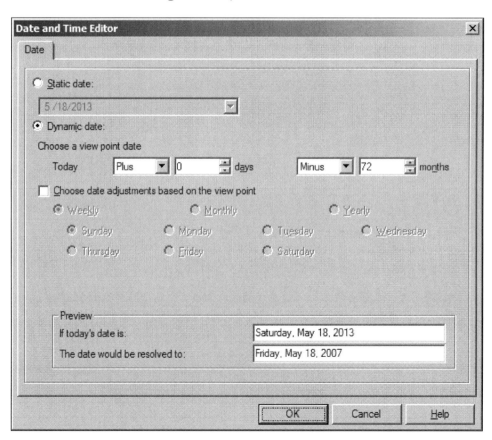

24. At the bottom of the window you can preview the calculated date. Click on **OK** and then on **OK** again.

25. Run the report, and look at the result. If you run this same report tomorrow, it will return a different day.

26. Save the report as `35 GBP Exchange Rates 6 years ago`, do not close it, and switch to **Design View**.

27. Now we want to filter a time span, not just a single date, so we modify the filter: where the **Operator** is **Exactly**, set it to **Between**. Another **Value** row appears, so with the **Date Editor** specify a dynamic date of **Minus 60 months**. (This number should be equal to the number of months you put in step 23 minus 12.)

28. Hit **OK** and then **OK** again, and run the report. Now we have one year of data. Save this report as `35 GBP Exchange Rates between 6 and 5 years ago`.

How it works...

Dynamic dates are a very powerful feature for data filtering, with the **Date and Time Editor** we can move back and forth in the calendar and create conditions: last Monday, two weeks ago, April 2nd of next year, and so on. Use the `Between` operator if you want to filter on periods of time.

Clicking on **Choose date adjustments based on the view point** allows us to set the dynamic date to the beginning of the week/month/year, in case you want to select data, for example, of last calendar month.

In this recipe, we used a many-to-many relationship between date and currency. MicroStrategy can handle this correctly, provided that we set the relationship type in the Attribute Editor.

There's more...

At this point of the project, we realize that the `SalesAmount` metrics (both from `FactInternetSales` and `FactResellerSales`) that we used, are in fact values expressed in several different currencies and we made a big mistake adding them all together.

> *"Oh, woe is me, T' have seen what I have seen, see what I see!"*.

> - William Shakespeare

More Info

In one of the next recipes we'll modify the fact tables to address this issue.

 You can watch a screencast of this operation at:
  ▶ `http://at5.us/Ch8V2`

Exercise 27

Looking at the image, can you create a report with `Date`, `Currency`, and `Sales Amount` from `FactResellerSales` converted to USD?

Date	Currency	Metrics	Sum SalesAmount from FactResellerSales	Minimum Exchange Rate	Currency adjusted Sum SalesAmount from FactResellerSales
7/1/2005	Canadian Dollar		115,361	0.681	78,568
	US Dollar		373,968	1.000	373,968
8/1/2005	Canadian Dollar		316,981	0.677	214,568
	US Dollar		1,221,427	1.000	1,221,427
9/1/2005	Canadian Dollar		205,641	0.689	141,675
	US Dollar		960,256	1.000	960,256
10/1/2005	Canadian Dollar		234,907	0.682	160,237
	US Dollar		609,814	1.000	609,814
11/1/2005	Canadian Dollar		381,806	0.681	260,122
	US Dollar		1,942,329	1.000	1,942,329
12/1/2005	Canadian Dollar		258,663	0.681	176,081
	US Dollar		1,444,282	1.000	1,444,282
1/1/2006	Canadian Dollar		163,780	0.668	109,435
	US Dollar		549,337	1.000	549,337
2/1/2006	Canadian Dollar		276,631	0.685	189,629
	US Dollar		1,624,158	1.000	1,624,158
3/1/2006	Canadian Dollar		335,344	0.677	227,152
	US Dollar		1,119,936	1.000	1,119,936
4/1/2006	Canadian Dollar		228,068	0.673	153,519

How would you do?

The ID form of the **Currency** attribute must include the **FactInternetSales** and **FactResellerSales** tables.

Changing the level of a metric filter

We already know how to create filters on metrics to restrict data returned by a query using a `HAVING` clause (*Chapter 4, Objects – Facts and Metrics*). In this recipe, we will go a step further; we want to filter on a metric value calculated at a different level than the report. Say that you want to know which products sold more than 1,000 units on a yearly basis all over the world, and you also want to see the countries where the products were sold. You have a report with `Year`, `Product`, and `Country`, so the `Sum OrderQuantity from FactResellerSales` metric is aggregated at year, product, and country level; but we need it to be aggregated only at year and product level for the filter to work. Here comes the qualification **Output Level**, as shown in the following screen capture:

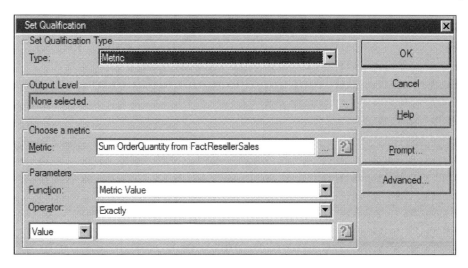

The qualification **Output Level** is independent from the report, it only affects the filter. You need to ask yourself a question: how do I want the metric to be aggregated before filtering the report? If we need the products that sold more than 1,000 units per year, we need the order quantity aggregated by year and product. It's like creating a pre-report with Year, Product, and the metric and then use the pre-report as a filter. Those combinations of Year and Product that pass the filter (greater than 1,000) are later displayed in the real report, together with Country.

Getting ready

First, we create a report with the year on pages, **Product** on rows and **OrderQuantity from FactResellerSales** on columns filtered on values greater than 1,000, as shown in the following image:

Year: 2006 ▼

Product	Metrics	Sum OrderQuantity from FactResellerSales
Sport-100 Helmet, Black		1,010
Sport-100 Helmet, Blue		1,057
AWC Logo Cap		1,388
Long-Sleeve Logo Jersey, L		1,432
Women's Tights, S		1,283
Women's Tights, L		1,231
Full-Finger Gloves, M		1,279
Full-Finger Gloves, L		1,942

You can see an example of the eight products that sold more than 1,000 units in the year 2006. We will use this report as a reference to check the results.

How to do it...

Now we create another blank report with these objects:

1. On page-by: **Year**.

2. On rows: **Country** and **Product**.

3. On columns: **Sum OrderQuantity from FactResellerSales**.

4. Now add the same metric to the report filter, **Set Qualification** appears.

5. In the **Output Level** group see that there's **None** selected, click on the ellipses button.

6. In the **Level** dialog box, click on the last radio button labeled **Calculate the output for the list of attributes**.

7. Then in the shopping cart select **Year** on the left and move it to the right.

8. Move the **Product** attribute also from left to right and confirm with **OK**.

9. Change **Operator** to **Greater than** and in **Value** type 1000.

10. Click on **OK** and run the report.

11. Notice that the numbers are indeed less than 1,000, that's because the filter considers only **Year** and **Product**, while the report groups by **Year**, **Product**, and **Country**.

12. We can easily confirm the correctness of the results thanks to dynamic aggregation. Click on the **Country** header and drag it onto the **Report Objects** list.

13. The Intelligence Server automatically aggregates the result, displaying the same numbers as in the reference report, as you can see in the following image:

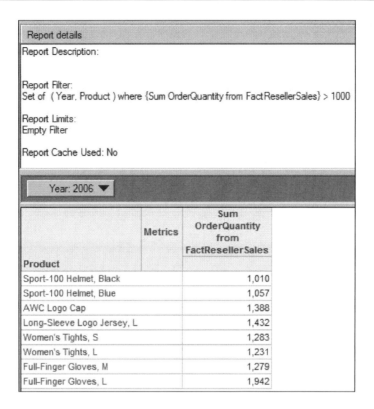

How it works...

In this type of filter, MicroStrategy runs a first SELECT with group by a11.ProductKey, a12.CalendarYear having sum(a11.OrderQuantity) > 1000, and stores the result in a temporary table. It then runs another SELECT, joining the fact table with the temporary table, this time grouping on a15.CountryRegionCode, a11.ProductKey, a12.CalendarYear.

I find this type of filter very useful and a big time saver.

There's more...

We can get to the same result creating a `Sum OrderQuantity from FactResellerSales (Year, Product)` level metric, removing Report Level and adding `Year` and `Product` in the dimensionality grid. As often there is not a single way to achieve the desired outcome, and if the numbers are correct, it really depends on how comfortable you feel with one solution or the other. Check the SQL view every now and then to assess the impact of a query also on the DBMS side.

Filtering a report based on a metric is different than putting a filter inside a metric definition (refer to *Chapter 4, Objects – Facts and Metrics*); a filter inside a metric only affects that particular calculation not the entire report.

You can watch a screencast of this operation at:

▶ `http://at5.us/Ch8V3`

Adding interactivity to filters using prompts

So, we have the sales amounts expressed in different currencies and we must address this issue before going too far. The CFO can't get any sleep until we fix the exchange rate adjustment, which is actually generating a distortion in the bottom line and undermining our CV.

The exchange rate is stored in a different fact table and is related many-to-many to both `FactInternetSales` and `FactResellerSales` tables. How to deal with that?

Well, I beg your pardon, I consider myself a practical person and sometimes lazy; as usual, different DBAs will have different solutions, more or less elegant. I personally prefer modifying the fact tables in this situation. Given that the exchange rate of a currency in the past doesn't change over time, and that multiplying one number by another is relatively easy in the ETL phase, I tend to pass this on the DBMS side. So, we will create an additional column in the two fact tables, named `USDSalesAmount` and populate them with `SalesAmount * EndOfDayRate`.

For those of you that have no free access to the data warehouse, may I suggest a logical table?

In this recipe, we introduce another type of MicroStrategy objects: the prompts. They serve a particular function asking the user for an input so that MicroStrategy can generate a customized SQL adding flexibility to the user's reporting needs.

Getting ready

To modify the fact tables in the `sqlcmd` utility, run these commands (find them in the companion code file):

```
ALTER TABLE FactResellerSales
ADD    USDSalesAmount money
go


update F set F.USDSalesAmount = SalesAmount * EndOfDayRate
from FactResellerSales F join FactCurrencyRate R
on F.OrderDateKey = R.DateKey and F.CurrencyKey = R.CurrencyKey
go


ALTER TABLE FactInternetSales
ADD    USDSalesAmount money
go


update F set F.USDSalesAmount = SalesAmount * EndOfDayRate
from FactInternetSales F join FactCurrencyRate R
on F.OrderDateKey = R.DateKey and F.CurrencyKey = R.CurrencyKey
go
```

Now the two fact tables include an extra column with the amount converted to US dollars. If you're a SQL rock star, feel free to add a column in your local currency also.

Next, create two new facts based on those columns and two metrics named, Sum USD SalesAmount from FactResellerSales and Sum USD SalesAmount from FactInternetSales respectively.

 You can watch a screencast of this operation at:
> `http://at5.us/Ch8V4`

How to do it...

We want to create a report where the user is prompted for one or more products before selecting data from the database:

1. Start by creating a blank report with **Product** on rows, **Year** on columns, and **Sum USD SalesAmount from FactResellerSales** on columns.

2. Run the report with no filter and see the result. Now minimize this window and switch back to the Desktop application.

3. Go to **Public Objects | Prompts** and create a new prompt. You'll see a window, like the following screen capture:

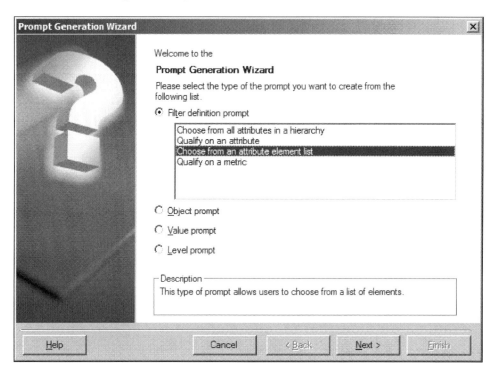

4. Select **Choose from an attribute element list** and click on **Next**.

5. Click on the ellipses button, pick the **Product** attribute, and click on **OK**.

6. Click on **Next** three times and then on **Finish**, save it with the name `Select one or more Products`.

7. Go to **Public Objects | Filters**, create a new empty filter.

8. In the Filter Editor, click on the **Public Objects** shortcut, browse to **Prompts**, click on the newly created **Select one or more Products** prompt and drag it onto the right filter definition part.

9. When you release the mouse button MicroStrategy creates a shortcut to the prompt inside this. Click on **Save and Close**, name it `Prompted Product Filter`.

10. Restore the **Report Grid** window and change it to **Design View**.

11. Drag the **Prompted Product Filter** object to the report filter, MicroStrategy creates a shortcut to the filter inside the report.

12. Execute the report. Before running the query, you are prompted to select one or more products from the left list. Choose some and move them to the right side of the cart, click on **Next** and then on **Finish**.

13. When the grid appears only the selected products are displayed.

14. Save this report as `38 Prompted Filter on Products`.

How it works...

Prompts allow the BI developer to create generic reports and let the user decide how to filter the results. There are several options when creating prompts, for example, the number of permitted answers, or if an answer is required. You may also set a default answer or allow the user to save their personal selection for the next executions. Please refer to the product manuals for more details.

There's more...

Pay attention when saving a report with a prompt. You'll see a dialog like the one shown in the following screen capture:

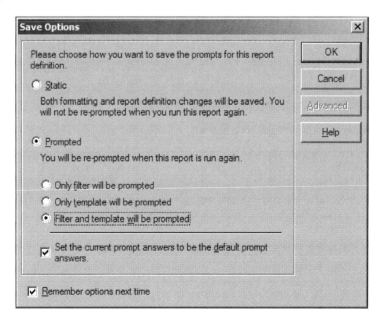

If you want the user to be prompted every time the report runs, select the second radio button (**Prompted**). Otherwise, your current prompt selection will be saved within the report definition and the prompt will never appear again.

 You can watch a screencast of this operation at:
> http://at5.us/Ch8V5

More Info

When looking at a prompted report, the user may want to change the current filter settings and select, for example, different products.

To do this, one must click on the **Re-prompt** button, which is almost invisible in the toolbar, and looks like a question mark between parentheses, as shown in the following icon:

 Prompted reports work in the same way both in Desktop and in the Web interface. There are minor visual differences between one environment and the other but the functionality is the same. Try it yourself: run this last report in the Web and see how it looks.

Using prompts as object selectors

We can use prompts to ask the user for attribute elements, but we can also ask the user to decide which objects he/she wants on the report template. How do we do? With a special type of prompt called object prompt.

The steps are similar to the previous recipe, but this time the users choose how to build the report.

Getting ready

You need to have completed the previous recipes to continue.

How to do it...

Go to the **Public Objects | Prompts** folder:

1. Create a new prompt.

2. In **Prompt Generation Wizard**, select the second radio button **Object Prompt**, click on **Next**.

3. With the first option **Use a pre-defined list of objects** selected click on **Add....**

4. From **Schema Objects | Attributes**, pick **Product**, **Product Subcategory**, **Product Category**, and **Year** and move them to the right.

5. Click on **Next** and then on **Finish**, and name it `Select one or more Attributes`.

6. Now create another new prompt. Again, select **Object Prompt** and click on **Next**.

7. This time, in the **Use a pre-defined list of objects** list add the metrics: **Sum OrderQuantity from FactResellerSales, Sum SalesAmount from FactResellerSales, and Sum USD SalesAmount from FactResellerSales.**

8. Click on **OK** and then on **Finish**.

9. Name this `Select one or more metrics`.

10. Now go to **My Reports** and create a blank new one.

11. In the Report Editor, click on the **Public Objects** shortcut and browse to the **Prompts** folder. Right-click on **Select one or more Attributes** and choose **Add to Rows**.

12. Right-click on **Select one or more Metrics** and choose **Add to Columns**.

13. Run the report. Now you will be prompted for the attributes that you want on the rows and the metrics that you want on the columns.

14. Select **Year**, **Product** from attributes, click on **Next** and select **Sum USD SalesAmount from FactResellerSales** for the metrics.

15. Click on **Finish** and look at the result.

16. If you want to modify the report, just hit the **Re-prompt** button.

17. Remember to save this report as `Prompted (Filter and Template will be prompted)`.

How it works...

This is a convenient way to create micro-wizards for the users. You select, among the attributes and metrics, a list of objects that belong to the same concept; then with a couple of prompts you can let the user build his/her own report with minimal effort. If they know how to use view filters, they'll probably never call you back again...well, unless some "snowball" query goes downhill.

There's more...

When creating these kind of DIY reports, it's wise to limit the number of attributes and metrics to a reasonable amount and use only objects that come from a single fact table.

Of course, it is also important that the objects are more than *sufficiently* documented and the calculation algorithm of the metrics is well-known to everybody.

 You can watch a screencast of this operation at:
- `http://at5.us/Ch8V6`

See also

- The *Setting up the Mobile Server* recipe in *Chapter 9, Mobile BI for Developers*

9

Mobile BI for Developers

In this chapter, we will cover:

- ▶ Setting up the Mobile Server
- ▶ Setting up mobile connection
- ▶ Installing and configuring the mobile client
- ▶ Adapting content to the iPad screen
- ▶ Using mobile views in documents
- ▶ Adding panels to mobile documents
- ▶ Creating panel selectors
- ▶ Adding details with pop-up windows
- ▶ Linking from one document to another

Introduction

During the last few years, the BI world has been experiencing a landslide movement towards mobile devices, and every major vendor of analytics software is adding to their catalog some sort of mobile solution.

The mind-blowing number of Apple and Samsung products sold so far, forces the BI players to rethink their strategies and prepare for the predictable extinction of the DesktopSaurus.

I personally have mixed feelings about this; but certainly the unstoppable shift of services—and soon personal desktops—to the cloud will leave a square and dusty empty space on our tables.

MicroStrategy was one of the first, if not the first, to offer full native client applications on mobile devices.

In this and the following chapter, we will explore the iPad version of the application, using the previously created reports, and creating new ones especially for the smaller screen of tablets. I must confess, I am not a tablet user, so we will discover the features together on the go.

Setting up the Mobile Server

MicroStrategy mobile deployments consist of two components: the Mobile Server, a web service running on IIS in case of Windows, or on a Java Servlet container in case of *nix environments, and the mobile clients installed on iPhone, iPad, BlackBerry, or Android.

The web service executes the reports and documents and serves the results in XML or JSON format, while the client takes care of the rendering, the prompts, the interactivity, and so on.

We start by configuring the web server part, which runs, in our case, on IIS 7.

Getting ready

For the following recipes to work, it is very important that we use a fixed IP address. If you're on a virtual machine, set the network card to be directly connected to the network (see in the screen capture the VMware network options):

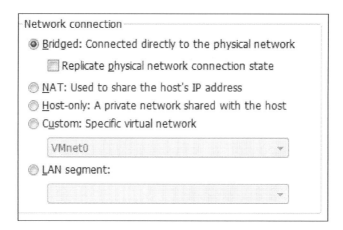

Then assign a fixed IP address to your Windows server, ask your network administrator for details. I will be using 192.168.1.89 for the examples, so whenever you see this address, change it with your corresponding one.

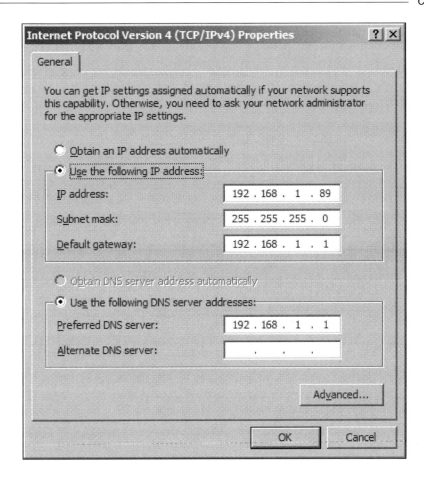

We will also need to know the hostname of the Windows server, and this can be easily seen by typing `hostname` in a command prompt window.

How to do it...

With the IP address and the hostname we can open the Mobile Administrator:

1. From **Start | All Programs**, go to **MicroStrategy | Mobile | Mobile Server | Mobile Administrator**. Click on **Continue** in the **User Account Control** window if it appears, and type the operating system account and password of the user `Administrator` if prompted.

2. Internet Explorer will show the **Administrator Page** with the message **No Intelligence Servers are currently connected**.

3. Click on the **Add a server manually** textbox and type the hostname of your Windows machine (in my case is `WIN-5KHTNPRO62T`).

4. Click on the **Add** button. You will be presented with the **Server Properties** page. In **Connect mode**, check the option labeled **Automatically connect to Intelligence Server when Mobile Server or Intelligence Server is restarted**.

5. Click on the **Save** button. Back on the **Connected servers** page, now you see that the server name of your machine appears in the list.

How it works...

Mobile Server connects to Intelligence Server; in order to do that, it needs to know the name of the server definition we created in *Chapter 1, Getting Started with MicroStrategy*. By default, and if you followed all the recipes, this name is the same as the machine name of the Windows server.

There's more...

Now that the Mobile Server is ready we need to set up the mobile connectivity. We'll do that in a minute, so unsheathe your iPad and read on.

By the way, I'm a little ashamed to say that I do not own an iPad. I borrowed one to do the tests.

 You can watch a screencast of this operation at:
 ▶ `http://at5.us/Ch9V1`

Setting up a mobile connection

Following from the previous recipe, we are now creating a configuration file with the connection settings that we can later distribute to our mobile users.

Configuration files are different depending on the device you are using; so there's one for iPad, one for iPhone, Android, and so on. The vast majority of the steps are similar from platform to platform; please refer to the product documentation *MicroStrategy Mobile Design and Administration Guide* for specific or nonstandard settings.

Mobile configuration can be done in two ways: automatically with a configuration file (like in this recipe) or manually on the mobile device itself. The advantage of the former method is that you can re-use the file for as many clients as you want.

Getting ready

Mobile devices communicate with the Mobile Server through HyperText Transfer Protocol (HTTP) much like an Internet browser does, therefore it is vital that they are connected to the network somehow, by means of Wi-Fi, 3G, 4G, or the like. It is not necessary to know the IP address of the iPad (in this case), as long as the device is able to communicate with the web server via HTTP.

You can try the connection by opening the Opera browser and typing the IP address of the web server (`192.168.1.89`) into the address bar. You should see an image logo of IIS.

How to do it...

From the **Administrator Page** inside Internet Explorer:

1. Click on **Mobile Configuration** on the top-right of the screen.

2. After a while, when the **Mobile Configuration Page** appears, click on the blue hyperlink labeled **Define New Configuration**, see screen capture:

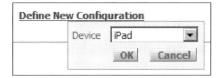

3. From the **Device** combobox, select **iPad** and click on **OK**.

4. Change the **Configuration name** value to `iPad_COOKBOOK`, and leave all the rest of options unchanged on this tab.

5. Click on the **Connectivity Settings** tab. The first combobox, **Authentication mode**, must be set to **Windows** (as we are using IIS, this is how we validate on the web server).

6. In the following **Login** and **Password** textboxes, put the operating system credentials that you use to open a session in Windows server and check the option **Overwrite user-specified credentials when applying configuration**.

7. Now click on the blue hyperlink named **Configure New Mobile Server**.

8. In **Mobile Server** name field, type the machine hostname you've given in step 3 of the previous recipe (in my case is `WIN-5KHTNPRO62T`).

9. Check the option box **Mobile clients access this server using the following external name:** this enables the next text field. Type here the IP address of your Windows server (192.168.1.89 in my case).

10. Leave the rest of parameters as they are and scroll down to the **Default Project Authentication:** header.

11. Notice that **Authentication mode** is set to **Standard**, which is ok; this is how we validate against the Intelligence Server.

12. In the next field **Login** type Administrator and in **Password** type the one that you've been using to open MicroStrategy Desktop.

13. Check **Overwrite user-specified credentials when applying configuration**.

14. Now click on the blue hyperlink **Configure New Project**.

15. Since we only have one, the **COOKBOOK** project should be already set in the **Project Name** combobox and the checkbox **Use default authentication** selected.

16. We're done with this tab, so we scroll back up to click on the **Home Screen** tab.

17. Set the radio button **Display the contents of a folder** and click on the small down arrow button to open a credentials dialog:

18. Again, this is the MicroStrategy username, so type Administrator and the corresponding password.

19. Click on the **Login** button to display another panel. Open the first combobox where it says **Shared Reports** and select **My Reports**. Then click on the **Current Folder** button.

20. Now hit the **Save** button. The configuration is stored and we can see the **iPad_COOKBOOK** line in the list.

21. There are four icons on the right: click on the one that looks like a globe (tool tip: **Generate URL**).

22. Here, in the first textbox change localhost to the IP address of the server (192.168.1.89 in my case).

23. Open **Authentication mode** and select **Windows**, and then click on **Save**.

24. Click again on the globe button to bring up the **Generate Configuration URL** dialog, this time click on **Generate URL**, and a text area will appear with a long string representing an address beginning with `mstripad://`.

25. This is the link that you need to open from an iPad to read the configuration file. The easiest way is to select all the content of this text area, copy and paste the entire URL into an e-mail message. Then send the message to yourself.

How it works...

The client configuration of a mobile device is not trivial. Given that we use a Windows server with IIS, we need to deal with the NT credentials first (step 6) in order to reach the web server, and then with the MicroStrategy username /password (steps 12 and 18), so that we can log in to the project.

In my setup, I used a VMware virtual machine connected to my home router. Since I do not have a DNS service running, I rely on class C private range IPs instead of DNS names. If you're a Net wiz, surely you can do better than this with your local network. I just wanted to keep things simple so that we can focus on BI.

While setting the Mobile Server name (step 8), we used the hostname of the Windows machine, although the option labeled **Mobile clients access this server using the following external name** (step 9) allows us specify a different name or an IP in case we are behind a NAT service or a load balancer, or simply we cannot rely on a working DNS server.

iPad users may change and store their credentials on the devices (they love to do it...); so the option labeled **Overwrite user-specified credentials when applying configuration** gives the possibility to overwrite those credentials in order to use only the username and password stored in the configuration file.

Needless to say, your production settings may be different and more complicated than this, involving proxies, different addressing, and so on. Ask your company network engineers when configuring the web server.

There's more...

The rest of the connection settings are usually good enough for a standard implementation. Refer to the manual and use them with common sense, for example, you may want to increase the memory limit or the network timeout in case you have very large datasets in your reports.

 You can watch a screencast of this operation at:
  ▶ `http://at5.us/Ch9V2`

Installing and configuring the mobile client

The client applications for iPhone and iPad are available for free on the Apple App Store:

Just search for the keyword `MicroStrategy` and install it as any other app.

When first launched, it will show a welcome page with demo projects from a public MicroStrategy server. You can tap **Explore the Product** to have an overview of the extraordinary capabilities built in to this client.

In this recipe, we will configure the client so that it can open our **COOKBOOK** project.

Getting ready

You need to have the MicroStrategy Mobile for iPad installed before going further.

How to do it...

Within your e-mail client, open the message you sent to yourself during the previous recipe:

1. Tap the hyperlink in the message beginning with **mstripad://**; the mobile application will open automatically and download the configuration file from the web server.

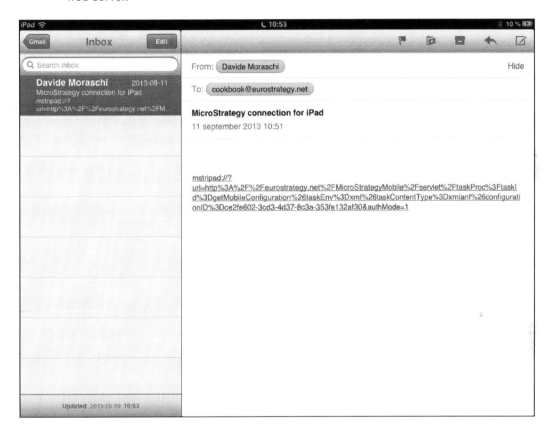

2. The IIS will ask for username and password:

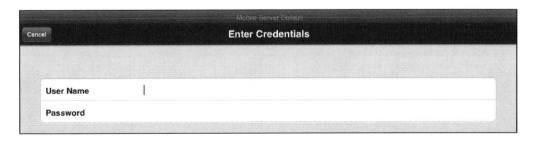

3. Type the operating system credentials you use to connect to Windows desktop.

4. Once the configuration file is downloaded and stored in the client application, the **COOKBOOK** project will be added and will contain the default folder that was specified in the previous recipe, in our case `My Reports`. You will see on the left the list of documents and reports we created so far.

5. Tap the first report in the list (**01 Countries**).

6. After a while the grid will display the result, congratulations! Your mobile configuration is complete!

How it works...

The configuration is actually an XML file that the iPad downloads via HTTP. Just out of curiosity you can open it with a text editor and see what's inside:

```
<taskResponse statusCode="200">
<cnf n="iPad_COOKBOOK" cid="164d6b93-baf3-4659-8bab-834aa56ac9bf"
v="1" bld="9.3.000.055J" dt="2" cntr="0"><lnk am="3" rt="0"
nm="192.168.1.89" po="80" ipo="true" bu="192.168.1.89:80/
MicroStrategyMobile/asp/TaskAdmin.aspx"/><cty><wsdc am="3"
lo="Davide moraschi" ps="********" ow="true"/><wsl><ws po="80"
pt="MicroStrategyMobile" ty="1" rt="0" udc="true" nm="192.168.1.89">
```

As you will soon realize, your operating system and MicroStrategy username/password are clearly stored inside this file, not bad from a security point of view. So, just to be safe, when you roll out your production environment, remember to use specific ad-hoc credentials.

There's more...

If, for any reason (including security), the configuration file is not an option in your environment, you can manually configure the client from the **Settings** menu. Look on the upper-right corner of the application, there is a round information icon: tap it, and from the menu select **Settings**. Use the previous recipe as a reference to fill in the Mobile Server, project, and account options.

More Info

Most of the errors in configuring the clients come from missing credentials, misspelled host names, or incorrect IP addresses; be sure to double-check them and to prove that the network connection between the web server and iPad is working.

Adapting content to the iPad screen

Mobile devices are different from desktop PCs; while you can open any report or document in an iPad, the best option is to design specific documents for small screens only. You will be able to leverage capabilities like swipe, tap-and-hold, rotate screen, and so on.

So, back to the drawing board, let's do some basic math. First and second generation iPads have a screen size of 1024 x 768 pixels, while third generation have 2048 x 1536. I will use the former for the recipes, and we need to account for the status bar (20 pixels), title bar (44 pixels), and the optional page-by bar (41 pixels). That leaves us, in landscape mode, roughly 1024 x 660 of usable space.

When the user rotates the device by 90 degrees, of course, the numbers change. MicroStrategy makes our life a lot easier when dealing with screen rotation, thanks to one of the best and most useful features: the views. We will explore them later.

Getting ready

The first thing we should do when developing mobile documents is to work with pixels as measurement unit, not inches nor centimeters.

How to do it...

We are using MicroStrategy Web for all the document development processes, so go to **Start | All Programs | MicroStrategy | Web | Web**, to bring up Internet Explorer:

1. Click on the **COOKBOOK** project and log in as usual.
2. Click on the upper-left red MicroStrategy logo, and select **Preferences**:

3. In the **User Preferences** page, under the **General** pane look for the **Language** header and click on **Show advanced options**.

4. Open the **Measurement Units** dropdown and select **Pixels**.

5. Click on the small floppy disk button on the top-left corner to save the preferences, and then hit the **Close** button to go back to the project's home page.

6. In the home page, click on **Create Document**; in the **Document Templates** choose **iPad Landscape**.

7. When the new empty document appears, click on the **Tools | Document Properties** menu.

8. On the left, under **Page Setup**, click on **Page**. See that the **Width** and **Height** values are displayed in pixels and already defined to fill the full iPad screen (with no page-by bar). Also the **Orientation** radio button is set to **Landscape**.

9. Now under **Layout Properties**, click on **Mobile**. There is a dropdown labeled **Supported Orientations**. This controls whether the screen will change or not when the user rotates the device.

   Notice that in this case the only orientation supported is **Landscape**.

10. Go back to the home page.

11. Repeat steps 6 to 10, this time use the **iPad Portrait** template.

How it works...

MicroStrategy offers several ready-to-use templates to create mobile devices dashboards. These are very convenient to design fixed-view documents.

There's more...

The **Supported Orientations** combobox allows you to decide which of the following modes the document will display in:

- ▶ **Portrait Only**
- ▶ **Landscape Only**
- ▶ **Portrait and Landscape**

Of course the challenge is to create auto-arranging views, so that the user can have different perspective in horizontal and in vertical orientation.

Exercise 28

Create two documents: one with the landscape template and another one with portrait.

In each document put a textbox saying something like "This is horizontal only", "This is vertical only", and see how they look on the iPad screen.

If you don't see a document in the list, try to close and re-open the MicroStrategy Mobile application. You should rotate your head together with the mobile device to see it correctly (ok, sorry about that...).

 You can watch a screencast of this operation at:
  ▶ `http://at5.us/Ch9V3`

Using mobile views in documents

One of my favorite features and probably the most useful from a development perspective is the ability to show different objects (or the same object with different sizes) depending on the available space on the screen. Imagine having multiple documents loaded at the same time, one above the other, only the topmost is visible, and they flip when you rotate the screen. The most appropriate document for the screen size is visible, while the others remain in the background. So, we can define a single document with multiple views: for landscape iPad, portrait iPad, smartphone, and so on. MicroStrategy will try to match the space of the device to the closest available view. No need to tilt your head anymore!

Getting ready

We will create a double-view document and see the result on the iPad screen.
You should have completed the previous recipes of this chapter to continue.

How to do it...

We start from the home page of our **COOKBOOK** project:

1. Click on **Create Document**, and select the **iPad Landscape** document template.

2. In design mode, open the **Tools** menu and click on **Document Properties...**.

3. From the left list, choose **Page Setup | Page** and set both **Width** and **Height** values to `1024`.

4. Go to **Layout Properties | Mobile**, in **Supported Orientations** select **Portrait and Landscape**, and then click on **OK**.

5. The canvas is now a 1024 x 1024 square. Open the **Tools** menu and choose **Manage views...**, you will see a dialog similar to this screen capture:

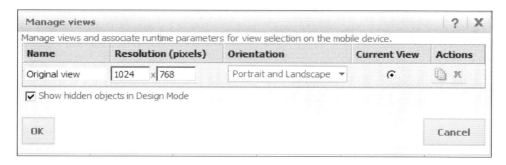

The default **1024 x 768** view is listed as **Current View**.

6. Under **Actions**, click on the **Duplicate** button to create a new line.

7. Rename the new view as `Portrait View` and change the **Resolution** to **768x1024**, in the **Orientation** dropdown pick **Portrait Only** and set previous **Original view** to **Landscape Only**.

8. Uncheck the option **Show hidden objects in Design Mode** and click on **OK**.

9. Open the **Insert** menu and select **Shape | Rectangle**. In the next message box, click on **No**.

10. Now draw a rectangle on the canvas and right-click inside it.

11. From the context menu, choose **Properties and Formatting...**.

12. Click on **Properties | Layout**, modify the **Position** value to 1 **Left** and 1 **Top** (pixels).

13. Set **Size Width: Fixed** to `1022` and **Height: Fixed** to `702`.

14. Next, go to **Format | Color and Lines**, change the **Fill | Color** to a light blue.

15. In the **Line and Shape Settings** area, modify **Style** to **Solid**, **Color** to dark blue and click on **OK**.

16. On to the **Tools | Manage views** window, we now switch to **Portrait View** by selecting the appropriate radio button under **Current View** and clicking on **OK**.

17. See that the blue shape disappears; we are now in **Portrait View**.

18. Repeat steps 9 to 15 to insert another shape:

  ❑ **Left**: 1 and **Top**: 1

  ❑ **Width**: `766` and **Height**: 958

  ❑ **Fill | Color**: Light Yellow

  ❑ **Line and Shape Settings | Style: Solid** and **Color**: Orange

19. When you're done go to interactive mode, see that only the current view is visible; to switch current view you need to go to design mode and open the **Tools | Manage views** menu.

20. Save the document as 40 iPad Landscape Portrait views.

21. Now bring up the mobile application on the iPad and open the document. Rotate the screen and notice how the different views are shown depending on the screen orientation.

How it works...

When a document has **Supported Orientations** set to **Portrait and Landscape**, if multiple views are available, MicroStrategy app will match the current orientation and resolution to the view that best fits the screen.

There's more...

You can add grids, graphs, and more to the views and decide if that particular object is always visible or it is shown only in the currently selected view. So, for example, if you have a company logo you can set this to appear in each view by answering **Yes** to this message:

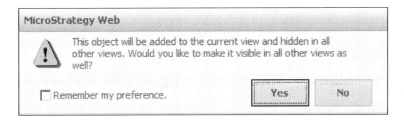

Exercise 29

Add two different grids on the document number 40; one in the Landscape layout and the other in the Portrait one. You can use different attributes, so that you give the user two different perspectives, for example, **Sales by Month** in one and **Sales by Category** in the other.

How would you add an image to both views? If the image doesn't fit in **Portrait View**, how would you resize it?

$$\Bigg[\qquad \text{You can watch a screencast of this operation at:} \qquad \Bigg]$$
> http://at5.us/Ch9V4

Adding panels to mobile documents

We saw already the use of panels in dashboards; the same technique can be applied to mobile development with an added feature: on mobile devices we can take advantage of the swipe gesture to change between a panel and the other. Additionally, we can design a small panel to be hidden at execution time, and display it as a pop-up information window with more details, for example, when the user taps an attribute.

Getting ready

We will modify the **40 iPad Landscape Portrait views** document from the previous recipe; so you need to have completed it before going further. Start by saving that document with a new name: `41 iPad Landscape Portrait with Panels`.

How to do it...

Open the document **41 iPad Landscape Portrait with Panels** in design mode:

1. Be sure that the landscape view is selected (that is, you see the light blue background). From the **Insert** menu click on **Panel Stack**.

2. In the warning message that appears click on **No**.

3. Drag the cross cursor to draw a rectangle, when you release the mouse button a new gray panel stack is created.

4. See that there's a toolbar just above the title of the stack, click on the next-to-last button with an **a|b** icon (tool tip: **Rename Panel**).

5. In the **Rename Panel** dialog, type `First Panel` as **Name** and click on **OK**.

6. Again, on the toolbar look for the fourth button from the left (tool tip: **Add Panel**) and click on it, notice that the title has changed.

7. Repeat steps 4 and 5 to name this as `Second Panel`.

8. Repeat step 6, then 4 and 5 to add a third panel and rename it (hum...) `Third Panel`.

9. With the second and third buttons on the stack toolbar (tool tips: **Display Previous Panel** and **Display Next Panel**) you can move between panels, go back to **First Panel**.

10. When the **Panel** is active, click on the button with a green plus icon on the left just below the title bar.

11. From the drop-down menu, choose **Shape** and then **Rectangle**, answer **No** to the warning.

12. A new dark gray rectangle is created and selected inside the **First Panel**, resize it so that it covers all the space inside this panel.

With the help of *Ctrl* key you can fine-size objects for your pixel-perfect pleasure...

13. Right-click inside the **Rectangle** shape and click on **Properties and Formatting....**

14. Go to **Format | Color and Lines**, set **Fill | Color** to **Dark Blue** and click on **OK**.

15. Move the cursor to the stack title bar and click it so that the stack toolbar appears.

16. Now go to the **Second Panel** and click the green plus icon below the title.

17. Repeat steps 11 to 14 using **Light Blue** as **Fill | Color** value.

18. Go to the **Third Panel** using the **Display Next Panel** button.

19. And yes...create another rectangle shape to fill the entire **Third Panel**, giving it the **Pale Blue** fill color.

20. Move back to the **First Panel** and save the document, overwriting the existing number 41, and run the newly saved document.

21. In the Web Interface, you can move between panels with the small arrows positioned on the right and left of the stack title bar.

22. In the iPad, you swipe your finger on the panel to switch from one to another. Isn't it cool?

How it works...

Panel stacks are another way of putting a lot of information on a document without crowding the interface, letting the user move around and flip through panels as they please. With the added capability of touch screens this component gets a lot easier to handle.

Each panel is actually a document in itself where you can put grids, graphs, and all other objects.

Designing documents in the Web Interface needs a little time to get used to the various controls, and—especially on small screens—a lot of patience for the correct positioning on the canvas.

The same result can be obtained from the desktop application, where you have a similar Document Editor. Try it yourself and decide which is more comfortable for you. Sometimes, you may need to use one or the other depending on your target platform and audience.

There's more...

Colors, transparencies, and fonts may have different rendering on mobile devices than on desktop monitors. This is due to the operating system, the display technology, the scaling, and other factors. Be sure to test the output on the final user's platform before releasing to production.

 You can watch a screencast of this and the next operation at:

  ▶ `http://at5.us/Ch9V5`

Creating panel selectors

We can swipe to move from one panel to another or we can add a panel selector to the bottom of the stack. Each panel can have its own set of objects, showing a different perspective of the data.

Getting ready

You need to have completed the previous recipe to continue.

How to do it...

We are now adding some content to the panels; go back to the design mode inside the Web Interface:

1. First of all, we create a panel selector. Click on the title bar of the stack to bring up the toolbar and right-click on the first button on the left (tool tip: **Select / Move**).

2. From the context menu choose **Create Panel Selector**. A drop-down list will be created on the top left of the stack.

3. Click on the panel selector and open its context menu with a right-click on the cross arrow button then select **Properties and Formatting...**.

4. In the **Properties | Selector** section, under the **Mobile** header, enable the checkbox labeled **Display selector docked to its panel stack** and confirm with **OK**.

5. Save, overwriting the document, and run it to test how the selector works.

6. Go back to design mode; we now need to add a dataset to the document, click on the button labeled **Please click on the button to add a dataset**.

7. In the **Select Dataset** dialog browse to **My Reports** folder and select the **28 InternetSales Dashboard** report, click on **OK**.

8. From the **Insert** menu, select **Grid** and answer **No** to the warning message; now drag the mouse cursor to draw a rectangle. When you release the cursor a new empty grid is created on the **First Panel**.

9. Open the **Properties and Formatting** window of this grid (right-click on the cross arrow) and set the following values:

    ❑ In **Properties | Layout**:

    Left: 20 and **Top**: 20

    Width: Fixed at 350 and **Height**: Fit to contents

    ❑ In **Properties | Grid**:

    Check **Remove extra column**.

10. Confirm with **OK**. Now drag the **Product Category** attribute to the **Drop objects here to add rows** area on the grid.

11. Drag the **Year** attribute to the **Drop objects here to add columns** area on the grid.

12. Drag **Sum SalesAmount from FactInternetSales** to the **Drop Metrics here to add data** area.

13. Bring up the context menu for the grid, right-clicking on the cross arrow button and select **Edit View Filter...**.

14. In the **VIEW FILTER** windows, click on **Add Condition**, open the **Filter On** dropdown and pick **Product Category**.

15. Next, click on the radio button named **Select** and move **Bikes** from the left to the right side of the shopping cart.

16. To confirm the selection you need to click on a small round button with a black checkmark (tool tip: **Apply**).

17. You should see now a line saying **Product Category In List (Bikes)**, close this window with the **OK** button.

18. Optionally rename the panel to Bikes. Right-click on the cross arrow to open the grid menu and select **Copy**.

19. Move on to the **Second Panel**, right-click inside the blue rectangle and choose **Paste**; a copy of the **First Panel** grid is created in the second one.

20. From the grid context menu select **Edit View Filter...** hit the **In List (Bikes)** hyperlink, and use the arrows in the shopping cart to remove **Bikes** and add **Clothing**. Click on **Apply** and close with **OK**.

21. Optionally rename the panel Clothing.

22. Move to the **Third Panel**, right-click inside it and paste another grid.

23. Again, using the **Edit View Filter...** option, modify the shopping cart so that the resulting condition would be **Product Category in List (Accessories)** and click on **OK**.

24. Optionally, rename this panel `Accessories`.

25. Move back to the first panel, save the document, overwriting the existing one and run it to see the result.

26. Try to flip through panels with both the small arrows and the selector. Open the document on the iPad and see the difference: here the panel selector is a bar on the bottom with three small white spots. Besides swiping, if you tap a spot you can move to a different panel.

How it works...

We created a grid with a view filter, then copied and pasted onto the other panels. The dataset contains sales amounts for all of the product categories, but every grid has a different view filter. We added a docked panel selector so it is easier to switch from one to another on a mobile device, provided that your fingertip is smaller than mine.

The **Remove extra column** option eliminates the **Metrics** cell from the grid, giving more space to the rest of the data.

There's more...

In the Web Interface:

1. Go to design mode and open the **Properties and Formatting** window of the panel selector.

2. In **Properties | General**, uncheck **Show Title Bar**.

3. In **Properties | Layout**, under the **Selector** header change **DHTML Style** to **Radio buttons** and **Orientation** to **Horizontal**.

4. Click on **OK**; now resize the selector so that it occupies the part above the title bar and has a width equal to the entire stack.

5. Save the document and run it. Much better now, you can point to the radio buttons in the Web Interface and still use the docked selector on the iPad:

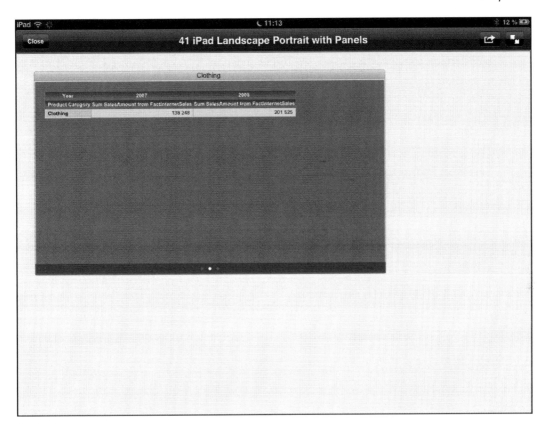

 You can watch a screencast of this and the previous operation at:
> http://at5.us/Ch9V5

Adding details with pop-up windows

Pop-up panels are another useful tool in the MicroStrategy Mobile client, we can use them to display additional details and add more interactivity to our documents. In the Web Interface pop up can be achieved with some JavaScript tricks, while on the iPad there is no need for that; just create a new panel and set it as an info window. Let's see how to do it.

Getting ready

You need to have completed the previous recipes to continue.

How to do it...

Open the **41 iPad Landscape Portrait with Panels** document in design mode:

1. Open the **Insert** menu and select **Panel Stack**.

2. Answer **No** to the warning message.

3. Draw a rectangle in an empty area of the **First Panel**.

4. When you release the mouse button a new panel stack with one panel is created. Rename the panel: `Details`.

5. Right-click on the cross arrow icon to open the stack context menu and select **Properties and Formatting...**.

6. In **Properties | General**, modify the **Name** to `Info Window`. Below the **Panel Stack** header check the option box labeled **Use as Information Window** and confirm with **OK**.

7. Now click on the green plus icon inside the **Details** panel and choose **Grid**.

8. Answer **No** to the message. Now there is a grid inside the **Details** panel.

9. Fill this grid with these objects:

    ❑   **Product Subcategory** on rows

    ❑   **Sum SalesAmount from FactInternetSales** on data

10. Open the context menu for the grid and select **Edit View Filter...**.

11. Add the condition `Product Category In List (Bikes)` and click on **OK** to save the view filter.

12. Hover to the grid on the left and place the cursor over the **Year** attribute header and right-click on it. From the menu that appears pick **Use as Selector**.

13. Right-click on it again and this time select **Edit Selector...**.

14. Verify that in the right part of the shopping cart, in the **Selected Targets** area, the **Info Window** panel stack is listed, and click on **OK**.

15. Save the document, overwrite the existing one, and run it.

16. In the Web Interface the **Info Window** panel stack is hidden.

17. Open the document in the iPad and tap one **Year** header (for example, **2008**); the **Info Window** panel stack will show the **Details** grid:

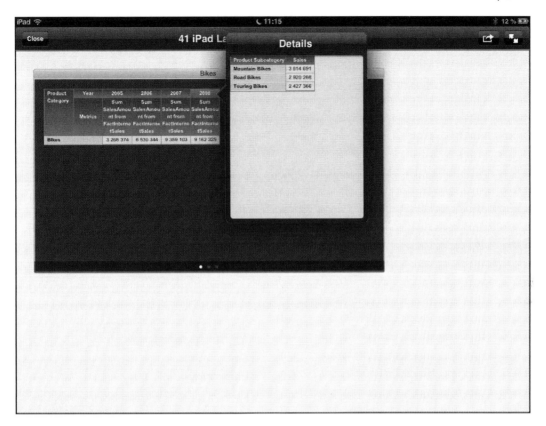

How it works...

Information windows are hidden when you open a document, but they function exactly as standard panels. So, they can be targeted by selectors and can use view filters, for example. You are not limited to grids, also graphs and other objects can be placed inside information panels. This feature adds a lot of details to a single document, and offers an impressive added value to static reports. Managers, CEOs, and decision makers will appreciate this feature, which—used consciously—saves a lot of extra gestures.

There's more...

In the Web Interface, there is a way to see information panels, if you run the document in express mode instead of interactive mode, and they function exactly as in the mobile client.

As with documents in the Web, the recommendation is to always put the least amount of datasets needed to display the results. I prefer to create one single ad-hoc dataset for each document instead of reusing previous reports that may contain extra unused columns or rows. Add to this that mobile devices often are connected over telephone networks with limited bandwidth. So, think twice before overloading a mobile dashboard with high-definition images or million-row grids: one document that on the PC may seem fast, could take minutes to download over a wireless connection. And, we know too well, our users on the go have no time or battery to spare.

 You can watch a screencast of this operation at:
   ▶   `http://at5.us/Ch9V6`

Linking from one document to another

Mobile BI should be attractive and a smooth ride experience. When looking at data riding a bumpy bus or commuting on a crowded train, every tap counts. Keep in mind how and where your users will engage with exploding pie charts or flying info windows. Have mercy, and provide an easy way to navigate from one report to the next; not every iPad travels in business class.

Getting ready

You should have completed the previous recipes to continue. In **My Reports** folder inside the Web Interface right-click on the document numbered 41 and select **Properties**. From the dialog box copy and write down the ID of the document (see the following screen capture):

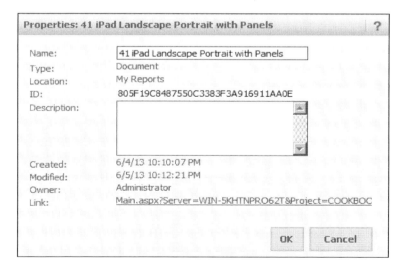

We will modify the **40 iPad Landscape Portrait views** document that we created in one of the previous recipes; so you need to have completed it before going further. Start by saving that document with a new name: 42 iPad Landscape Portrait Landing Page.

How to do it...

We are creating a home page with a link to the document number 41:

1. Open the document 42 in design mode, switch to the landscape view and from the **Insert** menu select **Shape | Rectangle**.

2. This time (very important) answer **Yes** to the warning message, so that the rectangle will be visible in portrait view as well.

3. Draw the rectangle and open its **Properties and Formatting...**.

4. Set these values:

   - In **Properties | Layout**:

     Left: 40 and **Top**: 40

     Width: Fixed at 160 and **Height**: Fixed at 160

   - In **Format | Color and Lines**:

     Fill | Color: (any color you like as long as it is Indigo)

5. Click on **OK** to confirm; now from the **Insert** menu choose **Text**.

6. Again, answer **Yes** to the message and draw the text area inside the indigo rectangle.

7. Type Tap to open the Category Dashboard inside the text area.

8. Click on the **Format** menu and use the toolbar to modify the color and the font of the text (set it Arial 18 points, white).

9. Now right-click on the text area and open the **Properties and Formatting...** and set:

   - In **Properties | Layout**:

     Left: 45 and **Top**: 45

     Width: Fixed at 150 and **Height**: Fixed at 150

10. Confirm with **OK**.

11. Switch to portrait view; note that the rectangle and the text did not maintain the layout, this is by design. We need to re-set the properties for dimension and location of the controls.

12. So, open **Properties and Formatting...** for the rectangle and set:

- ❑ In **Properties | Layout**

     Left: 40 and **Top**: 40

     Width: Fixed at 160 and **Height**: Fixed at 160

13. Repeat for the text:

- ❑ In **Properties | Layout**

     Left: 45 and **Top**: 45

     Width: Fixed at 150 and **Height**: Fixed at 150

14. Save the document, overwrite it, and run it.

15. Switch to design mode and change the view to landscape.

16. Open **Properties and Formatting...** for the text area (see screen capture):

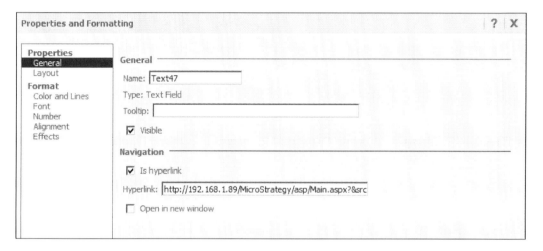

17. In **Properties | General**, check the option **Is hyperlink**, and type this URL (you can copy it from the companion code file):

    ```
    http://192.168.1.89/MicroStrategy/asp/Main.aspx?&src=Main.aspx.
    2048001&evt=2048001&currentViewMedia=2&documentID=805F19C848755
    0C3383F3A916911AA0E
    ```

18. Change the IP 192.168.1.89 with that of your machine and the ID 805F19C8487550C3383F3A916911AA0E with the ID of your document numbered 41, uncheck **Open in a new window** and confirm with OK.

19. Save the document, overwrite the existing one, and open it on the iPad to see it.

How it works...

With hyperlinks you can chain several documents together and create a consistent navigation path, so that the user will be redirected from one screen to another in a rational way.

There's more...

With hyperlinks you can create a custom home screen for your mobile users; open the MicroStrategy Mobile Administrator:

1. Click on **Mobile Configuration** in the top-right of the page.

2. Under the **Actions** header, click on the **Modify** icon, and then select the **Home Screen** tab.

3. Click on the radio button labeled **Display a custom home screen**, the option **Display a report or document** is already selected, then hit the small down arrow button to open the login information dialog for the **COOKBOOK** project.

4. Type Administrator and the corresponding password, then click on **Login**.

5. Navigate to **My Reports** folder and pick the document number 42.

6. Scroll to the bottom of the page and click on **Save**.

7. Back to the **Mobile Configuration** page click on the globe icon to open the **Generate Configuration URL** dialog box and click on **Generate URL**.

8. Copy the URL again and send it via e-mail to you iPad.

9. Open the link from your mobile device and MicroStrategy client will automatically open the landing document with the hyperlink to the dashboard.

 You can watch screencasts of this operation at:
  ▶ http://at5.us/Ch9V7
  ▶ http://at5.us/Ch9V8

See also

▶ The *Answering prompts in reports or documents* recipe in *Chapter 10, Mobile BI for Users*

10
Mobile BI for Users

In this chapter, we will cover:

- ▶ Answering prompts in reports or documents
- ▶ Sorting, drilling, and paging
- ▶ Adding notes and sharing
- ▶ When things go wrong

Introduction

Your company has given you a brand new iPad and the IT department has loaded a BI tool in it, so what's next? Install Angry Birds I suppose. I mean, after that.

How do we tap our way through hundreds of seemingly identical dashboards and reports, what is the best way to answer to a 10 thousands elements prompt, and do I have to swipe 800 times to reach to the end of the list? We'll try to answer that.

 The first time I borrowed my colleague's iPad, the icons on the home screen were trembling. A most welcome answer from Google directed me to the article *How to Stop the Icons on My iPad From Shaking*. That left me with a question: do shaking icons require more battery power?

Now after the kids have cut a reasonable amount of ropes and fed the little green monster at least until tomorrow, we can reach for the MicroStrategy icon and begin the journey.

Your BI administrator has configured the application so that you'll start from a home page or, most probably, a list of available documents in a public folder. This list is automatically refreshed when you open the app; if you don't seem to find the report you are looking for, the easiest thing to do is going back to the iPad home screen and open the tool again.

There is an **i** like information icon on the top-right corner of the screen. From here you can access the help page, MicroStrategy Express (which is a cloud version of the software, see *Chapter 13, MicroStrategy Express*), and the settings page. Feel free to explore the help and Express but please trust me when I tell you, "don't change anything in the settings page, your BI admin will be grateful".

To run a report simply tap its name, then on the **View** button.

Some reports contain prompts, which are questions that the user must answer before executing the query.

Answering prompts in reports or documents

The report number 38 named `Prompted Filter on Products` contains a prompt; this means that the user has to choose one or more products before the results are displayed. The list contains some 600 products.

Getting ready

You or your IT team need to have completed the previous chapter to continue.

How to do it...

Search through the list and find the report number 38. Select it, and tap **View** to open it:

1. After a few seconds, you'll see a list of products on the left, optionally some of the products may be already selected: the number between parentheses indicates how many, **(0/606)** in the case of the screen capture:

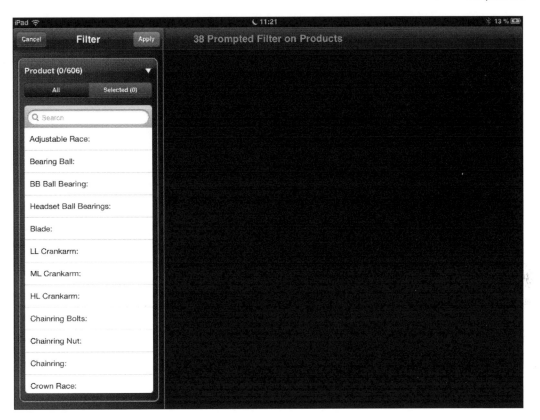

2. There are two tabs (**All** and **Selected**). Tap the second and uncheck all of the selected elements if any, then go back to the **All** tab.

3. In the search box, type Gloves. The list filters all the gloves, check all of them and then tap **Done**.

4. In the **Selected** tab, the number between parentheses reflects the number of gloves that we have checked.

5. You can repeat step 3 and add more products, for example, Brakes or Helmet. Always tap **Done** to confirm.

6. Now tap **Apply** and the report is executed. After a few seconds, you can see the results in a grid.

7. If you want to modify the selection, tap the **Filter** button to the right of the title and repeat the search.

How it works...

When we tap a prompted report, MicroStrategy loads the prompt, and only after the selection is applied the query runs on the database server with a `WHERE` clause to return the list of specified products.

There's more...

The same report may contain several prompts such as: date selection or geographic area or others. If there is no data that satisfies a specified selection, the result pane displays a message: **No data returned for this view. This might be because the applied filter excludes all data**. Try to filter only on `Caps` to see an example.

Sorting, drilling, and paging

Most of data manipulation techniques of the Desktop application can be used in the mobile app also; like ordering rows or going deeper in detail.

Getting ready

We will use the reports named **17 Internet Sales by Category, Country and Year** and **18 Dynamic Aggregation by Country and Product**. You need to have completed them to continue.

How to do it...

Open the mobile app and scroll the report list to find the number 17: this one has a page-by element:

1. Tap the report and run it, you will see the result page and a new bar with a button selector. In this case, the `Year` attribute is the page-by element.

2. Tap in the center of the grid and swipe, you will see an indicator showing the present year and the next (or previous) flashing for a brief moment. When the indicator fades away, the grid shows the results for another year.

3. Repeat the swipe to move back or forth in the page elements (depending on the sort order, the past years are to the right or to the left).

4. Another way to flip pages is to tap-and-hold the button in the page-by bar. Depending on the length of the attribute label and the size of the finger, this second option may be tricky, see the following screen capture. I've seen people doing this with a Bratwurst...:

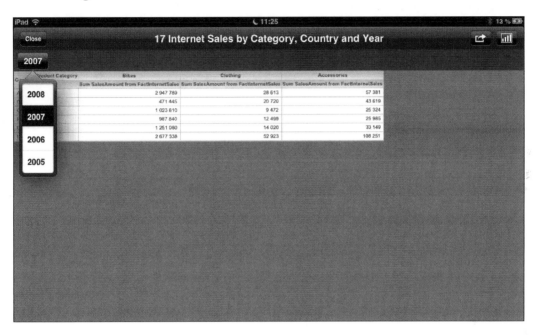

5. In the drop-down list that opens, tap the year you want to switch to.

6. Now close this report and run the number 18.

7. When the grid appears, tap-and-hold the **Bikes** element, when you release, a new context menu pops up with the option to drill. Tap the menu to see the drill interface. Use the swipe movement on the drill path selector to highlight the direction where you want to go, for example, **Product Subcategory**.

8. When the **Product Subcategory** is highlighted, tap it and tap again **Update**.

9. See that the grid is now filtered on the **Bikes** category and displays the subcategory on the rows.

10. Look for **Germany** in the first group (**Mountain Bikes**). Tap-and-hold, then release and select **Drill**. Drill to **City**: now you see the list of cities in Germany where we sold mountain bikes. Wunderbar!

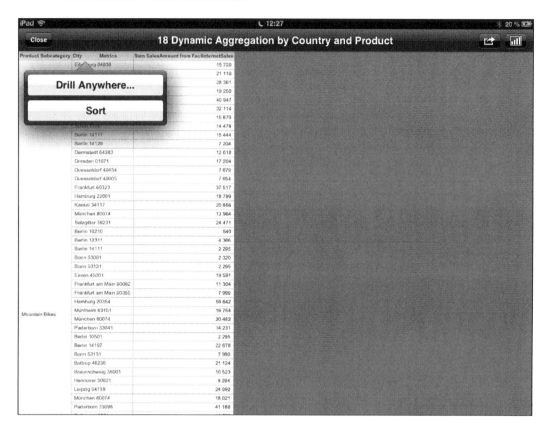

11. Now we want to sort the cities by name. Tap-and-hold the **City** column header (not the city name) and release so that the context menu appears. Select **Sort** and then **Ascending**.

12. The cities are now sorted by name.

How it works...

When the user navigates to a different attribute (from country to city) the request is sent to the Mobile Server and the result is retrieved, while in the case of sorting the operation is performed on the app. Care must be taken when drilling to a completely different path as the request may be very complex. It's the developer's responsibility to prepare easy-to-explore reports and predefined exploration routes with the use of, for example, document links.

There's more...

On the title bar, there is a small graph button, tap this to quickly switch the view from grid to graph. Try it with report number 17 to see how easy it is to change from a table view to a chart.

The other button on the title bar, a curved arrow, is the action button. If you tap it and select **Email Screen**, you can share the current view of the report by e-mail.

Adding notes and sharing

MicroStrategy Mobile allows you to add comments, notes, and freehand drawings to a report view. Let your creativity enrich the otherwise monotonous information from the BI tool:

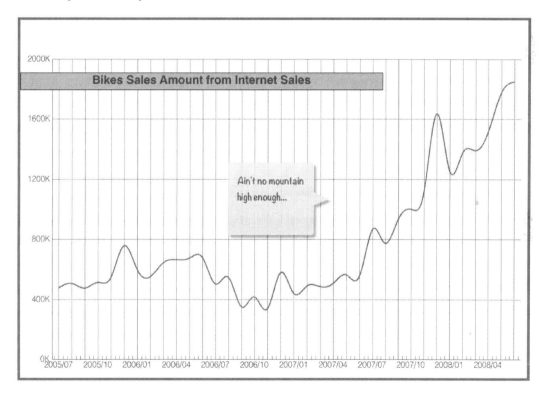

Getting ready

We will use the report named **23 Bikes Internet Sales by Month**. So, you need to have it ready before going further.

How to do it...

Open the report number 23 on your mobile device:

1. Tap the action button on the right-hand side of the title bar.

2. Select **Annotate and Share**, this will open a screenshot of the report.

3. Use your finger to draw freehand shapes or write polite comments.

4. Tap your masterpiece and choose **Add Comment**.

5. You can type text inside the box that is shown. Comment boxes can be moved by tapping-and-dragging them around; or even resized by dragging their corners.

6. Once you're ready to share, tap the action button again and then on **Email Screen**.

How it works...

Annotations and comments are not saved with the report. So, when you close and reopen it, your drawings are gone.

There's more...

If you want to store a snapshot of the report for your personal records without sending it by mail, from the action button select **Annotate and Share**, then tap again the same action button icon and select **Save in Photos**.

When things go wrong

It doesn't happen very often, does it?

Sometimes we find ourselves in a meeting where the iPad refuses to work; besides the standard checks on the battery and the Wi-Fi coverage, what can we do? Misbehaving reports can be due to many different reasons. Most of the time, if nothing was changed the night before, it could be a network issue or just a wrong answer to a prompt. If—beyond any reasonable attempt—the report refuses to deliver its payload, it's time to pick up the phone and dial IT support.

I have been, for many years, that guy on the other end of the phone, with the sleepy voice and an evasive attitude.

In the unlikely event of an IT problem, be prepared to give the following data:

▸ Make and model (version of operating system if applicable) of the mobile device: the MicroStrategy clients vary a lot from one another, and it's useful to know beforehand which tablet/smartphone you are using

▸ IP address of the device (if known) to detect network issues

▸ Name of the Intelligence Server, project, and report you are trying to access and the answers selected in every prompt; so that the IT guy can repeat your exact steps to reproduce the problem

Mobile clients have a diagnostic log that can be accessed for troubleshooting purposes. Messages in the log page may help the IT guy diagnose the problem.

Getting ready

You need to have experienced one or more errors to continue.

How to do it...

To simulate a malfunction, you may stop the virtual machine we've used through the course of the book; in this way, we artificially create a service outage. Open a report on the iPad and wait for it to time out with an error:

1. Open the information menu and tap **Parameters**.

2. In the **Parameters** page, select **Advanced Settings**.

3. The last option in the **Advanced Settings** page is **View Log**, tap it.

4. The almost incomprehensible messages here are bad things that happened behind the scenes:

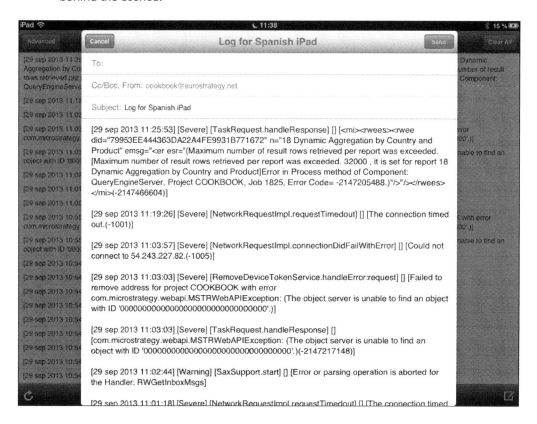

5. Tap the icon at the bottom-right corner and a new e-mail message will be created with the log content. Send it to the IT guy. I know: had the problem been the Wi-Fi connection you wouldn't be able to send it, in that case, unfortunately, there is very little to do on the mobile side.

How it works...

It's important to know where to look in case of error. The MicroStrategy Mobile app offers a detailed log in the **Advanced Settings** page that can help troubleshoot less-than-optimal performance.

There's more...

The logging level can be set on the same page: you, or the IT support, may select from **Warning**, **Errors**, **Messages**, or **All**.

See also

▶   The *Creating virtual attributes with consolidations* recipe in *Chapter 11, Consolidations, Custom Groups, and Transformations*

11
Consolidations, Custom Groups, and Transformations

In this chapter, we will cover:

- ▸ Creating virtual attributes with consolidations
- ▸ Aggregating results with custom groups
- ▸ Creating bands on metrics (custom groups banding)
- ▸ Month-to-date and year-to-date transformations

Introduction

With this chapter, we start the advanced part of our BI project. The objects that we will learn in this section are intended to answer specific requirements while developing reports. As far as I'm concerned, I use them occasionally, when no other technique can accomplish the task or when the data warehouse is a complete closed box and there is no way to modify the design of the tables.

Sometimes, especially in large companies or convoluted public institutions, the responsible of the database server is an unreachable entity and trying to persuade the multiple layers of IT decision makers to do a modification in the design it's simply not worth the time.

In those cases, the multiple manipulations that MicroStrategy offers come in very handy to work around Byzantine corporate structures and star schemas carved in stone.

I often like to repeat that there is no single solution to a reporting requirement: depending on the skillset of the programmer, the tools available, and the time allotted to develop, there may be more than one correct path that leads to the desired result. Each of them is more or less elegant, performing, scalable, and comprehensible but as long as the numbers are correct, they're all plausible. Stick to your preferred method; or, in other words, there is no need to use a feature just because it's there. It is nevertheless important to know that the feature exists, so that we can rely on it when we're out of silver bullets.

Creating virtual attributes with consolidations

This type of object is useful, fast, and it is calculated on the Intelligent Server side so it doesn't put load on the database. As the name suggests, it serves the purpose of consolidating row values. This means not only adding one row to another, but also doing row-to-row calculations.

Remember from previous chapters that there are multiple `London` or `Paris` elements in the `City` attribute, the schema was designed this way to respond to a specific requirement: allow the reports to display separate ZIP codes in large cities. Now we want to have a look at how much we sell in the entire city of London, but we don't have such an element in the `City` attribute.

So, we create our own virtual attribute to show, in one single row, a consolidated value for all the elements that represent the city of London and another row with the values for the rest of the UK.

Getting ready

You need to have completed the preceding chapters before going on.

How to do it...

We will create a consolidation in **My Objects** folder:

1. In MicroStrategy Desktop application, open **My Objects** folder, right-click on the empty area on the right and select **New | Consolidation** from the context menu.

2. Leave the default **Empty Consolidation** and click on **OK**.

3. We are in the Consolidation Editor, very similar to other editors we used already, maximize this window to have sufficient space and click on the text element **Click here to add new consolidation element**.

4. Change the text **New Derived Element** to `London Area`, the red row below says **Empty Expression**.

5. In the **Object Browser** pane, double-click on the **Geography** hierarchy to explore the attributes that belong to it.

6. Double-click on the **Country** attribute, then on the **United Kingdom** element and on the **City** attribute.

7. Now you see a list of city elements, you can sort them by clicking on the **DESC** header. Use *Shift* + click to select all the London elements (there should be 14 of them) and drag them onto the expression text area in the lower-right part of the Consolidation Editor.

8. Move to the upper part and hit **Click here to add new consolidation element**.

9. Rename this element as Rest of UK.

10. Now select all elements in the city list from **Abingdon** to **Liverpool** and drag them to the expression pane. Repeat the step with all elements from **Maidenhead** to **York YO15**. By default, MicroStrategy adds a **+** sign between elements.

11. Click on **Save and Close**, name it UK Areas. Let's put it to the test.

12. Go to **My Reports** folder and create a blank new one.

13. Add **Sum SalesAmount from FactResellerSales** to columns; now click on **My Personal Objects** shortcut and open **My Objects** folder.

14. **Add to rows** the recently created consolidation and run the report.

15. Save the report as 50 UK Sales but do not close it.

16. From the **Data** menu, click on **Grand Totals**—what happens? ...Ouch! Nothing, no total here. By default, consolidations do not allow subtotals.

17. Save and close the report, move to **My Objects** folder and double-click on **UK Areas** to edit.

18. Right-click on any of the elements, for example, **Rest of UK**, in the context menu there is a **Subtotals** option, click on **Enabled** (see the following screen capture):

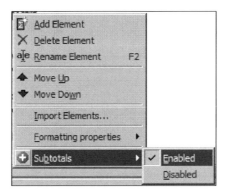

19. Save and close the consolidation and re-run the report.

20. Now the **Total** row shows **4279009**.

How it works...

If you look at the SQL view, you'll see what happens behind the scenes:

```
where a12.GeographyKey in (244, 245, 246, 247, 248, 249, [...]group
by a12.GeographyKey
```

MicroStrategy generates a query with all the UK elements in the WHERE clause, grouping by GeographyKey, which is the ID of the City attribute; the result is retrieved, then the consolidation is performed by the Intelligence Server (the part that does the calculation is called Analytical Engine as opposed to the SQL Engine, which generates the SELECT).

See the last sentence of the SQL view:

```
[Analytical engine calculation steps:
   1.   Calculate consolidation: <UK Areas>
   2.   Perform cross-tabbing
]
```

This means that the RDBMS knows nothing about UK Areas, we created our virtual attribute without having to modify the database schema.

One drawback of this technique is that you need to know your elements beforehand; you cannot dynamically select all London elements without prior knowledge of how many London(s) are there. See the custom groups later in the chapter for an alternative.

There's more...

We want to add more rows to the grid, and look at how London compares to the rest of the UK. Consolidations allow us to perform this kind of inter-row operations, such as London / Rest of UK. Follow these steps:

1. Close the report and open the **UK Areas** consolidation, add a new consolidation element.

2. Give the new element the name London / UK.

3. Drag the first consolidation element, named **London Area**, onto the lower part of the screen, in the **Enter your expression here** area. The resulting expression is **[London Area]**.

4. Click on the division button labeled with a forward slash, which is right above the expression and then drag the second consolidation element named **Rest of UK** and drop it after the / so that the resulting expression is: **([London Area] / [Rest of UK])**.

5. Click on **Save and Close**. Right-click on the report named **50 UK Sales**, select **Purge Report Cache** and run the report again. What a surprise, the new row **London / UK** shows **1** and the total row **4279010**. Hmmm... something's not working as expected.

More Info

What is happening is that we have a ratio (`London / UK`), which should be formatted as a percentage, but it's not; since we are showing no decimals, the number is rounded to `1`.

Then in the **Total** row we have a sum of all the values in the consolidation, that's why the number shown is **4279010** instead of **4279009**.

This is a very common mistake when using this type of object, and we should always keep in mind that, if we want a total here, we should create another element with the sum of the appropriate values only, in this case:

```
([London Area] + [Rest of UK])
```

One extremely useful feature of consolidations is that we can give different formats to different rows. It is worth noting that the format will be used for any metric used in conjunction with the consolidation (in the example, we are applying it to a `SalesAmount` metric, but could be any other metric); it is up to the developer of the report to use it appropriately. So, let's change that format and add a total:

1. Edit the consolidation.
2. Right-click on **London / UK**, select **Formatting properties | Element Values...**.
3. In the **Format Cells** dialog, under the **Number** tab, choose **Percent**, select the first option from **Negative numbers** and click on **OK**.
4. Add a new consolidation element and name it `UK Total`.
5. Use the formula (`[London Area] + [Rest of UK]`), see image:

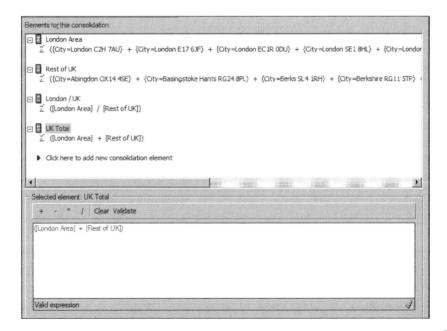

6. Click on **Save and Close**, and re-run the report.

7. To disable the **Total** line, go to **Data** menu and then **Subtotals** and click on the button **Clear All**. Now you have a proper result.

Exercise 30

Change the header and value of **UK Total** so that they display in bold.

 You can watch a screencast of this operation at:
▶ `http://at5.us/Ch11V1`

Aggregating results with custom groups

Custom groups are another type of object that allow us to aggregate results on a report or document. They differ from consolidations in several aspects, the most important being that the SQL needed to calculate custom groups is executed on the RDBMS side.

Unlike consolidations, custom groups cannot perform row-level calculations; but they offer a lot of flexibility when defining the elements. A custom group element is a set of rows identified by a name and a filter condition. Thinking about the previous example: instead of manually picking all the 14 London elements of the `City` attribute, we would create a filter that restricts only those elements with the `DESC` form beginning with London.

Additionally, in the filter definition of a custom group element, we can use metrics, like in "Products of the Bike Category that sold more than 1500 units", and display results in bands like in "Bikes that sold from 1000 to 1199 units, from 1200 to 1299, 1300 units or more, etc."

Furthermore, we can expand the custom group elements and see, for example, every bike inside a band.

It is useful to think about custom groups as a collection of mini-reports stacked one above the other, each mini-report having its own filtering conditions.

Getting ready

You need to have completed the previous recipe to continue.

How to do it...

In this recipe, we will create the same UK Areas as we did before, so that we see the difference in generated SQL; later we'll move on to create a more complex custom group:

1. Go to **My Objects** folder, right-click on an empty area, and select **New | Custom Group** from the context menu. Leave default **Empty Custom Group** and click on **OK**.

2. This is the Custom Group Editor (similar to the Filter Editor); maximize the window to have sufficient space.

3. In the **Object Browser** pane on the left, double-click on **Geography** to list the attributes in the hierarchy.

4. The right part of the editor is the **Custom Group definition** pane. Drag the `City` attribute from the left list and drop it onto the area on the right with the text **Double-click here or drag an object from the object browser to add a custom group element**.

5. A new custom group element is created with an attribute qualification on **City**; in the lower-right part of the screen click on the **Qualify on** drop-down list and select **DESC**.

6. From the **Operator** list, choose **Begins with**.

7. Leave the **Value** option selected, and in the textbox to the right type `London`, then confirm with **OK**. Now the Custom Group Editor shows one element named **Custom Group Element1** containing a filter definition **City (DESC) Begins with London**.

8. Right-click on **Custom Group Element1** and from the context menu that appears select **Rename**. Type `London Area`.

9. Move to the left and double-click on the **Country** attribute to see the list of countries, pick the **United Kingdom** element, drag it to the right and drop it on the line that says **Double-click here or drag an object from the object browser to add a custom group element**, the **Custom Group element2** is created with a filter definition **Country in list (United Kingdom)**.

10. In the **Object Browser** pane, click on the button with the icon that resembles a folder with a green up arrow (tool tip: **View contents one level up**):

11. We're back in the attribute list, click on **City**, drag-and-drop it to the red **[Add Qualification]** line just below the **Country in list (United Kingdom)** to create a second filter definition on **City**.

12. Repeat steps 5, 6, and 7. A new filter definition **< Default > - City (DESC) Begins with London** is added with the **AND** operator.

13. Right-click on **AND**, select **Toggle Operator** from the menu and choose **AND NOT**.

14. Right-click on the **Custom Group Element2** line and rename it as Rest of UK.

15. The final **Custom Group definition** should look like the image:

```
Custom Group definition

⊟ •♦ London Area
         ⚙ City ( DESC )  Begins with London
         ▶ [Add Qualification]
⊟ •♦ Rest of UK
         ⚙ < Default > - Country In list (United Kingdom)
      AND NOT
         ⚙ < Default > - City ( DESC )  Begins with London
         ▶ [Add Qualification]
   ▶ Double-click here or drag an object from the object browser to add a custom group element.
```

16. Click on **Save and Close**. Go to **My Reports** folder, create a blank new report.

17. Click on **My Personal Objects** shortcut, double-click on **My Objects**, then right-click on **UK Areas Custom Group** and select **Add to Rows**.

18. Browse to **Public Objects | Metrics** and add **Sum SalesAmount from FactResellerSales** to columns. Run in **Grid View** and check the numbers with the report we did in the previous recipe.

19. Save the new report without closing it and name it 50 UK Sales with Custom Groups.

20. Switch to **SQL View**. Note the difference between this report and the previous in terms of SELECT statements. Close both reports.

How it works...

Custom groups generate at least one query per element. In this case you can see the first SELECT filtering on:

```
where (a13.City + ' ' + a13.PostalCode) like N'London%'
```

And the second statement with:

```
where (a13.CountryRegionCode in (N'GB')
 and (not (a13.City + ' ' + a13.PostalCode) like N'London%'))
```

In the previous report, the consolidation used a single SQL to produce the same result.

From a RDBMS perspective consolidations are more efficient; but custom groups offer a lot more flexibility.

There's more...

Now we want to see all the London elements that belong to the `London Area` element in the same report, but we don't need such a detail for the `Rest of UK` element.

A very handy feature of custom groups is the ability to detail the single item that fit into a group element. Let's see how it works:

1. After closing all reports, move to **My Objects** folder, and double-click on **UK Areas Custom Group** to edit.

2. Right-click on the first element named **London Area**, from the context menu select **Show Display Options**.

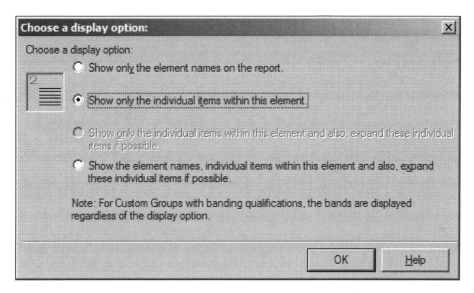

3. Click on the second option **Show only the individual items within this element**, and confirm with **OK**.

4. Click on **Save and Close**.

5. Run the **50 UK Sales with Custom Groups** report, and see the results.

More Info

Subtotals in custom groups, like in consolidations, are not enabled by default. You may enable them in the Custom Group Editor from the menu **Custom Group | Options**:

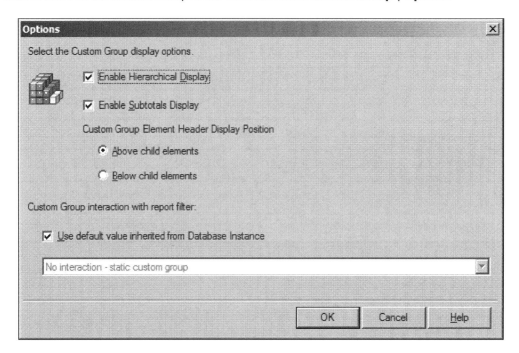

There is a checkbox labeled **Enable Subtotals Display**.

 My personal advice with custom groups and totals is to create a new separate element, as we did in the previous recipe, in order to avoid miscalculations and/or double counting.

If, on the other hand, you plan to use subtotals with custom groups, which by the way is perfectly understandable, please read on the following exercise.

Exercise 31

Do the following:

1. Edit the **UK Areas Custom Group**, right-click on **London Area**, and click on **Show Display options**.

2. Click on the last radio button, as shown in the following screen capture:

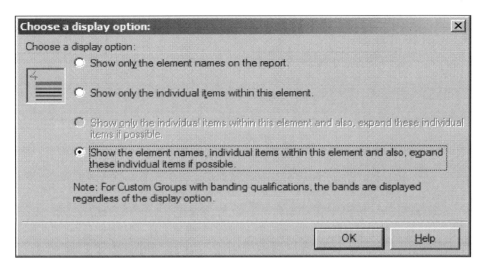

3. Click on **Save and Close**, then run the **50 UK Sales with Custom Groups** report.

How much is the grand total?

Can you tell why?

 You can watch a screencast of this operation at:
▸ `http://at5.us/Ch11V2`

Creating bands on metrics (custom groups banding)

Elements inside custom groups act like separate and independent filters; they add different WHERE and GROUP BY clauses to the SQL statement generated by the report. The filtering condition can be an attribute qualification as in the previous example, a metric qualification, or other objects. Metric qualifications work like filters on metrics (see *Chapter 4, Objects – Facts and Metrics*, and *Chapter 8, Dynamic Selection with Filters and Prompts*, for more details).

I personally use custom groups because they offer a high level of flexibility and may be modified over time, when reporting requirements change, with no need to touch the database schema. As a plus, you can give different formats to different elements.

Another very interesting feature of custom group is the **custom banding**.

Custom bands are a way to create sets of rows depending on the values of a metric. Typical use can be segmenting customers by purchase brackets or clustering products by number of units sold.

Getting ready

You need to have completed the previous recipe to continue.

How to do it...

In this recipe we are creating a custom group and a report showing the best-selling bikes that sold more than 1000 units, more than 1200, and so on:

1. Go to **My Objects** folder and right-click on the empty area to the right, select **New | Custom Group** and click on **OK**.

2. Double-click on the line that says **Double-click here or drag an object from the object browser to add a custom group element**.

3. The new element is created and named **Custom Group Element1**, rename it as Best selling Products.

4. Double-click on the red colored **[Add Qualification]** text, now in the lower part of this screen select the fifth radio button labeled **Add a Custom Group Banding qualification** and click on **OK**.

5. Click on the ellipses button next to the **Metric** textbox and select the **Sum OrderQuantity from FactResellerSales** metric, confirm by clicking on **OK**.

6. Click on the **Level...** button. In the shopping cart that appears move the **Product** attribute to the **Selected objects** list and click on **OK**.

7. Open the **Banding type** drop-down list and pick **Banding Points**, you will see a row in a white area with a band named **Band 1**, as shown in the image:

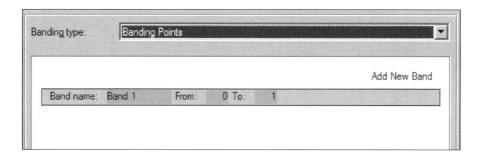

8. Click on **1** displayed next to the **To** header and change it to 1200.

9. Then click on the **0** value displayed next to the **From** header and type 1000.

10. Lastly, click on the **Band 1** text and name this band as More than 1000 units.

11. Click on the **Add New Band** text.

12. Band number 2 already has a **From** value set to **1200** in the lower limit, modify the **To** value and write 1400.

13. Rename **Band 2** to `More than 1200 units` and click on **Add New Band**.

14. Change upper limit **To** of the third band to a very high number such as `100000` and name the band `More than 1400 units`. Click on a white area to confirm the name, the editor should look like the following screenshot:

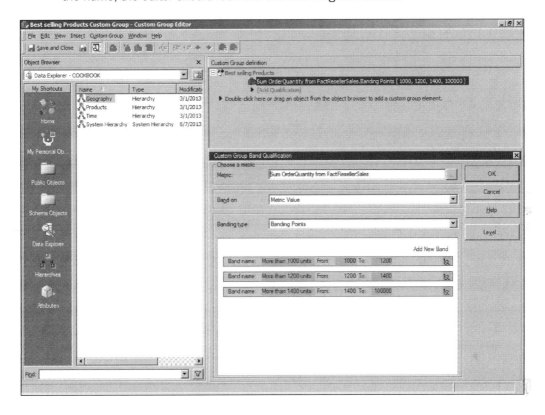

15. Close this pane with the **OK** button, click on **Save and Close**, name it as `Best selling Products Custom Group` and click on the **Save** button.

16. Go to **My Reports** and create a blank new one.

17. Browse to **My Objects** in **Object Browser** and add to rows the **Best Selling Products Custom Group**.

18. Go to **Public Objects | Metrics** and add to columns the **Sum OrderQuantity from FactResellerSales**.

19. Click on the **Data Explorer** shortcut, double-click on the **Products** hierarchy and then on **Product Category** and drag the **Bikes** element to the report filter area.

20. Run the report in **Grid View**, observe that we have the three bands each one with its `OrderQuantity` and a total for the custom group element `Best selling Products`.

21. Save this report as `51 Best selling Bikes Bands`.

How it works...

The name of the custom group element—Best selling Products—will appear at the top of the first column, then in a hierarchical view, all the names of the bands will appear in a second column.

It's worth noting that lower limits are inclusive while upper limits are not: so the first band in our example is actually between 1000 and 1199, the second between 1200 and 1399, and so on. Adjust the values of the textboxes according to the expected results.

Another aspect that may lead to confusion is that the bands always go from small numbers to big numbers. There is no way to create them in reverse order that is from a higher to a lower value (at least until version 9.3.0).

The Level is actually the GROUP BY clause of the query: is the Level at which we calculate the OrderQuantity before filtering those Products that pass the 1000 threshold. Go to **SQL View** to see how the HAVING clause is used to restrict the result set.

There's more...

What if we want to sort the banded products by OrderQuantity in descending order? It actually makes sense to have the top bikes first in the report grid. Try this:

1. In **My Objects** folder, double-click on **Best Selling Products Custom Group** to edit.
2. Right-click on the name of the first element to bring up the context menu, click on **Show display options**.
3. Select the second radio button **Show only the individual items within this element** and click on **OK**.
4. Click on **Save and Close**, go to **My Reports**.
5. Open the report number 51 in **Design View** and browse to **Attributes**.
6. Add the **Product** attribute to rows and run the report.
7. When the grid appears, right-click on the **Sum OrderQuantity from FactResellerSales** header and from the context menu select **Sort rows by this column | Descending**.
8. Now the bands are in reverse order, save the report as 51 Best selling Bikes Bands DESC.

Exercise 32

Create a new fact: OrderQuantity from FactInternetSales

Create a new metric: Sum OrderQuantity from FactInternetSales

Modify **Best Selling Products Custom Group**, rename the first element to `Best selling Products (Resellers)`, and create a second element `Best selling Products (Internet)` with similar bands (1000-1200, 1200-1400, 1400-100000) based on the `Sum OrderQuantity from FactInternetSales` metric.

Build the report `52 Best Selling Products Reseller and Internet`, like the one in the following image:

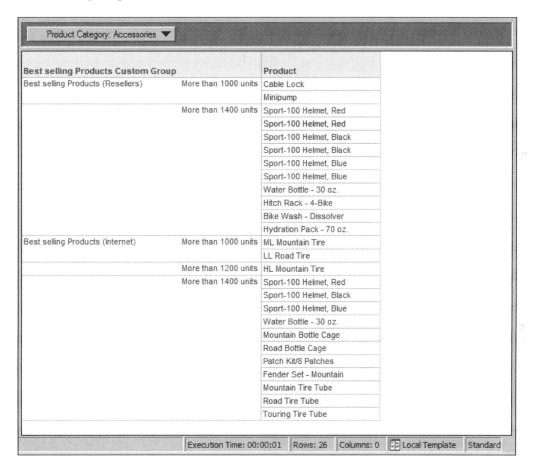

Remember to update the schema and to set the custom group element display options.

You can watch screencasts of these operations at:

▸ `http://at5.us/Ch11V3`

▸ `http://at5.us/Ch11V4`

Month-to-date and year-to-date transformations

A frequent requirement in reporting is to compare daily numbers with running monthly or yearly aggregates. These numbers are often referred to as **MTD** (**month-to-date**) and **YTD** (**year-to-date**) respectively. As always, there are more than one correct paths to get to the right values.

The technique explained in this recipe is one of them. It involves creating a reference table with two columns: the first contains the date we are referring to (let's call it the current date) and the second column holds every date that is needed to obtain the running total referred to the current date, for example all the days from the beginning of the month in case of the MTD.

#	DateKey	MTD_DateKey
01	20050701	20050701
02	20050702	20050701
03	20050702	20050702
04	20050703	20050701
05	20050703	20050702
06	20050703	20050703
07	20050704	20050701
08	20050704	20050702
09	20050704	20050703
10	20050704	20050704
11	20050705	20050701
12	20050705	20050702
13	20050705	20050703
14	20050705	20050704
15	20050705	20050705
16	20050706	20050701
17	20050706	20050702
18	20050706	20050703
19	20050706	20050704
20	20050706	20050705
21	20050706	20050706
22	20050707	20050701
23	20050707	20050702
24	20050707	20050703
25	20050707	20050704
26	20050707	20050705
27	20050707	20050706
28	20050707	20050707

Looking at the image, if I want to calculate a month-to-date metric for July 3, 2005, I need to sum the three days: first, second, and third of July. The same applies to the YTD with (easy-to-guess) a lot more rows.

Think about it, in dimensional modeling words, as a helper table for a many-to-many relationship between DimDate and itself.

We already used transformations in *Chapter 4, Objects – Facts and Metrics*, to do a "this month versus previous month" analysis (a one-to-one relationship); in this recipe we will learn how to use them in a many-to-many case.

Getting ready

Some preparation is needed before going further; the helper tables. Open the `sqlcmd` command interface, change to the `AdventureWorksDW2008R2` database and issue the following instruction:

```
with calendar as
    (
        select cast('2005-07-01' as datetime) DateValue1
        union all
        select DateValue1 + 1
        from    calendar
        where   DateValue1 + 1 < '2010-11-30'
    )
,monthtodate as
    (
        select cast('2005-07-01' as datetime) DateValue2
        union all
        select DateValue2 + 1
        from    monthtodate
        where   DateValue2 + 1 < '2010-11-30'
    )
select cast(convert(varchar, DateValue1, 112) as integer)
DateKey, cast(convert(varchar, DateValue2, 112) as integer)
MTD_DateKey
into DimDate_MTD
from    calendar, monthtodate where DateValue1 >= DateValue2
and DateValue2 >= DateAdd(mm, DateDiff(mm,0,DateValue1),0)
order by DateValue1, DateValue2
OPTION (MAXRECURSION 0)
```

The full statement is available in the companion code file.

Execute it with the command:

go

We are using a feature present in Microsoft SQL Server and other RDBMS called **common table expression** (**CTE**) with a recursive query.

A CTE is a temporary named result set that you can reference within a `SELECT` sentence; a kind of fake table that only exists during the execution of the statement.

In SQL Server a CTE can reference itself recursively, so what we do here is generate two lists of dates from a lower limit (2005-07-01) to an upper limit (2010-11-30) and join them to produce a final result set into a new table named `DimDate_MTD`. The limits are the minimum and maximum dates available in the `DimDate` table.

And, before you ask: yes, I Googled it. But the copy-and-paste that followed was very difficult.

How to do it...

Let's begin with the month-to-date:

1. Open **Schema | Warehouse Catalog...** menu and move the table **DimDate_MTD** from the left to the right of the shopping cart, then click on **Save and Close**.

2. Go to **Schema Objects | Attributes** folder and double-click on **Date**.

3. In the Attribute Editor, with the **ID** form selected, click on **Modify**.

4. In the **Modify Attribute Form** window, check the **DimDate_MTD** table in the **Source tables:** list and confirm with **OK**.

5. Click on **Save and Close**, and update schema.

6. Move to the **Schema Objects | Transformations** folder, right-click on an empty area, and select **New | Transformation**.

7. We're in the **Select a Member Attribute** dialog, pick **Date** and click on the **Open** button.

8. In the **Define a new member attribute expression** window, open the **Table:** drop-down list and select **DimDate_MTD**.

9. Click on **MTD_DateKey** in the **Available columns** list and drag it to the **Enter expression here** text area. Confirm with on **OK**.

10. In the lower part of the Transformation Editor there are two radio buttons under **Transformation mapping type**, click on the second one, labeled **Many to many**.

11. Click on **Save and Close**, name it `Month to Date`. And update schema.

12. Go to **My Reports** folder, and create a blank report.

13. Add the **Date** attribute to rows and **Sum SalesAmount from FactInternetSales** to columns. Run the report in **Grid View**.

14. Right-click on the **Sum SalesAmount from FactInternetSales** header. From the context menu, select **Insert | Transformations | Month to Date | Normal**.

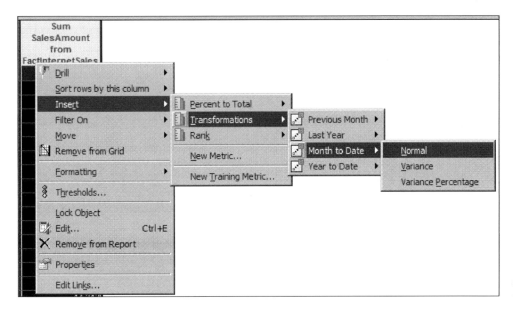

15. Answer **Yes** to the message box saying that the report will be re-executed.

16. Look at the result set; now you have a new column with the running total for each month.

17. Save and close the report, name it as `52 Internet Sales Month to Date`.

How it works...

Transformations can be applied on-the-fly to any metric by performing steps 14 and 15; the resulting column is a new metric that is only available in the current report (derived metric).

Looking at the SQL view:

The first `SELECT` statement calculates the first column (the real metric) grouping on `OrderDateKey`.

The second `SELECT` statement joins the fact table to the `DimDate_MTD` table on:

`(a11.OrderDateKey = a12.MTD_DateKey)`

And then groups on `DateKey`. Since there are many `MTD_DateKey` for each `OrderDateKey`, the numbers in the second column contain an aggregate of all the calendar days from the beginning of the month until the `OrderDateKey`.

The magic of the transformation is that, once it is built and proved correct, we can apply it on other metrics as well, with no additional effort other than right-clicking several times.

There's more...

If you want to re-use the same transformed metric in more reports, you can embed the transformation directly into a metric definition as we learned in *Chapter 4, Objects – Facts and Metrics*:

1. Go to **Public Objects** | **Metrics** folder.

2. Edit the **Sum SalesAmount from FactInternetSales** metric.

3. Save a copy of this metric as `Sum SalesAmount from FactInternetSales (MTD)`.

4. On the upper-right pane of the Metric Editor, click on the line that says **Transformation = (nothing)**.

5. From the **Object Browser** pane on the left, drag the **Month to Date** transformation onto the list on the right.

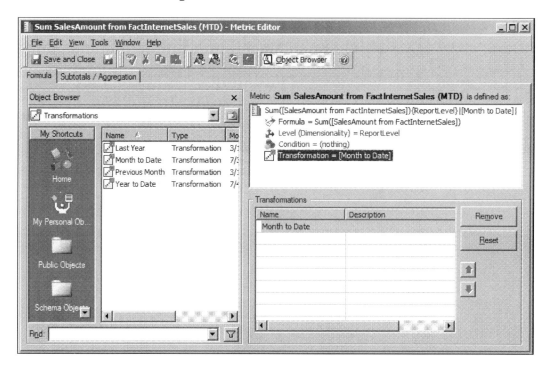

6. Click on **Save and Close**, go to **My Reports** folder and add the newly created metric to the report number 52.

7. Now you can remove the derived metric in the second column. Right-click on its header, select **Remove from Report** and answer **Yes** to the re-execute warning.

8. Save and close the report.

Exercise 32

Using the code in the companion file create first the helper table `DimDate_YTD` then the year-to-date transformation.

Create a transformation metric based on `Sum SalesAmount from FactInternetSales` and the year-to-date transformation.

Create a new report like the one in the image:

	Metrics	Sum SalesAmount from FactInternetSales	Sum SalesAmount from FactInternetSales (MTD)	Sum SalesAmount from FactInternetSales (YTD)
Date				
24-Jan-2007		13,759	355,357	355,357
25-Jan-2007		6,298	361,655	361,655
26-Jan-2007		20,301	381,956	381,956
27-Jan-2007		5,275	387,231	387,231
28-Jan-2007		11,451	398,682	398,682
29-Jan-2007		13,474	412,156	412,156
30-Jan-2007		9,240	421,397	421,397
31-Jan-2007		17,469	438,865	438,865
01-Feb-2007		18,138	18,138	457,003
02-Feb-2007		19,624	37,762	476,627
03-Feb-2007		11,302	49,064	487,929
04-Feb-2007		30,851	79,915	518,780
05-Feb-2007		16,835	96,750	535,615
06-Feb-2007		22,601	119,351	558,217
07-Feb-2007		15,938	135,289	574,154
08-Feb-2007		17,216	152,505	591,370
09-Feb-2007		20,491	172,996	611,862
10-Feb-2007		14,937	187,934	626,799
11-Feb-2007		8,351	196,285	635,150
12-Feb-2007		18,597	214,882	653,747
13-Feb-2007		20,360	235,242	674,107
14-Feb-2007		18,595	253,837	692,702
15-Feb-2007		18,592	272,429	711,294
16-Feb-2007		8,241	280,670	719,535

Year: 2007 ▼

Execution Time: 00:00:00   Rows: 365   Columns: 3

Note that the MTD Metric restarts on February 1, while the YTD does not.

You can watch screencasts of these operations at:
- ▸ http://at5.us/Ch11V5
- ▸ http://at5.us/Ch11V6

See also

▸   The *Creating a cube from an existing report* recipe in *Chapter 12, In-Memory Cubes and Visual Insight*

12
In-Memory Cubes and Visual Insight

In this chapter, we will cover:

- ▸ Creating a cube from an existing report
- ▸ Building a new cube
- ▸ Scheduling data refresh
- ▸ Creating reports and documents based on a cube
- ▸ Exploring data with Visual Insight
- ▸ Using the network visualization

Introduction

MicroStrategy's in-memory technology is the most important part of the Intelligence Server extension named OLAP Services.

The OLAP Services' main advantage is the ability to perform very fast queries using desktop, web, and mobile clients without the need to overload the RDBMS server. It also allows for slicing and dicing data directly in the Intelligent Server memory without having to re-execute the SQL statement against the data warehouse.

Formerly known as **Intelligent Cubes** and now rebranded In-Memory cubes, this technology improves the efficiency and performance of reports, documents, and Visual Insight analyses. In previous chapters we already took advantage of some OLAP features like page-by, pivoting, dynamic aggregation, and view filters; we are now exploring the use of multidimensional datasets to leverage the fast response times and the MOLAP capabilities of In-Memory cubes.

Some other advantages of cubes:

- ▶ Can be shared and used by many reports/documents
- ▶ Can be refreshed on a scheduled basis during off-peak hours
- ▶ Support drilling
- ▶ Allow self-service data analysis

You can think about In-Memory cubes as a big, fast cache that is stored in the memory of the Intelligence Server. There are exceptions to that, in fact, cubes can be unloaded and saved to disk when not used and memory is needed for other cubes. Since direct memory access is several times faster than disk I/O, it is easy to guess that the benefits of fast executions are seriously impacted by the swapping to/from disk. It is the administrator's responsibility to properly size the memory on the Intelligence Server in order to minimize this impact. Please refer to the administration manuals in the product documentation for more details on how to monitor memory usage.

So, the In-Memory cube is a static copy of result data that can be shared among many different reports. Static means that, until refreshed, the cube contains the same numbers; depending on your data warehouse ETL policy, you can decide when and how often these numbers need to be recalculated, daily, hourly, or else.

All reports and documents that read from the cube will have the same version of the truth, and this is a very nice-to-have side effect. We can restrict users' access in such a way that they can only view data inside a cube and never escape from there. This is a tremendous help to prevent snowball SQL.

On the other hand, for the advanced users, it is possible to allow drill functionalities outside the cube, so that they can navigate from the aggregate multidimensional data (MOLAP) to the underlying detailed RDBMS tables (ROLAP). This is another very useful perk to lure business analysts and give them full control over the results.

I don't need to remind you that an empowered BI user, after a training period, becomes independent, self-sufficient, and is able to satisfy his/her data needs without IT support. And this is a very, if not the most, important benefit of In-Memory cubes.

Having said that, a good in-memory strategy can make our life easier. The drawback is that we can't just "cubify" everything. There are cases when the benefits are more evident than others. For example, frequently accessed reports with a very large number of returned rows are good cube candidates; reports that run only once a month, or return a very limited set of rows, may not give added value if cubified. If you have a business user complaining that every day he/she has to spend 15 minutes waiting for the invoice report to pop up, well, that's a clear example of a candidate cube!

One last remark before we continue: according to MicroStrategy's benchmarks for scalability and response time, the best cubes are those that are smaller than 5 GB in size.

Creating a cube from an existing report

There is an increasing demand, from users across all organizations, for higher BI performance, driven by the rapid growth of data volumes and number of users. In this recipe, we will see how to transform a report into a cube.

In-Memory cubes help reduce data transfer between the RDBMS and the Intelligence Server, thus decreasing network bandwidth utilization.

A faster response helps improve user satisfaction, and ultimately, wide adoption of the platform and productivity.

When we execute an In-Memory cube, no data is displayed. The query is run and the result set is stored in memory ready to be used by reports, documents, or Visual Insight analyses (starting from 9.3.1 analyses are called dashboards). The process of executing a cube is known as **publishing**. A cube cannot be used if it is not published.

Probably the easiest way to build a cube is converting an existing report. It is a convenient way to see and validate the actual dataset that will be included before publishing it.

Getting ready

You need to have completed the preceding chapters to continue.

How to do it...

We will convert the report named **28 InternetSales Dashboard**:

1. Go to **My Reports** folder and right-click on the report number 28; from the context menu, select **Edit** to open the Report Editor.

2. Open the **Data** menu and click on **Intelligent Cube Options | Convert to Intelligent Cube**; you will see the icon in the title bar of this window changing to a little blue cube.

3. Click on **File | Save As...** and name it 28 InternetSales Cube.

4. From the toolbar, click on the **Run Report** button to execute it.

5. A message will appear saying that execution is complete and result data has been published as an Intelligent Cube. Click on **Save and Close**.

6. In **Folder List** on the left, navigate to **Administration | System Monitors | Caches | Intelligent Cubes**; right-click on **28 InternetSales Cube** and select **Quick View** from the context menu.

7. In this window you can see interesting information about the recently created cube like the size, the number of rows, and the last update time.

How it works...

You can right-click on **28 InternetSales Cube** in **My Reports** and open the **SQL View**. The SELECT statement sent to the RDBMS is the same as the original report, but the data is stored in memory and on disk for later use (you can find it under C:\Program Files\ MicroStrategy\Intelligence Server\Cube\<machine name>\<some more strange chars>\<Intelligent Cube Instance ID>.cube).

There's more...

Cubes can be unloaded from memory to make more space available when they're not used, and reloaded from the context menu by right-clicking on the cube icon in the **Administration | System Monitors | Caches | Intelligent Cubes** folder. See the screen capture:

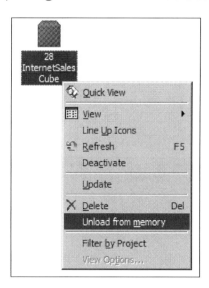

To revert the action and load the cube back in memory, right-click again and choose **Load in memory**:

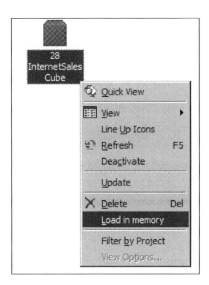

 You can watch a screencast of this operation at:
> `http://at5.us/Ch12V1`

Building a new cube

Creating a new cube is very similar to creating a report. We use the same editor and the same objects. There are restrictions on which objects can be used inside a cube; for example, consolidations and custom groups cannot be added to the cube definition. However, there are alternative techniques that provide the same functionalities like derived elements (check the product documentation). Now that we learned how to transform a report into a cube, we will try to create a new one from zero. And this time we want it bigger.

Getting ready

Out of the box the limit for a cube dataset is 32,000 rows. We need to change that in order to do this recipe. Go to the **Project Configuration** window (right-click on the project name in the Desktop application) and set the **Governing Rules | Default | Result Sets** parameters (as in the following screen capture):

- ▶ **Intelligent Cubes**: `128000`

- ▶ **All other reports**: `128000`

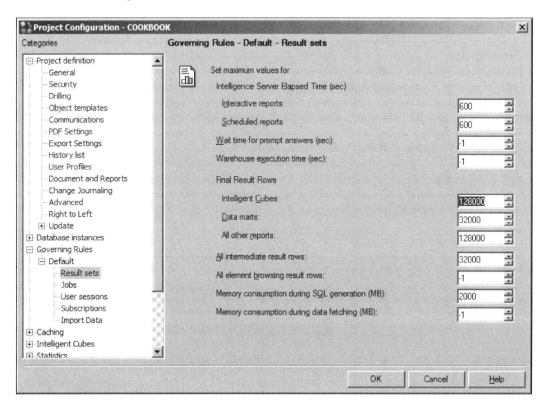

This setting will allow us to create a cube bigger than 32,000 rows.

 Please note that in MicroStrategy Desktop, the report grids only display the first 65,000 rows, independently from the real number of rows returned in the result set.

How to do it...

Before building the cube, we create two additional metrics:

1. In the **Public Objects | Metrics** folder, right-click on **Sum USD SalesAmount from FactResellerSales** and select **Edit** from the context menu.

2. In the Metric Editor, click on **File | Save As...** and type `Sum USD SalesAmount from FactResellerSales Previous Month`. Click on **Save**.

3. Now click on the line that says **Transformation = (nothing)** on the right and drag the **Previous Month** transformation from the **Object Browser** section onto the grid labeled **Transformations**.

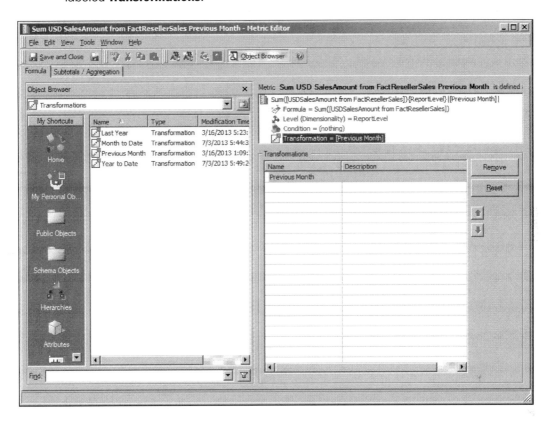

4. Save and Close this new metric.

5. Repeat steps 1 to 4 with **Sum OrderQuantity from FactResellerSales** to create a new metric named `Sum OrderQuantity from FactResellerSales Previous Month`.

6. Go to **My Personal Objects | My Reports** folder, right-click on an empty area on the right and select **New | Intelligent Cube**.

7. Leave **Empty Intelligent Cube** selected and hit **OK**.

8. The Intelligent Cube Editor is very similar to the Report Editor. Click on the **Public Objects** shortcut and navigate to the **Metrics** folder.

9. Add the following metrics to columns:

   ❑ **Sum USD SalesAmount from FactResellerSales**

   ❑ **Sum USD SalesAmount from FactResellerSales Previous Month**

□ **Sum OrderQuantity from FactResellerSales**

□ **Sum OrderQuantity from FactResellerSales Previous Month**

□ **Sum Freight from FactResellerSales**

□ **Sum TaxAmt from FactResellerSales**

10. Open the **Data | Report Data Options...** menu and go to the **Metric Join Type** category.

11. Set every **Metric Join Type** to **Outer**, like in the following screen capture, and confirm with **OK**:

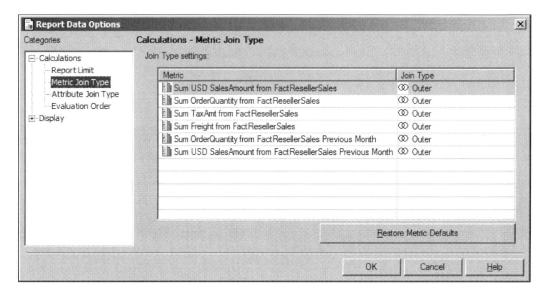

12. Click on the **Attributes** shortcut and add the following attributes on rows:

□ **Currency**

□ **Employee**

□ **Month**

□ **Product**

□ **Product Category**

□ **Product Subcategory**

□ **Promotion**

□ **Reseller**

□ **Salesterritory Reseller**

□ **Year**

13. Open the **File** | **Save As...** menu and name it 54 ResellerSales Cube.

14. Click on the **Run Report** button. This time it will take considerably longer than other previous reports.

15. At the end, you will see a message saying that the result data has been published as Intelligent Cube <54 ResellerSales Cube>.

16. Close this window and go to the **Administration** | **System Monitors** | **Caches** | **Intelligent Cubes** folder.

17. Right-click on the cube 54 and select **Quick View**. Note down the **Total number of rows** and close this window.

18. Now open MicroStrategy Web from **Start** | **All Programs** | **MicroStrategy** | **Web** | **Web**.

19. Click on the **COOKBOOK** project and log in with Administrator and the corresponding password.

20. Open **My Report** folder and scroll down to find the cube number 54.

21. Right-click on the cube and from the context menu select **Create Analysis** (starting from 9.3.1 this will be **Create Dashboard**).

22. After a while you will be presented with a dialog box titled **Select a Visualization**. Click on the round **X** on the top-right corner of this dialog, we will select a visualization later:

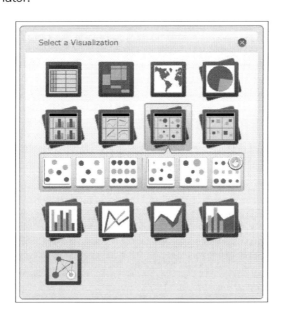

23. Welcome to the Visual Insight window. Move the cursor over the VI toolbar (not the MicroStrategy one) and click on the second button from the left (tool tip: **Show Dataset Objects**).

24. You will see a new pane (titled **Dataset Objects**) on the left with all the attributes and metrics included in the cube plus an extra **Row Count** metric.

25. Click on the **Row Count** metric and drag it to the second pane (titled **Grid**) inside the **Columns** area. Note that the border of the area turns green and the cursor changes to a plus symbol shape (white on green).

26. When you drop the object, the right part of the screen changes to a grid named **Visualization1**, and the **Row Count** value matches the number that we noted down in step 17. See the following screenshot:

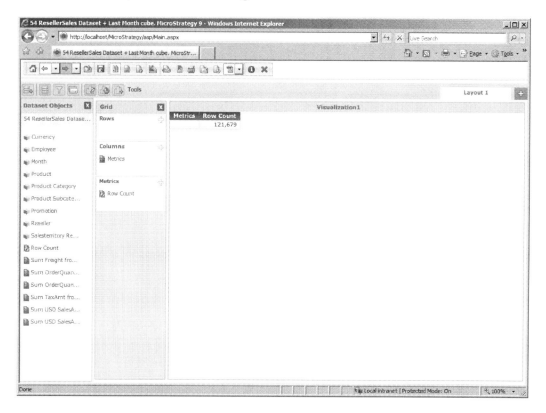

27. You can close the browser window without saving.

How it works...

We created a cube with many attributes and metrics, and published it. Once published, a cube can be used as a source dataset for reports, documents, and Visual Insight analyses. You may have noticed that all the objects contained in the cube come directly from one single fact table (**FactResellerSales**) or are hierarchically related to the fact table, like the **Month** and **Year** attributes. What we have done here is, in fact, denormalized data mart from a star schema. MicroStrategy stores the dataset in binary format and adds a row counter to the cube.

From the web browser, we created a new analysis with Visual Insight to check that the cube was correctly built and available.

There's more...

From the **Administration** | **System Monitors** | **Caches** | **Intelligent Cubes** folder, you can right-click on a cube and choose **Delete**. The cube will be removed from memory and from the disk, but the cube definition will not be deleted from the metadata. You can still find the cube in **My Reports** folder; if you re-execute, it will be published and available again.

 You can watch a screencast of this operation at:
> `http://at5.us/Ch12V2`

Scheduling data refresh

As we learned before, cubes are a big cache in the Intelligence Server memory. Their data is static. We need to update them when new data is available, typically after an ETL job is run.

Refreshing a cube's data involves connecting to the data warehouse and re-executing the underlying SQL statements. Normally, the best time to do it is during off-peak hours, and since BI developers like to sleep at night, there must be a way to automate that.

MicroStrategy offers a scheduling mechanism to automate cube updates very similar to cron on *nix or the Task Scheduler on Windows.

In order to automate a cube refresh, we need two objects: a **schedule** and a **subscription**.

A schedule is just a recurring timer, like every day at 3 A.M., or every Monday; it does not perform any action. A subscription is an object that binds a report, document, or cube to a schedule and a **delivery type**. There are several delivery types in MicroStrategy, such as e-mail and printer; in our case we will use a special delivery type called **Cube Refresh**.

Subscription can be used to automatically mail data to users on a schedule basis; or execute long running reports before working hours (so that they are already cached); or—like in our case—to execute and publish cubes after a data load. Let's see how to do it.

Getting ready

You need to have completed the previous recipe to continue.

How to do it...

Imagine that our ETL jobs run from 1 A.M. until 2:30 A.M. daily. We need to create a subscription to refresh the cube 54 at 3 A.M. every day:

1. In the Desktop application, navigate to the **Administration | Configuration Managers | Schedules** folder.

2. Right-click on an empty area on the right and select **New | Schedule** from the context menu.

3. On the welcome screen, click on **Next**.

4. In the **Name** textbox, type `Every day at 3AM` and hit **Next**.

5. Leave **Time-triggered** selected and click on **Next**.

6. Leave the default validity range, click on **Next**.

7. In the **Recurrence Pattern** window, in the **Time to trigger** group, modify **Execute at** to `3AM` and click on **Next**.

8. You will be presented with a list of next occurrences. Click on **Next** and again on **Finish**.

9. Now that we have a schedule we move to the **Administration | Configuration Managers | Subscriptions** folder.

10. Right-click on the empty area and select **Subscription Creation Wizard** from the context menu.

11. Click on **Next** on the welcome page.

12. On the **Specify Characteristics** page the first combobox already has the **COOKBOOK** project selected, open the second one labeled **Choose a delivery type** and pick **Cube Refresh**. Hit **Next**.

13. On the **Choose Reports/Documents** page, browse to **My Personal Objects | My Reports** and move **54 ResellerSales Cube** to the right of the shopping cart, and click on **Next**.

14. The **Schedule** combobox should already be set to **Every day at 3AM**, **Next**.

15. Hit **Next** again and click on **Finish**, the subscription is ready to trigger; every morning at 3 A.M. the cube 54 will be refreshed.

How it works...

The time—trigger works with the system clock of the Intelligence Server. In case you work for an international company across several time zones, plan your schedules carefully to make sure the cubes are refreshed at times when no one is using them.

It has happened to me more than once that the data got refreshed one hour later due to daylight saving time in summer; I discovered the hard way how to explain to an Oracle server that in most European countries we move the clock one hour ahead from spring to autumn in order to save energy and bring misery to ETL jobs.

There's more...

Cubes can be published based on a schedule or manually. The amount of memory needed to publish a cube is approximately double the size of the cube itself. This is another good reason for updating them when the load on the Intelligence Server is very low.

 You can watch a screencast of this operation at:
  ▶ `http://at5.us/Ch12V3`

Creating reports and documents based on a cube

Reports and documents based on a cube give fast access to the data and are very similar to their data warehouse counterparts. The main difference is that the objects available are only those attributes and metrics present in the cube.

Of course, we can use features such as sorting, totals, prompts, and view filters as we did in previous chapters with standard reports and documents.

Drilling is limited to the objects included in the cube unless you specifically allow reports to drill outside.

Getting ready

You need to have completed the preceding recipes to continue.

How to do it...

To create a report based on a cube:

1. Open the Web Interface and go to **My Reports** folder.
2. Scroll down to find the **54 ResellerSales Cube** and right-click on it.
3. Click on **Create Report**. Note that the list of report objects reflects the content of the cube.

4. Click on **Reseller Attribute**, drag-and-drop it to the area labeled **Drop objects here to add rows**.

5. Click on the **Year** attribute, drag-and-drop it to the area labeled **Drop objects here to add columns**.

6. Lastly, put the **Sum USD SalesAmount from FactResellerSales** metric in the data area.

7. In the toolbar, click on the first button (tool tip: **Run Report**) to see the result. The grid appears almost immediately and no round trip to RDBMS is performed.

8. Click on the first button on the toolbar (tool tip: **Save As...**) and name this 55 Sales by Reseller and Year. Click on **OK** and again on **Run newly saved report**.

9. Click on the red MicroStrategy star logo on the upper-left corner and then hit **My Reports**.

10. Again, scroll down to find the cube number 54 and right-click on it.

11. From the context menu, select **Create Document**. Note that the list of dataset objects reflects the content of the cube.

12. Right-click on the **Promotion** attribute and select **Add to Grouping**. A new section named **Promotion Header** is created.

13. Click-and-drag the **Promotion** attribute to the **Promotion Header** section, when a yellow border appears around the section drop the object.

14. Resize the **{[Promotion]}** text field by dragging the small white squares, so that it occupies the whole section width.

15. You may optionally drag the **Detail Header** gray bar up a little to reduce the white space below the **{[Promotion]}** text field.

16. Right-click on the **Detail Header** gray bar and select **Properties and Formatting...** from the context menu.

17. Click on **Layout** on the left and enable the checkbox labeled **Height can shrink** below the **Size** headline. Click on **OK**.

18. Drag the **Salesterritory Reseller** attribute to the area labeled **Drop objects here to add rows**. Then drag the **Sum USD SalesAmount from FactResellerSales** metric to the area labeled **Drop Metrics here to add data**.

19. Right-click on the cross arrow icon on the top left of the grid and choose **Properties and Formatting...** from the context menu.

20. Click on **Layout** on the left and set the radio button **Fit to contents** under **Height** in the **Size** headline, confirm with **OK**.

21. Switch to the interactive mode by clicking on the appropriate toolbar button (tool tip: **Interactive Mode**).

22. Note that in the **GROUPING** pane, the combobox named **Promotion** has **No Discount** automatically selected. Click on the dropdown and choose **(All)**.

23. Now you can scroll the document and see the sales amount for each **promotion**.

24. Click on **Save As...** and name it 56 Promotions by Sales territory, click on **OK** and again on **Run newly saved document**.

How it works...

If you open the **SQL View** of the report number 55, you'll see the difference between a standard data warehouse query and a cube. In this case the SQL is:

```
select   [Reseller]@[ResellerKey],
  [Reseller]@[ResellerName],
  [Year]@[CalendarYear],
  sum([Sum USD SalesAmount from
      FactResellerSales])@{[Reseller],[Year]}
from  54 ResellerSales Cube
```

And the result grid appears sensibly faster than in other reports.

There's more...

If you want your users to be able to navigate and drill outside the cube (for example, to the **Date** attribute in our case), you need to edit the cube and open the menu **Data | Configure Intelligent Cube**.

From the **Intelligent Cube Options** window, uncheck **Use default settings** in the **Drilling** group, and select the checkbox labeled **Allow reports to drill outside the Intelligent Cube**, see screen capture:

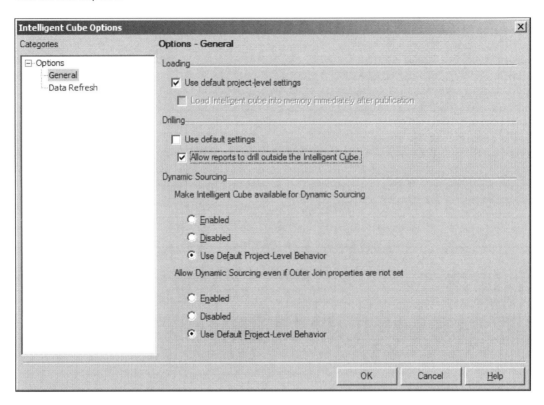

Remember to re-execute the cube in order to publish it with the new settings.

 You can watch a screencast of this operation at:
  ▸ http://at5.us/Ch12V4

Exploring data with Visual Insight

Visual Insight or VI is a new technology intended to empower business users and give them the ability to analyze and explore data without the intervention of IT people. It allows them to manipulate grids, graphs, and advanced visualizations and to see immediate results without the need to go back and forth between design and run mode.

VI can use cubes as a dataset in order to achieve high performance during the process of discovering and designing graphical data analysis.

The aim of this technology is to change the classic data reporting workflow that involves asking the IT group for data, manual extraction, spreadsheet distributions, and other sometimes non-standard practices.

VI and In-Memory cubes are intended to offer an easy, fast, reliable mechanism to manipulate large datasets, create interactive visualizations, and distribute them.

Being more visual and immediate, Visual Insight analyses have a lower time-to-proficiency factor. I mean, it takes less time to get to the point where you can produce good results.

Getting ready

You need to have completed the preceding recipes to continue.

How to do it...

We are creating a new analysis based on **54 ResellerSales Cube**:

1. In the Web Interface, go to **My Reports** folder and right-click on the cube number 54, then select **Create Analysis** (**Create Dashboard** starting from 9.3.1) from the context menu.

2. When the **Select a Visualization** dialog appears, click on **Grid**.

3. The analysis is prepopulated with some objects, but we want to remove them. Starting from the left of the screen, note there's a **Filter** pane and a **Grid** pane.

4. Hover with the mouse on the header of the **Grid** pane until a small down arrow button appears. Click on that button to open the context menu:

5. Choose **Remove All Objects** and click on **OK** when prompted "Are you sure...?".

6. The result pane is now empty. Move the cursor to the toolbar and click on the second button from the left (tool tip: **Show Dataset Objects**). A new pane appears on the left with all the attributes and metrics in the cube.

7. Now hide the **Filters** pane by clicking on the small **X** button (tool tip: **Close**) on its header.

8. Select the **Product Category** attribute in **Dataset Objects**, drag-and-drop it onto the **Rows** area in the **Grid** pane. Notice that the cursor changes to a black arrow with a green plus marker.

9. Similarly, drag the **Sum USD SalesAmount from FactResellerSales** metric to the **Metrics** area in the **Grid** pane.

10. See that the results are immediately visible, with no need to switch from design to view.

11. Hover the mouse on the name of the metric in the **Grid** pane until a small down arrow icon appears:

12. Click on the arrow to open the context menu and select **Rename**, in the textbox type `Sales` and hit *Enter*.

13. We can also rename the visualization title, which is now **Grid**. Open the context menu of the result pane in the top-right corner just below the **Layout 1** tab:

14. Click on **Edit Title**, type Sales by Category, and hit *Enter*.

15. Now move the cursor to the toolbar and click on the last button before **Tools** (tool tip: **Insert Visualization**).

16. A new **Visualization2** pane appears, click on the big **Select a Visualization** image.

17. When the **Select a Visualization** dialog appears, click on the **Vertical Bar – Standard** thumbnail, the first one in the matrix of bar graphs group (refer to the following screen capture):

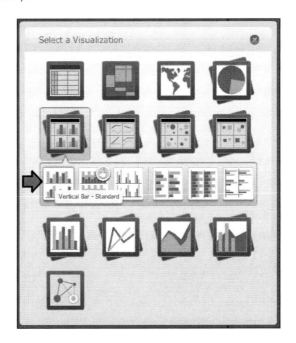

18. The graph is automatically populated with some data and what before was the **Grid** pane has changed to the **Graph Matrix** pane with the settings for the chart.

19. Open the context menu of the **Graph Matrix** pane and click on **Remove All Objects**. Click on **OK** on the confirmation message.

20. Click-and-drag the **Product Subcategory** attribute to the **Graph Matrix | MATRIX | Rows** area and drop it.

21. Open the context menu for the recently added attribute and rename it `Subcategory`.

22. Click on the **Month** attribute, drag-and-drop it into the **Graph Matrix | GRAPH AXIS | X Axis** area. Note how the chart changes instantly, but we're not done yet.

23. Drag the **Sum USD SalesAmount from FactResellerSales** metric in the **Graph Matrix | GRAPH AXIS | Y Axis** area and rename it `Sales`.

24. Drag the **Product Subcategory** attribute from the **Dataset Objects** onto the **Graph Matrix | MARKER | Color By** area.

25. At this point we have a graph matrix that (for each subcategory) shows a bar chart with the sales by month giving each subcategory a different color marker. Yet, it is difficult to read.

26. Open the context menu of the first visualization pane named **Sales by Category**, by clicking on the small down arrow in its title bar, and click on **Use as filter...**.

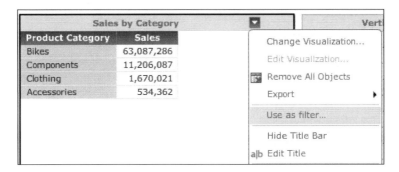

27. In the **Filtering Options** dialog that appears, select the **Vertical Bar – Standard** checkbox. Then open the **Also filter targets when selecting elements of** combobox and pick **Product Category**. Check the option **Allow users to clear all selections** and confirm with **OK**.

28. Now click on the **Bikes** element in the **Sales by Category** grid. Bingo! The chart automatically filters only the selected category; still we can improve a little more the visibility.

29. Move the cursor and place it between the two panes, exactly on the white space that separates them. Notice that it changes to a double-arrow shape; click-and-drag to the left to resize the left pane.

30. Move to the legend on the right pane and hide it by clicking on the small gray arrow (tool tip: **Hide Legend**).

31. Save this analysis. Click on the **Save As...** button in the MicroStrategy toolbar on the top of the screen, and name it 57 Visual Insight Analysis. Click on **OK** and again on **Run newly created analysis**.

How it works...

The chart we used in this analysis is different from the standard charts we saw earlier, in the fact that it is indeed a matrix of several charts stacked onto each other. We can partition the matrix by rows and columns using attributes; in this recipe we used the subcategory. Inside the matrix, every single chart has an X and Y axis, where usually the Y represents a metric and the X an attribute. The marker in this case is a bar and we assigned a different color to a different subcategory.

There's more...

The marker has a **Size by** property, useful to represent another metric. If you want to try it, drag the **Sum OrderQuantity from FactResellerSales** metric to the **Graph Matrix | MARKER | Size By** area. The bars now have different widths, representing the number of ordered quantity: thin bar = low quantity and thick bar = high quantity. Cool!

We can further improve the usability of the visualization with a page-by control.

1. On the toolbar, click on the fourth button from the left (tool tip: **Show Page-by**).

2. From the **Dataset Objects**, drag the **Year** attribute and drop it in the **Page-by** row. A series of buttons is created.

3. Hover on the **Layout 1** tab, open its context menu and rename it `Grid and Graph`.

4. Save the analysis, overwriting the existing one, and run it.

> You can watch a screencast of this operation at:
> ▸ `http://at5.us/Ch12V5`

Using the network visualization

The new network visualization is useful to detect a relationship between two attributes, or the lack thereof. It shows circles (or nodes) representing elements of the attributes and lines (or edges) connecting elements to each other depending on the value of a metric.

To make an example we will review the connection between employees and products in our **ResellerSales** cube; this will give us an idea of which type of product each employee sells. To do that, we can use the **Employee** and **Product Subcategory** attributes and associate them with the **Sum OrderQuantity from FactResellerSales** metric.

Getting ready

You need to have completed the preceding recipes to continue.

How to do it...

We want to look at the relationship between our employees and the products they sell:

1. From **My Reports** in the Web Interface, run the analysis **57 Visual Insight Analysis**.

2. Hit the top-right blue plus button right next to the **Grid and Graph** tab (tool tip: **Add Layout**).

3. A new layout is created with a blank visualization, click on **Select a Visualization** and from the dialog box choose the last thumbnail (tool tip: **Network**).

4. Close the **Filters** pane by clicking on its small **X** button near the title.

5. There's a pane named **Network**, open its context menu and click on **Show Properties**; this is the **Properties** pane for the network visualization:

6. Check the **Show node label** setting. Open the context menu and click on **Show Properties** once again to go back to the **Network** pane.

7. From the context menu of the **Network** pane, select **Remove All Objects** and confirm with **OK** when prompted.

8. Now enable the **Page-by** row by clicking on the fourth button in the toolbar (tool tip: **Show Page-by**).

9. Drag the **Product Category** attribute to the **Page-by** row:

10. Add the following objects to the **Network** pane:

    ❑ **Employee** into **NETWORK | From item** area

    ❑ **Product Subcategory** into **NETWORK | To item** area

    ❑ **Sum OrderQuantity from FactResellerSales** into **COLOR AND SIZE | Node Size**

11. When you hover the cursor over a node, the corresponding edges are highlighted to show which products each employee has a relation to.

12. You can use the tool on the left of the visualization to pan and zoom:

13. Move the mouse cursor over employee **Syed Abbas**. Mmmmh, looks like he's not selling any **Road Bike**. This requires more investigation and maybe a call to Syed's manager.

How it works...

The network visualization needs at least two attributes and one metric. You may add up to two additional metrics and use them to change the color and the size of the lines.

There's more...

If you click on the **Select** button, the dashed rectangle in the visualization tool, you can draw a selection area. The nodes inside the area will be highlighted and a small down arrow button will appear when you hover on one of them: click on that button to filter on the selection. In the context menu that appears, you can choose to keep only, or exclude, those elements.

To clear the filter, click on the small funnel icon on the left of the visualization title bar.

Additionally, you may want to try the **Layout** button of the network visualization to change from circular to linear to "spider web" views. This last one is very popular for social network and marketing data. This is shown in the following image:

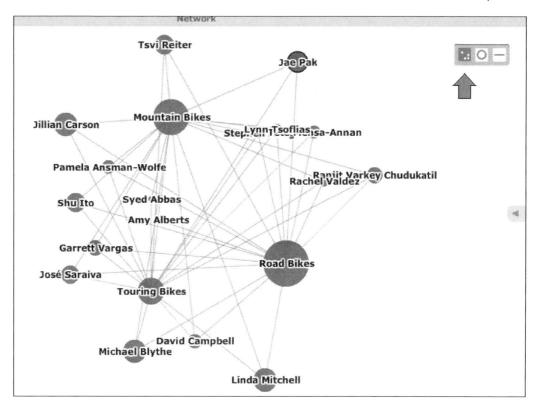

Exercise 34

In this same layout, modify the network visualization to analyze the relationship between **Promotion** and **Product** attributes based on the sales amount.

You can watch a screencast of this operation at:

▶ `http://at5.us/Ch12V6`

See also

▶ The *Creating an Express account* recipe in *Chapter 13, MicroStrategy Express*

13
MicroStrategy Express

In this chapter, we will cover:

- ▶ Creating an Express account
- ▶ Importing Excel data
- ▶ Using filters
- ▶ Importing cross-tabbed data
- ▶ Connecting to a RDBMS
- ▶ Refreshing dashboard data
- ▶ Sharing a dashboard by e-mail

Introduction

Express is the latest BI solution from MicroStrategy, and it is based on the cloud. It differs from the solution we covered in preceding chapters mainly because there is nothing to download or install, there is no desktop interface, and everything is done via a web browser.

From the UI and usability point of view, it is very similar to Visual Insight and offers access to both on-premise and cloud-based data sources.

One of the benefits of a cloud-based solution is that it doesn't need any infrastructure or hardware, and obviously cuts down the implementation time considerably.

Experienced desktop BI developers may feel that they lose the control and the fine-tuning possibilities of the in-house design; nevertheless the cloud Gold Rush has begun and this will undoubtedly modify the way we do our job; sooner or later, a customer will ask for a cloud-based solution and we'd better be prepared.

The capabilities of Express go beyond the data discovery tool; it is also a mobile design platform where you can combine dashboards, documents, and multimedia content into a mobile branded application. It also allows distributing and sharing information via e-mail, on social networks or by embedding visualizations in websites, blogs, and so on.

Express is available, as many cloud solutions, as a freemium platform. When you create an account, you get access to the personal features at no cost and by paying a small subscription you can unlock premium capabilities such as Advanced Templates, Database Connectivity, and Automated Deliveries among others.

We will start with the free account and then explore the premium components. There is a 30-day trial that you can activate in your account, which is just enough for getting an idea of the possibilities of this solution.

Creating an Express account

First, we need to create an account. The process is very straightforward and takes a few minutes. The user account will be created by default with only the free features enabled, so no charge will be applied.

Getting ready

MicroStrategy Express uses Adobe Flash technology so be sure to visit the Adobe page and update to the latest version of Flash. You will also need a supported web browser:

In the following recipes I will use Internet Explorer 9 and Chrome 28, you can download them from: http://at5.us/Ch13U1 and http://at5.us/Ch13U5 respectively.

How to do it...

Follow these steps:

1. Open Internet Explorer and go to `http://at5.us/Ch13U2`

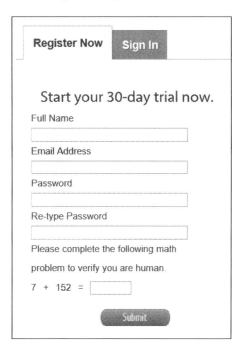

2. Fill in the form with name and e-mail address and click on **Submit**.
3. You will receive a message saying **Please verify your email address**. Open the e-mail and follow the instructions to activate your MicroStrategy Express account.
4. Once your e-mail is verified, go to `http://at5.us/Ch13U3`, type your e-mail and password and click on **Sign In**.
5. The Flash application will take a few seconds to load the first time, then after filling in a personal detail form, you'll see a welcome page.

How it works...

Express is essentially a cloud version of the entire MicroStrategy platform. Premium users have access to documents and dashboards, while personal accounts can only use the Visual Insight data discovery.

If you look at the URL in your browser address bar, you'll see that we are actually connected to a J2EE MicroStrategy Web.

There's more...

There is a button on the right below your name, labeled **Help & Resources**. Click on it
and select **Video Help**.

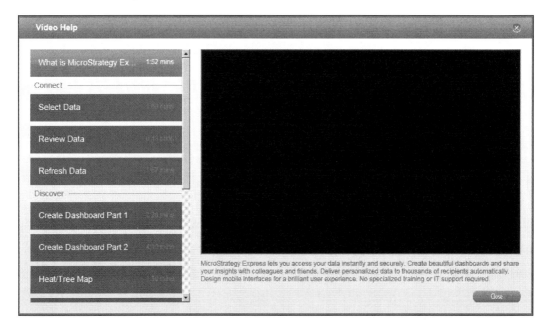

You can watch some useful video training here, or come back as needed for reference. As of
writing, this document `http://at5.us/Ch13U8` is the most recent manual for Express. For
details about the visualizations, you can also refer to *Chapter 4* in *Report Services Document
Analysis Guide*.

> You can watch screencasts of this operation at:
> ▶ `http://at5.us/Ch13V1`
> ▶ `http://at5.us/Ch13V2`

Importing Excel data

Importing data from Excel is the easiest way to start with Express. There are plenty of good examples and free data sources on the Web, you can pick your favorite or just upload an Excel file of yours.

Excel files may contain more than one sheet of data, but only one sheet can be imported at a time, and they must comply with a few rules:

- ▸ Only one table per worksheet is allowed
- ▸ The first worksheet cannot be empty
- ▸ Worksheets must contain data in the first 20 rows

I prepared a worksheet for these recipes from the World Bank data; it contains some indicators from years 2000 through 2010 for every country of the world. You can download the data from `http://xls.apphb.com/Ch13X1.xlsx` to have a look at it before going on.

Getting ready

The Excel file can be on the local computer or stored on the Web and accessible via HTTP, HTTPS, or FTP. Please review this document for guidelines and tips about preparing your own Excel data at `http://at5.us/Ch13U4`.

How to do it...

We will now import a file from the Web:

1. Close MicroStrategy Express welcome page by clicking on the round red **X** icon.
2. Click on **New Dashboard...**, the application loads the **Select Data** page.
3. From the left list, choose the radio button labeled **Use File from URL** and enter the `http://xls.apphb.com/Ch13X1.xlsx` address in the **Enter a URL for Excel/ CSV File** text area.
4. Click on **Continue**, Express loads the first 50 rows of data and displays the **Review Data** page. From here, we can decide which columns are attributes and which are metrics.

5. Move the cursor over the first column header (**Country Name**), a small down arrow icon appears, click on it to open the context menu.

6. This column has already been detected as an attribute; we only need to specify that is a country. In the context menu, select **Attribute**; in the list that pops up, click on **Country** and then on **OK**, like in this image:

7. Moving to the second column (**Date**), open the context menu and select **Attribute** and uncheck everything but **Year** and click on **OK**, see image:

8. Third and fourth columns were detected as metrics, very well. Move to fifth column (**Business: Mobile Phone Subscribers**), this was detected as an attribute but it is really a metric, so open its context menu and click on **Metric**.

9. From here onwards, the columns should all be metrics, so scroll right and change all the columns that were identified as attributes (blue) to metrics (orange).

10. When you're done, click on **Continue**. Express saves the definition and starts importing all the data. This phase can take a while. At the end of the import, you'll be presented with a **Select a Visualization** dialog.

11. Click on the first thumbnail in the top left (tool tip: **Grid**), a new dashboard is created with some data. This interface looks very familiar...

12. Click on **Save & Close**, in the **Save As** dialog, type `World Bank Indicators` in the **Name** text field and click on **OK**.

You will be redirected to the main page and your new dashboard will appear in the list.

How it works...

Behind the scenes MicroStrategy Express has loaded the Excel file, created attributes and metrics, and populated the dataset that serves as a source for the dashboard.

There's more...

When the data changes, we can refresh the dataset:

1. From the main Express window, move the cursor on the name of the dashboard (**World Bank Indicators**) and click on the **Refresh data** hyperlink.

2. Click on the **Review data** checkbox on the right, and hit **Continue**.

3. You can inspect the data for correctness and click on **Finish**.

4. When a message appears that **Data refresh was successful**, click on **Exit** to be redirected back to the main page.

You can watch screencasts of this operation at:

   ▶   `http://at5.us/Ch13V3`

   ▶   `http://at5.us/Ch13V4`

Using filters

In *Chapter 12, In-Memory Cubes and Visual Insight*, we learned how to control a visualization from another using the first as a filter. Now we will create a filter that affects all the visualizations in the same panel.

Getting ready

You need to have completed the preceding recipe to continue.

How to do it...

From the Express main page, click on the dashboard that we saved in the last recipe to open it:

1. Open the context menu of the visualization pane named **Grid** (on the right, in the title bar just before the red **X**), and select **Change Visualization....**

2. Click on the group named **Matrix** of bar graphs (first on the left of the second row) and pick the first thumbnail named **Vertical Bar – 100% Stacked**.

3. Open the context menu of the pane titled **Graph Matrix**, and choose **Show Properties**.

4. In the **Properties** pane, change **Shape** to **Line**. Go back to the **Graph Matrix** pane by closing the **Properties** pane with the **X** button.

5. Move to the **Filters** pane: we need to remove the default filter. Hover the cursor on the **Year of Date** header and open its context menu, click on **Remove filter**.

6. Repeat step 5 with the other objects in the pane until it is completely empty.

7. Drag the **Country Name** attribute to the **Graph Matrix | MATRIX | Rows** area.

8. In the **Graph Matrix | GRAPH AXIS | X Axis** area, there is a **Metrics** placeholder, click on it and drag it to the **Graph Matrix | MATRIX | Rows** area just below the **Country Name** attribute.

9. Move the mouse to **My Data** pane and find the metric named **Finance: GDP Per Capita (current Us$)**, pick it and move it to the **Graph Matrix | GRAPH AXIS | Y Axis** area, overlapping the existing metric. When the cursor changes to a black arrow with a blue indicator, drop it to replace the underlying object.

10. In **My Data** pane select **Country Name**, drag-and-drop it into the **Filters** pane. See that a new **Country Name** selector is created with a textbox.

11. Open the context menu of **Filters | Country Name** and choose **Display Style | Check Boxes**.

12. Uncheck **(All)** and type `Brazil` in the **Search...** textbox and check **Brazil**, the line chart changes instantly.

13. Repeat the search with `Italy` and check it. Now type `Russian` and add **Russian Federation** to the graph. There is a clear decline in 2008 that affected both Italy and Russia but less so in Brazil.

14. Click on the context menu of the **Vertical Bar - 100% Stacked** visualization and rename it `GDP per capita`.

15. Now click on the insert visualization button on the toolbar (third from the left, tool tip: **Insert Visualization**).

16. A new **Visualization2** pane appears. Click on **Select a Visualization** and pick **Vertical Bar - 100% Stacked**.

17. Modify the **Graph Matrix** pane adding and removing objects until it looks like the following screen capture:

18. Rename this pane `Internet Users`.

19. Click on the **Tools** menu in the toolbar and select **Insert Text Field**.

20. When the new text field appears, change it to `World Bank data 2000 - 2010`.

21. Click on the **Save** button in the lower part of the screen.

Congratulations! You can now analyze data of different countries just by changing the filter.

How it works...

Selections in the filter pane affect every visualization in the layout, both existing and new ones. If you need to create a visualization not affected by the filter, you can add a new layout (white on blue plus button top right).

There's more...

To clear the filter, use the small funnel with red **X** icon next to the filter title (**Clear All Filters**) or near the object header inside the pane (**Clear Filter**).

 You can watch a screencast of this operation at:
  ▶ `http://at5.us/Ch13V5`

Importing cross-tabbed data

Data files do not always come in tabular shape; more often than not they are cross-tabbed with some attributes on columns and others on rows. A very typical scenario is a worksheet with a time dimension in the columns headers (months, years...) like this one: `http://xls.apphb.com/Ch13X2.xlsx`, which represents the total expenditure per capita on health in different countries from 1995 to 2010. As you can see there are country names on rows and years on columns. The metric name is actually in cell A1.

MicroStrategy Express has the option to uncross this kind of files, pivoting the year on rows, and converting it to an attribute.

Getting ready

From now on, I will use the Chrome browser instead of IE, the main reason is that Chrome has better support of HTML5, which we'll need in the next recipes. So, if you don't have it already, please download and install it from `http://at5.us/Ch13U5`. In Chrome (as in other browsers), you can use the *F11* key to toggle between full screen and windowed mode.

How to do it...

Open Express in Google Chrome and optionally switch to full screen:

1. From the main page, select **New Dashboard...**.

2. Under **Select Your Data Source**, click on **Use File from URL**, and type `http://xls.apphb.com/Ch13X2.xlsx` into the **Enter a URL for Excel/CSV File** textbox and click on **Continue**.

3. When the data preview appears, in **Select a data format:** check the radio button labeled **Crosstabbed** and enable the checkbox labeled **No Metric Headers.**

4. The data grid is now surrounded by a selection rectangle with small black squares on the edges. Move the cursor to the top-left black square.

5. Click-and-drag the cursor until only the values are selected (see the following screen capture):

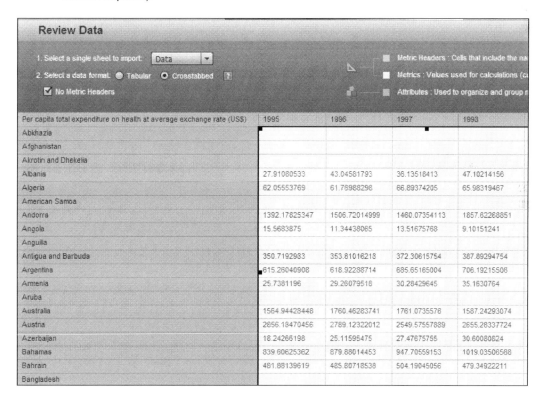

6. The blue background indicates that both the country names and the years are considered attributes, click on **Continue**.

7. Inspect the data: first two columns are attributes and the third is a metric. Rename the columns using their context menu:

    ❑ First column: `Country`

    ❑ Second column: `Year`

    ❑ Third column: `Per Capita Total Expenditure on Health`

8. Click on **Continue**. After a few seconds you will see the **Select a Visualization** dialog, click on the group **Area** and then **Vertical Area - Stacked**.

9. Show the **Filters** pane by clicking on the **Show | Filters** toolbar menu.

10. Drag the **Country** attribute from **My Data** to the **Filters**. A new textbox appears under the **Country** header, type `Belgium` and click on the small gray tag that pops up labeled **Belgium**.

11. The graph automatically reflects the selection. Now under the **Graph | GRAPH | Vertical axis** pane, open the context menu of the **Per Capita Total Expenditure on Health** metric and rename it `Health Expenditure`.

12. Lastly, add some more countries using the **Filters** pane. For example, `France`, `United Kingdom`, and `Germany`, to see which spends less per capita on health.

13. When you're done hide **My Data** and **Graph** panes clicking on their respective **X** icons next to the title (tool tip: **Close**). Rename the **Vertical Area - Stacked** header to `Health Expenditure per capita`, and change the **Layout 1** tab title to `Stacked Area Graph`.

14. Click on **Save & Close** and name it `Health Expenditure`.

How it works...

By pivoting columns to rows, we are able to use cross-tabbed Excel files that would otherwise need some ETL massaging, which is time consuming and—of course—prone to errors.

There's more...

You can export a visualization:

Open the context menu next to **Health Expenditure per capita** and select **Export | Image**.

A new PNG file will be downloaded from the browser to your PC.

 You can watch a screencast of this operation at:
> `http://at5.us/Ch13V6`

Connecting to a RDBMS

From this recipe on, we are exploring the subscription-based version of Express. You can use the free 30 days trial to test drive the premium features described henceforth. As of writing, I have no pricing information regarding the subscription; a quick Google search pointed me to this FAQ document: `http://at5.us/Ch13U6`, which simply says you need to contact the company for details.

The list of different databases that can be accessed from Express includes DB2, Oracle, SQL Server, MySQL, Informix, and more; both on-premise and cloud hosted.

When accessing a database in your company network, you need to have a public facing IP address to connect to (remember that while Express runs as a Flash application in your browser, you're actually using an Intelligence Server on the cloud); there may be network restrictions in your company and firewall rules that prevent this, therefore please refer to your network administrator and discuss the implications of opening an external access to the RDBMS: Express will disclose you the fixed IP address used to enter your LAN.

When accessing a database hosted in the cloud, you should configure the access to it, and depending on the provider you may have different degrees of control over the external accessibility. During this recipe, anyway, you can use a small SQL Server that I set up just for training purposes: it contains a single table with data about vehicles and consumption (source: `http://www.fueleconomy.gov`).

Getting ready

You need to enable the premium features trial in Express:

1. Log in to Express and from the main page click on **New Team...**.
2. On the welcome page, click on the button labeled **Start Free Trial**.

3. In the **Create New Team** dialog, type Cookbook as **Name** and click on **OK**.

4. Your team is being created. After few seconds, you'll be redirected to the welcome page for your team.

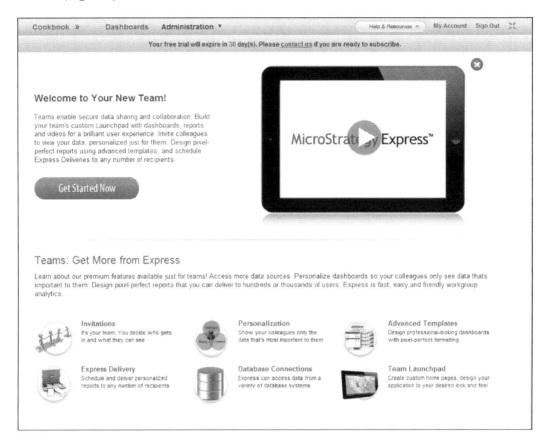

You can increase the available space by hiding the **Teams** pane on the left and clicking on the full screen icon on the top right.

How to do it...

We are now creating a new connection and a new dashboard:

1. Close the welcome page by clicking on the red **X** button. Click on **New Dashboard...**, the **Select Your Data Source** page appears.

2. Select **Database**, read the instructions on the right, and note down the IP address in case you need to open firewall access. Click on **Continue**.

3. You will see a **Quick Tips** page; hit **Close** to continue.

4. In the following page, there are three areas: **Database connections, Available tables**, and an empty area on the right (query designer). Move to the title bar of **Database connections** and click on the green plus icon to create a new one.

5. In the **Database connection** dialog, open the first dropdown labeled **Select** and choose **SQL Server**. The rest of the controls change accordingly.

6. In the second dropdown labeled **DBMS**, pick **Microsoft SQL Server 2008**; fill the four following textboxes with these values (I know they look weird but they're real, you can copy and paste them from the companion code file):

   ❑ **Server, Port:** a8dcbfcc-ff1a-43e0-8955-a20b014d110c.sqlserver.sequelizer.com

   ❑ **Database Name:** dba8dcbfccff1a43e08955a20b014d110c

   ❑ **User:** ifgyjwiiswzigybz

   ❑ **Password:** jcyTY35ZeufL8LzCMx4mZCFgi3UB4KAmpo6VQCgypx3bXPugAzPXeYcPDrK5hB6A

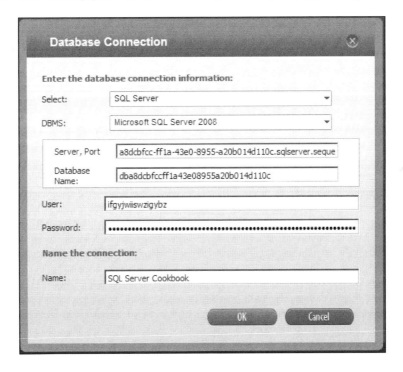

7. Name the connection SQL Server Cookbook and press **OK**.

8. Now in the **Database connections** group, select **SQL Server Cookbook** to see a list of available tables. There is only one, named **Vehicles**. Click on the plus sign on the left of the name to see its columns.

9. Click on the table name (**Vehicles**) and drag it to the right empty pane, the table will appear on the query design canvas.

10. In the query designer, scroll down the table until you find the field named **fuelType1**.

11. Placing the cursor on the **fuelType1** field activates two buttons, click on the first one with a green plus icon. This adds the column **[Vehicles. fuelType1]** to the result pane in the lower part of the screen.

12. Scroll down and repeat step 11 to add the columns named **make** and **model**. Then scroll back up to find the field named **co2TailpipeGpm**. Add this one also.

13. Click on the green right arrow on the top of the designer to execute the query. The result pane now shows the first few lines of the dataset.

14. Move to the header of the **Co2tailpipegpm** column on the result pane and open its context menu. Select **Metric**; the result pane should look like this screen capture:

Fueltype1	Make	Model	Co2tailpipegpm
Regular Gasoline	Alfa Romeo	Spider Veloce 2000	423.190476190476
Regular Gasoline	Ferrari	Testarossa	807.909090909091
Regular Gasoline	Dodge	Charger	329.148148148148
Regular Gasoline	Dodge	B150/B250 Wagon 2WD	807.909090909091
Premium Gasoline	Subaru	Legacy AWD Turbo	467.736842105263
Regular Gasoline	Subaru	Loyale	403.954545454545
Regular Gasoline	Subaru	Loyale	355.48
Regular Gasoline	Toyota	Corolla	370.291666666667
Regular Gasoline	Toyota	Corolla	341.807692307692
Regular Gasoline	Toyota	Corolla	355.48
Regular Gasoline	Toyota	Corolla	341.807692307692
Regular Gasoline	Volkswagen	Golf III / GTI	423.190476190476
Regular Gasoline	Volkswagen	Golf III / GTI	370.291666666667

15. Click on **Continue**.

16. Click on **Select a Visualization**, pick the second icon (tool tip: **Heat Map**). A new dashboard with a Heat Map will be created.

17. Open the **Show** menu and choose **Page-by**.

18. From **My Data** pane, drag the **Fueltype1** attribute to the **Page-by** row.

19. Click on the **Make** attribute in **My Data** and drag it to the **Heat Map | Grouping** area. Place it right over the existing **Fueltype1** attribute; when the two overlap, you will see the cursor changing to a black arrow with a small blue icon: this means the **Make** attribute will substitute **Fueltype1**.

20. From the **Heat Map | Color By** area, drag the **Row Count** metric to the **Heat Map | Size By** area and substitute the existing **Co2tailpipegpm** metric.

21. Now move to **My Data** pane and open the context menu of the **Co2tailpipegpm** metric. Select **New Metric | Average**. This will create a new average (**Co2tailpipegpm**) metric.

22. Drag the new metric to the **Heat Map | Color By** area and substitute the existing **Row Count**. Try to click on the **Page-by** button and you'll see the Heat Map changing accordingly.

23. Now move the cursor to the **Heat Map | Color By** area. Click on the square with four colors next to the header (tool tip: **Thresholds...**).

24. In the **Thresholds** dialog, open the first dropdown and select **Red-Orange-Green**.

25. Open the second dropdown labeled **Based On** and pick **Highest %**. Press **OK**.

26. Rename this visualization as `tailpipe CO2 in grams/mile for fuelType1`, and change the **Layout 1** title to `Heat Map`.

27. Click on **Save & Close** and name this as `Vehicles CO2 emissions`.

How it works...

Looking at the following image:

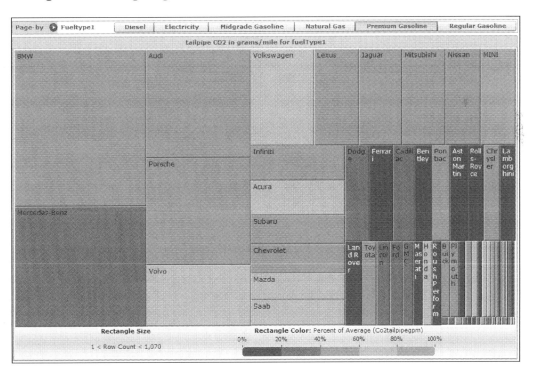

We can see that high averages of CO2 emissions are shown in red (**Ferrari**, not surprisingly) and low values in green (**MINI**). The size of the boxes represents the number of rows in the dataset per each car brand. With the Page-by buttons, the Heat Map switches from a fuel type to another.

In this particular recipe, the connection to the RDBMS is performed from the Intelligence Server hosted on MicroStrategy data centers to a test SQL Server hosted by a cloud provider. Your case may be different.

It is important to have a clear view of your network architecture and how to access it from outside. Different database vendors can have different settings (port, server name, user, and so on); have all the relevant information at hand before connecting from Express. MicroStrategy support (support@microstrategy.com) can help you configure the access or set up a VPN tunnel if needed.

There's more...

Filters can be applied to Heat Maps just like other visualization: show the **Filters** pane and drag an object to it.

Adding more attributes to the **Heat Map | Grouping** area creates more boxes.

Exercise 35

Add the **Model** attribute and filter on the **BMW** brand in the **Premium Gasoline** page.

Modify the threshold so that light blue is environment friendly, deep blue is not. Now you know which will be your next car.

 You can watch screencasts of this operation at:

- ▶ `http://at5.us/Ch13V7`
- ▶ `http://at5.us/Ch13V8`
- ▶ `http://at5.us/Ch13V9`

Refreshing dashboard data

Data changes over time and, after every new load, cached datasets must be refreshed. Express accesses your RDBMS the first time you create a dashboard, and then stores a copy of the results for later analysis. Whenever the data changes on the data warehouse, Express must reload an updated copy. This can be done manually or on a schedule.

The manual process is the same as we used in the preceding recipe; just select database connection, tables, and fields; in this recipe, we will look at how the whole procedure can be automated to run unattended.

When automating schedules in Express, the time is always set according to GMT clock. This means that the daylight saving time is not taken into account, and your loads will run at a different time in summer (in case your country observes DST). For example, a 2 A.M. GMT load would run at 3 A.M. in Rome during winter, and 4 A.M. during summer.

 Bookmark this URL `http://www.timeanddate.com/time/dst/events.html` just in case, and be prepared to receive nightly calls...

Getting ready

You need to have completed the previous recipe to continue.

How to do it...

To set a schedule:

1. Open Express and go to your team main page.
2. Move the cursor to **Vehicles Co2 emissions**, click on the **Refresh data** option.
3. From the drop-down menu, choose **Set Schedule**.
4. In the **Select a schedule below** dialog, click on the radio button labeled **Weekly**.

5. Change the day to **Sunday** in the first dropdown and the hour to 3 A.M. in the second (or any time you prefer).

6. Press the **OK** button, the schedule is now set. It will automatically trigger next Sunday at 3 A.M. GMT.

How it works...

When trigger fires, the data will be loaded from the source database and the dataset cache will be recreated.

There's more...

To modify the schedule, click on the round clock icon next to the dashboard name and press the **Modify** button.

You can watch a screencast of this operation at:

▶ `http://at5.us/Ch13V10`

Sharing a dashboard by e-mail

You can deliver your dashboard to members of your team by sending them an e-mail with a link to Express or an attached PDF.

Since we only have one user in our team, for simplicity in this recipe we will send a message to ourselves.

Getting ready

In order to see Flash contents in a PDF document, you need to install a separate Flash player (see article `http://at5.us/Ch13U7`). This is a standalone install, not the web browser plugin; download the appropriate version for your operating system and install it.

How to do it...

We are now sending a dashboard via e-mail:

1. Once you have the Flash player installed go to the main team page. Move the cursor over **Vehicles Co2 emissions**, and click on the **Share** option.

2. From the drop-down menu, select **Deliver**.

3. A page named **Delivery Settings** opens, click on the **To** button and in the **Select Recipients** dialog select your name in the **Users** list. Then press **OK**.

4. Enable the checkbox labeled **Include a portable dashboard in PDF format**.

5. Open the **Frequency** dropdown and choose **One time, immediately**.

6. Press **OK** and check your e-mail.

7. Open the message and download the copy of `Vehicles Co2 emissions.pdf`.

8. Open the file in Adobe Reader. Once it loads try to click on the page-by buttons to change the Heat Map.

Wow!

How it works...

The PDF contains a copy of the entire dashboard in Flash format. When the Adobe reader finds Flash content in a file, it loads the Flash player to render it. We are actually looking at an embedded SWF inside a PDF document.

There's more...

You can schedule a delivery too. Instead of choosing **One time, immediately** on step 5, pick **On the following schedule** and fill the **Select a schedule below** dialog box.

You can watch a screencast of this operation at:
> `http://at5.us/Ch13V11`

Sharing from the free account

Dashboard sharing is also available for the personal accounts. It doesn't allow to schedule a delivery but you can send a link via e-mail or embed an IFRAME into your web page or blog, which is an extremely useful feature.

The procedure is very similar: in the personal main page, hover the cursor on a dashboard name and click on **Share**. Then select from the available options the last one: **Embed (Social)**. This provides you with the HTML code to embed the dashboard in a standard web page.

See also

▶ *Appendix C, Cloudera Hadoop*

▶ *Appendix D, HP Vertica*

Solution to Exercises

Exercise 1

Run this code in the `sqlcmd` console:

```
use AdventureWorksDW2008R2
go
select count(1) from FactCurrencyRate
go
```

The SQL Server returns: **14264**

```
select count(1) from FactResellerSales
go
```

The SQL Server returns: **60855**

```
select count(1) from DimGeography
go
```

The SQL Server returns: **655**

```
select count(1) from DimDate
go
```

The SQL Server returns: **1188**

```
select count(1) from DimCurrency
go
```

The SQL Server returns: **105**

Exercise 2

From the **Warehouse Catalog** window, select the desired tables by pressing *Ctrl* + click and move them to the right-hand side of the shopping cart.

Once you're done, click on **Save and Close**.

Update the schema.

Exercise 3

One-to-many relationship.

DimCustomer, **DimDate**, and **DimSalesTerritory** are parent; **FactInternetSales** is child; **DimProductCategory** is parent of **DimProductSubcategory**, which is parent of **DimProduct**, which is parent of **FactInternetSales**; **DimGeography** is parent of **DimCustomer**.

I'd say "normalized".

Exercise 4

We won't use those tables during the following chapters, so you can do them as an exercise or just skip this one. The important point is to create all the column objects with the same name and the same data type: `EmployeeKey`, `ParentEmployeeKey`, `SalesTerritoryKey`, `FirstName`, `LastName`, and `DepartmentName`.

Exercise 5

You can download a screencast of this exercise from:

> ▶ `http://at5.us/Ch3V4`

Exercise 6

It's a foreign key.

It relates to the primary key of the table **DimGeography**.

Add **DimCustomer** as a source table for the **City** ID and add the **Customer** attribute as a child of **City** (one-to-many).

Exercise 7

No special instructions here; just follow the steps of the recipe. In the **Modify Attribute Form** window, type EMAIL in the **Name** textbox of the **Form** general information group, and select **Email Type** in the **Form** format group.

Exercise 8

No special instructions here; just create a new hierarchy and follow the recipe steps with the Product Category, Product Subcategory, and Product attributes. Save the hierarchy and name it Products.

Exercise 9

No special instructions here; just create a new hierarchy and follow the recipe steps with the Country, StateProvince, City, and Customer attributes. Save the hierarchy and name it Geography. The Customer attribute should be child of City (see *Exercise 6*).

Exercise 10

In **Frankfurt 91480**, there are 30 customers.

Exercise 11

Create a new filter with the attribute qualifications:

- ▸ **Attribute: Product Category**
- ▸ **Qualify On: Elements**
- ▸ **Operator: In list**
- ▸ **Element List**:
  - ❏ **Bikes**
  - ❏ **Accessories**

Create a new filter with the attribute qualifications:

- ▸ **Attribute: City**
- ▸ **Qualify On: Elements**

▶ **Operator**: **In list**

▶ **Element List**:

    ❑ **Paris 75002**

    ❑ **Paris 75003**

    ❑ **Paris 75005**

    ❑ **Paris 75006**

    ❑ **Paris 75007**

    ❑ **Paris 75008**

    ❑ **Paris 75009**

    ❑ **Paris 75010**

    ❑ **Paris 75012**

    ❑ **Paris 75013**

    ❑ **Paris 75016**

    ❑ **Paris 75017**

    ❑ **Paris 75019**

    ❑ **Paris La Defense 92081**

Exercise 12

Create the fact according to the screen capture:

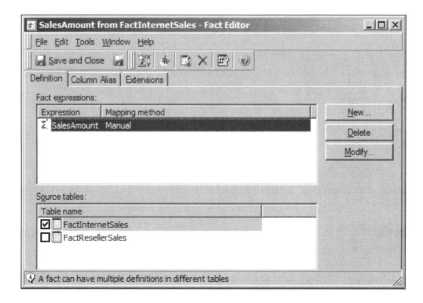

Then the metric:

Exercise 13

Ooops, no.

Check the result with this query in `sqlcmd`:

```
select sum(SalesAmount) from FactInternetSales
```

The SQL Server returns:

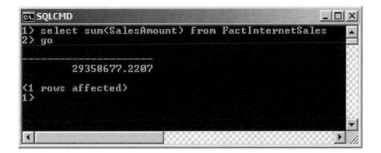

Exercise 14

The two metrics come from the same fact table, so in the SQL view there is just one SELECT statement with both count(1) and sum(all.SalesAmount).

See the image for results:

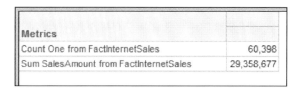

Metrics	
Count One from FactInternetSales	60,398
Sum SalesAmount from FactInternetSales	29,358,677

Exercise 15

The report has the Customer attribute on rows and Sum SalesAmount from FactInternetSales on columns.

Exercise 16

See the fact expression in the following screen capture:

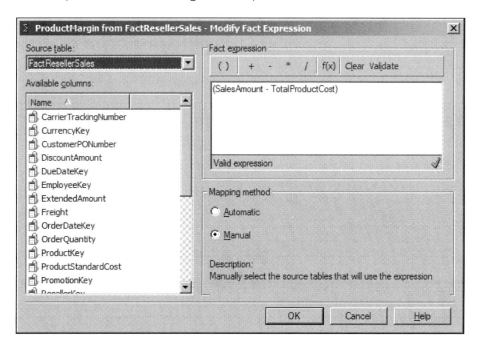

See the source table in the following image:

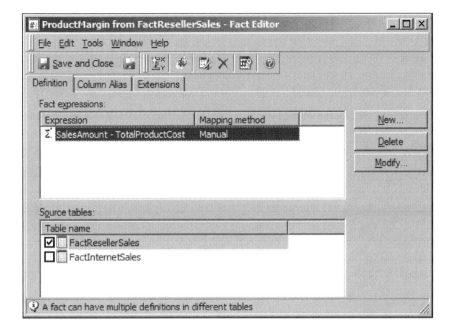

Exercise 17

No special instructions here; just be sure to have all the underlying facts before creating the metrics. Leave the default aggregation function Sum().

Exercise 18

Since all the metrics created in *Exercise 17* come from the fact table FactResellerSales; MicroStrategy issues a single SELECT query to get them all.

You can move the metrics from columns to rows (pivot) using the context menu that appears when you right-click on the header.

Exercise 19

Use the RankProductMargin from FactResellerSales DESC metric and filter on the metric (**Function: Metric Value, Operator: Less than or equal to, Value: 5**). Run the report and in the grid view, sort the rank metric column in ascending order.

Exercise 20

Repeat the steps in the recipe to create a metric at Country level using a copy of Sum SalesAmount from FactInternetSales. Then create another metric with the formula:

  ([Sum SalesAmount from FactInternetSales] / [Sum SalesAmount from FactInternetSales (Country Level)])

Use those metrics in a report with the Country and StateProvince attributes.

Exercise 21

The numbers now reflect the 2007 year only, when the **Touring-1000 Promotion** was active; we lost sales data of 2005, 2006, and 2008.

To solve this error, we need to set **Join Type** to **Outer** in the **Sum SalesAmount from FactResellerSales** metric (or both the metrics if you prefer), see screen capture:

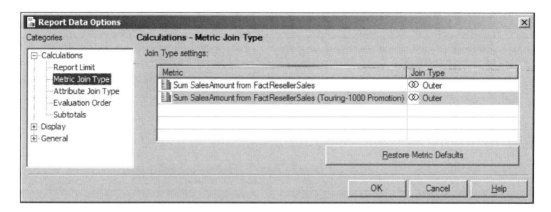

Exercise 22

It's the same problem as in the previous exercise; correct it by setting **Metric Join Type** to **Outer**.

Exercise 23

See the following image for the **View filter** conditions:

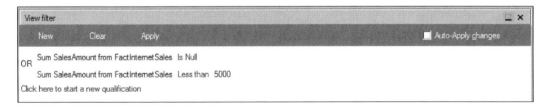

Exercise 24

This is a joke more than an exercise. It's a **Pie:Ring** graph and the sugar coating is done with a pattern in the **Series | Fill | Background type:** option.

Exercise 25

In the document header, or if I want it to be displayed on each page in the page header.

Exercise 26

We use the metric to force the SQL generator to use the fact table FactResellerSales; otherwise, MicroStrategy would use the lookup (DimEmployee), which is smaller and faster, but, in that case, we won't have the correct result.

Exercise 27

Yes, creating a metric with this formula:

```
([Sum SalesAmount from FactResellerSales] * [Minimum Exchange Rate])
```

Exercise 28

No special instructions here; just follow the steps in the recipe.

Exercise 29

From the **Insert** menu, choose the **Image** button. Answer **Yes** to make it visible in all views.

By dragging an image corner or changing its properties in the appropriate view, all the others views will retain their original settings.

Exercise 30

Right-click on the **UK Total** element and select **Formatting properties** (**Element header** or **Element values**).

Exercise 31

6,214,739.

London Area is double counted.

Exercise 32

Use `Product Category` as a page-by attribute.

Set the display option of the new element, as shown in the screen capture:

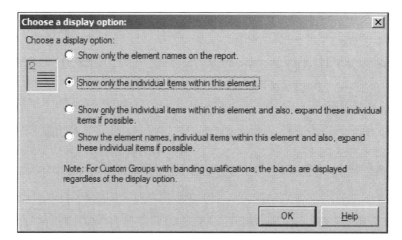

Exercise 33

Create the transformation, as shown in the screen capture:

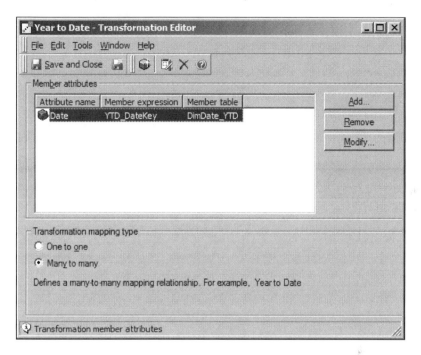

Then create the metric:

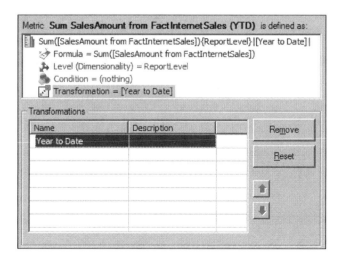

Place the Date attribute on rows, metrics on columns, and page-by year.

Exercise 34

Place **Promotion** in **NETWORK | From item** and **Product** in **To item**. Place **Sum USD SalesAmount from FactResellerSales** in **COLOR AND SIZE | Node Size**:

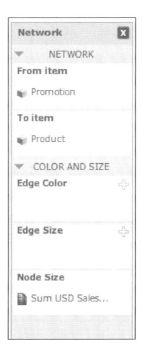

Exercise 35

No special instructions here; just set the **Thresholds** according to this screen capture:

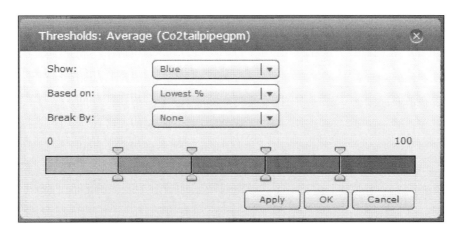

B

Where to Look
for Information

Some useful online resources with information on MicroStrategy.

Online resources

There are many places online where you can find information about MicroStrategy, ask questions, and network with fellow users.

The MicroStrategy official website `http://www.microstrategy.com/` is the first and most important place where you can find official information, marketing materials, and institutional videos.

Another tool that I strongly recommend is the free learning management system available at `https://resource.microstrategy.com/education/CourseCatalog.aspx`. You will need a MicroStrategy account (also free) to get in; click on **Online Courses** and follow several very interesting slideshows about different product aspects.

Next, for sure, are the extensive knowledge base and discussion groups where you will almost certainly find a solution to your problem, or a shoulder to cry on, and a helping alternative from another developer:

- `https://resource.microstrategy.com/support/`
- `https://resource.microstrategy.com/Forum/`

There is a growing community of BI users on LinkedIn; just browse the groups and join some of them:

- ▶ `http://www.linkedin.com/groups?gid=3028129`
- ▶ `http://www.linkedin.com/groups?gid=2832295`
- ▶ `http://www.linkedin.com/groups?gid=2901258`

In Google Groups, you can join:

- ▶ `https://groups.google.com/forum/#!forum/microstrategy-experts`

Blogs

When talking about MicroStrategy blogs, the first and most complete one is written by Bryan Brandow (MCEP). It is safe to say that he is the most knowledgeable MicroStrategy developer in the blogosphere:

- ▶ `http://www.bryanbrandow.com/`

Brian is part of the great MicroStrategy group at Facebook in Menlo Park, CA.

Another very interesting and focused on SDK is the one that David Ureña Cot (MCEP) is writing:

- ▶ `http://www.microstrategysdkbooster.com`

David is currently working as BI developer at Sony in London.

A worth mentioning and very complete blog is:

- ▶ `http://www.microstrategyblog.com/`

Where several contributors write excellent content and home of the famous Metadata Browser.

Tiwari Ashish and Sorin Suciu, two long time MicroStrategy users and very skilled writers are among the authors of:

- ▶ `http://www.microstrategy101.com/`

And last, but not least, the MicroStrategy Learning Forum at:

- ▶ `http://microstrategytechbuzz.blogspot.com.es`

Maintained by Raja Vel.

Books

I hope the one you're holding will stay close to your keyboard for a long time; besides that, `https://itunes.apple.com/us/artist/microstrategy-university/id445962707?mt=11` has a list of official MicroStrategy curriculum books available on iTunes. Of course, the product documentation is always the most updated source of information, especially for new features.

Lastly, a little off-topic but a really interesting book, about how to deal with customers and members of the board, when things go downhill:

Thank You for Arguing: What Aristotle, Lincoln, and Homer Simpson Can Teach Us About the Art of Persuasion by *Jay Heinrichs*. It is available at:

▶   `http://www.amazon.com/dp/0307341445`

C

Cloudera Hadoop

In this appendix, we will cover:

- ▸ Connecting to a Hadoop database

Introduction

Hadoop is one of the names we think about when it comes to Big Data. I'm not going into details about it since there is plenty of information out there; moreover, like somebody once said, "If you decided to use Hadoop for your data warehouse, then you probably have a good reason for it". Let's not forget: it is primarily a distributed filesystem, not a relational database. That said, there are many cases when we may need to use this technology for number crunching, for example, together with MicroStrategy for analysis and reporting.

There are mainly two ways to leverage Hadoop data from MicroStrategy: the first is Hive and the second is Impala. They both work as SQL bridges to the underlying Hadoop structures, converting standard SELECT statements into jobs. The connection is handled by a proprietary 32-bit ODBC driver available for free from the Cloudera website.

In my tests, Impala resulted largely faster than Hive, so I will show you how to use it from our MicroStrategy virtual machine.

 Please note that I am using Version 9.3.0 for consistency with the rest of the book. If you're serious about Big Data and Hadoop, I strongly recommend upgrading to 9.3.1 for enhanced performance and easier setup. See MicroStrategy knowledge base document *TN43588: Post-Certification of Cloudera Impala 1.0 with MicroStrategy 9.3.1*.

The ODBC driver is the same for both Hive and Impala, only the driver settings change.

Connecting to a Hadoop database

To show how we can connect to a Hadoop database, I will use two virtual machines: one with MicroStrategy Suite and the second with Cloudera Hadoop distribution, specifically, a virtual appliance that is available for download from their website.

The configuration of the Hadoop cluster is out of scope; moreover, I am not a Hadoop expert. I'll simply give some hints, feel free to use any other configuration/vendor, the procedure and ODBC parameters should be similar.

Getting ready

Start by going to `http://at5.us/AppAU1`

The Cloudera VM download is almost 3 GB (`cloudera-quickstart-vm-4.3.0-vmware.tar.gz`) and features the CH4 version. After unpacking the archive, you'll find a `cloudera-quickstart-vm-4.3.0-vmware.ovf` file that can be opened with VMware, see screen capture:

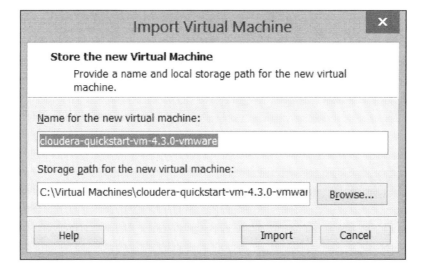

Accept the defaults and click on **Import** to generate the **cloudera-quickstart-vm-4.3.0-vmware** virtual machine.

Before starting the Cloudera appliance, change the network card settings from **NAT** to **Bridged** since we need to access the database from another VM:

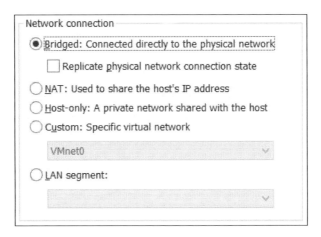

Leave the rest of the parameters, as per the default, and start the machine.

After a while, you'll be presented with a graphical interface of Centos Linux. If the network has started correctly, the machine should have received an IP address from your network DHCP. We need a fixed rather than dynamic address in the Hadoop VM, so:

1. Open the **System | Preferences | Network Connections** menu.

2. Select the name of your card (should be something like **Auto eth1**) and click on **Edit...**.

3. Move to the **IPv4 Settings** tab and change the **Method** from **Automatic (DHCP)** to **Manual**.

4. Click on the **Add** button to create a new address. Ask your network administrator for details here and fill **Address**, **Netmask**, and **Gateway**.

5. Click on **Apply...** and when prompted type the root password `cloudera` and click on **Authenticate**. Then click on **Close**.

6. Check if the change was successful by opening a **Terminal** window (**Applications | System Tools | Terminal**) and issue the `ifconfig` command, the answer should include the address that you typed in step 4.

7. From the MicroStrategy Suite virtual machine, test if you can ping the Cloudera VM.

    When we first start Hadoop, there are no tables in the database, so we create the samples:

8. In the Cloudera virtual machine, from the main page in Firefox open **Cloudera Manager**, click on **I Agree** in the **Information Assurance Policy** dialog.

9. Log in with username `admin` and password `admin`.

10. Look for a line with a service named **oozie1**, notice that it is stopped. Click on the **Actions** button and select **Start...**.

11. Confirm with the **Start** button in the dialog. A **Status** window will pop up, wait until the **Progress** is reported as **Finished** and close it.

12. Now click on the **Hue** button in the bookmarks toolbar.

13. Sign up with username `admin` and password `admin`, you are now in the **Hue** home page.

14. Click on the first button in the blue **Hue** toolbar (tool tip: **About Hue**) to go to the quick **Start Wizard**.

15. Click on the **Next** button to go to **Step 2: Examples** tab.

16. Click on **Beeswax (Hive UI)** and wait until a message over the toolbar says **Examples refreshed**.

17. Now in the **Hue** toolbar, click on the seventh button from the left (tool tip: **Metastore Manager**), you will see the default database with two tables: **sample_07** and **sample_08**.

18. Enable the checkbox of **sample_08** and click on the **Browse Data** button. After a while the **Results** tab shows a grid with data. So far so good.

19. We now go back to the Cloudera Manager to start the Impala service. Click on the **Cloudera Manager** bookmark button.

20. In the **Impala1** row, open the **Actions** menu and choose **Start...**, then confirm **Start**.

21. Wait until the **Progress** says **Finished**, then click on **Close** in the command details window.

22. Go back to **Hue** and click on the fourth button on the toolbar (tool tip: **Cloudera Impala (TM) Query UI**).

23. In the Query Editor text area, type `select * from sample_08` and click on **Execute** to see the table content.

Next, we open the MicroStrategy virtual machine and download the 32-bit Cloudera ODBC Driver for Apache Hive, Version 2.0 from `http://at5.us/AppAU2`.

Download the `ClouderaHiveODBCSetup_v2_00.exe` file and save it in `C:\install`.

How to do it...

We install the ODBC driver:

1. Run `C:\install\ClouderaHiveODBCSetup_v2_00.exe` and click on the **Next** button until you reach **Finish** at the end of the setup, accepting every default.

2. Go to **Start | All Programs | Administrative Tools | Data Sources (ODBC)** to open the 32-bit ODBC Data Source Administrator (if you're on 64-bit Windows, it's in the `SysWOW64` folder).

3. Click on **System DSN** and hit the **Add...** button.

4. Select **Cloudera ODBC Driver for Apache Hive** and click on **Finish**.

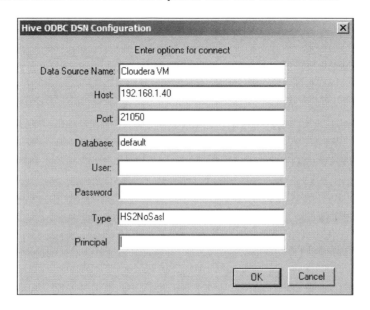

5. Fill the **Hive ODBC DSN Configuration** with these case-sensitive parameters (change the **Host** IP according to the address used in step 4 of the *Getting ready* section):

   ❑ **Data Source Name**: Cloudera VM

   ❑ **Host**: 192.168.1.40

   ❑ **Port**: 21050

   ❑ **Database**: default

   ❑ **Type**: HS2NoSasl

6. Click on **OK** and then on **OK** again to close the ODBC Data Source Administrator.

7. Now open the MicroStrategy Desktop application and log in with administrator and the corresponding password.

8. Right-click on **MicroStrategy Analytics Modules** and select **Create New Project…**.

9. Click on the **Create project** button and name it HADOOP, uncheck **Enable Change Journal for this project** and click on **OK**.

10. When the wizard finishes creating the project click on **Select tables from the Warehouse Catalog** and hit the button labeled **New…**.

11. Click on **Next** and type Cloudera VM in the **Name** textbox of the **Database Instance Definition** window.

12. In this same window, open the **Database type** combobox and scroll down until you find **Generic DBMS**. Click on **Next**.

13. In **Local system ODBC data sources**, pick **Cloudera VM** and type admin in both **Database login** and **Password** textboxes.

14. Click on **Next**, then on **Finish**, and then on **OK**.

15. When a **Warehouse Catalog Browser** error appears, click on **Yes**.

16. In the **Warehouse Catalog Options** window, click on **Edit…** on the right below **Cloudera VM**.

17. Select the **Advanced** tab and enable the radio button labeled **Use 2.0 ODBC calls** in the **ODBC Version** group.

18. Click on **OK**. Now select the category **Catalog | Read Settings** in the left tree and enable the first radio button labeled **Use standard ODBC calls to obtain the database catalog**.

19. Click on **OK** to close this window. When the **Warehouse Catalog** window appears, click on the lightning button (tool tip: **Read the Warehouse Catalog**) to refresh the list of available tables.

20. Pick **sample_08** and move it to the right of the shopping cart. Then right-click on it and choose **Import Prefix**.

21. Click on **Save and Close** and then on **OK** twice to close the **Project Creation Assistant**.

22. You can now open the project and update the schema.

From here, the procedure to create objects is the same as in any other project:

1. Go to the **Schema Objects | Attributes** folder, and create a new **Job** attribute with these columns:

   ❑ **ID**:

   Table: **sample_08**

   Column: **code**

   ❑ **DESC**:

   Table: **sample_08**

   Column: **description**

2. Go to the **Fact** folder and create a new **Salary** fact with salary column. Update the schema.

3. Go to the **Public Objects | Metrics** folder and create a new **Salary** metric based on the **Salary** fact with Sum as aggregation function.

4. Go to **My Personal Objects | My Reports** and create a new report with the **Job** attribute and the **Salary** metric:

	Metrics	Salary
Job		
All Occupations		42,270
Management occupations		100,310
Chief executives		160,440
General and operations managers		107,970
Legislators		37,980
Advertising and promotions managers		94,720
Marketing managers		118,160
Sales managers		110,390
Public relations managers		101,220
Administrative services managers		79,500
Computer and information systems managers		118,710

There you go; you just created your first Hadoop report.

How it works...

Executing Hadoop reports is no different from running any other standard DBMS reports. The ODBC driver handles the communication with Cloudera machine and Impala manages the creation of jobs to retrieve data. From MicroStrategy perspective, it is just another `SELECT` query that returns a dataset.

There's more...

Impala and Hive do not support the whole set of ANSI SQL syntax, so in some cases you may receive an error if a specific feature is not implemented:

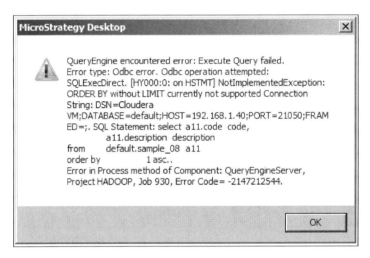

See the Cloudera documentation for details.

You can watch screencasts of this recipe at:

> ▶ http://at5.us/AppCV1
>
> ▶ http://at5.us/AppCV2
>
> ▶ http://at5.us/AppCV3

See also

> ▶ The *Connecting to a Vertica database* recipe in *Appendix D, HP Vertica*

D
HP Vertica

In this appendix, we will cover:

  ▸   Connecting to a Vertica database

Introduction

Vertica Analytic Database is grid-based, column-oriented, and designed to manage large, fast-growing volumes of data while providing rapid query performance. It features a storage organization that favors SELECT statements over UPDATE and DELETE plus a high compression that stores columns of homogeneous datatype together.

The Community (free) Edition allows up to three hosts and 1 TB of data, which is fairly sufficient for small to medium BI projects with MicroStrategy. There are several clients available for different operating systems, including 32-bit and 64-bit ODBC drivers for Windows.

Connecting to a Vertica database

As in the previous appendix, we will use a virtual appliance with the Vertica software and the MicroStrategy machine. The procedure is similar, just the ODBC driver changes.

Getting ready

You need to create a username and log in to the https://my.vertica.com website before downloading; then go to address http://at5.us/AppDU1, and click on the **VMWare Server 2.0 and Workstation 7.0 (vmdk)** link.

When you unzip the archive, you'll find a Vertica 6.1.2 x64 for VMWare folder, open the Vertica 6.1.2 x64 for VMWare.vmx file. The network card should already be bridged, and there is no need to change it.

Power on the machine; it will boot (see the following screenshot) and stop at a row that says **Starting sendmail**:

```
▶ Hide Details                                                                    Starting E-Mail

Setting hostname vertica:                                           [  OK  ]
Setting up Logical Volume Management:                               [  OK  ]
/: clean, 124461/11567104 files, 1176973/11558767 blocks
/boot: clean, 35/26104 files, 15235/104388 blocks
Remounting root filesystem in read-write mode:                     [  OK  ]
Mounting local filesystems:                                        [  OK  ]
Enabling local filesystem quotas:                                  [  OK  ]
Enabling /etc/fstab swaps:                                         [  OK  ]
INIT: Entering runlevel: 5
Entering non-interactive startup
Applying Intel CPU microcode update:                              [  OK  ]
Starting sysstat: Calling the system activity data collector (sadc):
                                                                   [  OK  ]
Starting background readahead:                                     [  OK  ]
Checking for hardware changes                                      [  OK  ]
Bringing up loopback interface:                                    [  OK  ]
Bringing up interface eth0:
Determining IP information for eth0... done.
                                                                   [  OK  ]
Starting auditd:                                                   [  OK  ]
Starting system logger:                                            [  OK  ]
Starting kernel logger:                                            [  OK  ]
Starting irqbalance:                                               [  OK  ]
Starting portmap:                                                  [  OK  ]
Starting RPC idmapd:                                               [  OK  ]
Starting system message bus:                                       [  OK  ]
Starting PC/SC smart card daemon (pcscd):                          [  OK  ]
Starting HAL daemon:                                               [  OK  ]
Starting hidd:                                                     [  OK  ]
Starting sshd:                                                     [  OK  ]
ntpd: Synchronizing with time server:                             [  OK  ]
Starting ntpd:                                                     [  OK  ]
Starting sendmail: █
```

At this point, one may be tempted to shut it down. Don't lose your patience; it is not stuck. I did the same error many times before finding the solution.

Looks like a DNS problem, after about 10 to 20 minutes, when the sendmail daemon times out, the boot will continue.

When the graphical interface appears, we can change the IP address and get rid of the failing services:

1. Open the **System | Administration | Server Settings | Services** menu.

2. When prompted, in **Password for root**, type `password`.

3. In the **Service Configuration** window, **Background Services** tab, scroll down to find **ntpd**, and deselect its checkbox. Scroll down to **sendmail** and uncheck this as well.

4. Click on the **Save** button in the toolbar and close this window.

5. Now open the **System | Administration | Network** menu; here, you'll find a couple of lines with two devices named **eth0.bak** and **eth0**, select **eth0** and click on the **Edit** button.

6. In the **Ethernet Device** window, enable the radio button labeled **Statically set IP address**.

7. Ask your network administrator for details here, and fill in the **Address**, **Subnet mask**, and **Default gateway address** fields.

8. You may need to move up the window to see the bottom; click on **OK** (the rightmost).

9. Now go to the **Hosts** tab, select the line with **Vertica** and click on **Edit**.

10. Change the **Address** field and write the same IP that you used in step 7, then click on **OK**.

11. From the **File** menu, select **Save** and click on **OK**, and then close this window.

12. Open **System | Shutdown** and hit **Restart**.

13. When the machine reboots, go to **System | Administration | Network**.

14. Check that the **DNS** tab reflects the correct **Primary DNS** for your network, change it if needed, as shown in the following screen capture:

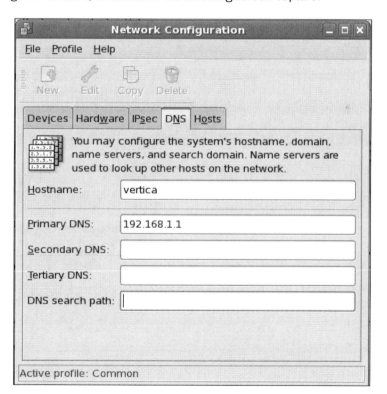

15. Reboot the machine. When it restarts open the **Applications | Accessories | Terminal** menu.

16. In the **Terminal** window, type `admintools`.

17. In the blue screen that appears, use the arrow keys to select the row **Accept** and press the Space bar to check it; then press the *Enter* key.

18. In the **Main Menu** tab of this window, select **Exit** and press *Enter*.

19. When you're back to the command prompt, type:

    ```
    /opt/vertica/sbin/install_example VMart
    ```

20. The example data installation can take a little while, when it's finished, type the following command:

    ```
    /opt/vertica/bin/vsql
    ```

21. This is the Vertica database command-line SQL utility. Now type:

    ```
    Select count(*) from store.store_sales_fact;
    ```

22. The result shows a row count of 5 million. Type `\q` to quit vsql and close the terminal with `exit`.

Open the MicroStrategy virtual machine and test if you can ping the Vertica appliance, then download the HP Vertica Client Package for the Community Edition from:

▸   `http://at5.us/AppDU1`

Select the Windows 32-bit `vertica-client-6.1.2-0.32.exe` file and save it in `C:\install`.

How to do it...

We install the ODBC driver:

1. Run `C:\install\vertica-client-6.1.2-0.32.exe` and click your way to the end of the installation accepting the defaults and click on **Finish**.

2. Go to **Start | All Programs | Administrative Tools | Data Sources (ODBC)** to open the 32-bit ODBC Data Source Administrator (if you're on 64-bit Windows, it's in the `SysWOW64` folder).

3. Click on **System DSN** and hit the **Add...** button.

4. Select the Vertica driver and click on **Finish**, you'll see the following dialog box:

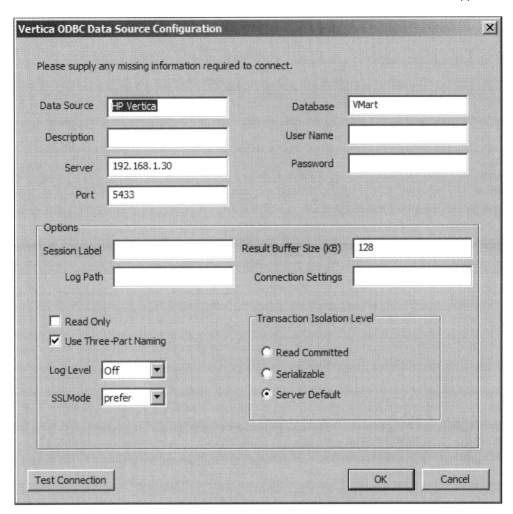

5. In the **Vertica ODBC Data Source Configuration** dialog, type these case-sensitive parameters (change the IP according to your network, as per step 7 in the *Getting ready* section):

   ❑ **Data Source**: HP Vertica

   ❑ **Server**: 192.168.1.30

   ❑ **Port**: 5433

   ❑ **Database**: VMart

6. Click on **OK** and then on **OK** again to close the ODBC Data Source Administrator.

7. Now open the MicroStrategy Desktop application and log in with `Administrator` and the corresponding password.

8. Right-click on **MicroStrategy Analytics Modules** and select **Create New Project...**.

9. Click on the **Create project** button and name it `VERTICA`, uncheck **Enable Change Journal for this project** and click on **OK**.

10. When the wizard finishes creating the project, click on **Select tables from the Warehouse Catalog** and hit the button labeled as **New...**.

11. Click on **Next** and type `HP Vertica` in the **Name** textbox of the **Database Instance Definition** window.

12. In this same window, open the **Database type** combobox and scroll down until you find **Vertica 6.0**. Click on **Next**.

13. In **Local system ODBC data sources**, pick **HP Vertica** and type `dbadmin` in **Database login** and `password` in the **Password** textbox.

14. Click on **Next**, on **Finish**, and then on **OK**.

15. When the **Warehouse Catalog** window appears, pick **customer_dimension, product_dimension** and **store_sales_fact**, and move them to the right of the shopping cart. Then select all the three tables in the right side, right-click on them and choose **Import Prefix**.

16. Click on **Save and Close** and then on **OK** twice to close the **Project Creation Assistant**.

17. You can now open the project and update the schema.

From here on the procedure to create objects is the same as in any other project:

1. Go to the **Schema Objects | Attributes** folder, and create a new **Product** attribute with these columns:

   ❏ **ID**:

      Tables: **product_dimension** (lookup) and **store_sales_fact**

      Column: **product_key**

   ❏ **DESC**:

      Table: **product_dimension** (lookup)

      Column: **product_description**

2. Create a new **Category** attribute with this column:

   ❏ **ID**:

      Table: **product_dimension** (lookup)

      Column: **category_description**

3. Set the **Product** attribute as a child of **Category**.

4. Go to the **Fact** folder and create a new **Sales Dollar Amount** fact with the `sales_dollar_amount` column from the `stores_sales_fact` table.

5. Go to the **Public Objects | Metrics** folder and create a new **Sales Dollar Amount** metric based on the **Sales Dollar Amount** fact with `Sum` as aggregation function.

6. Update the schema.

7. Go to **My Personal Objects | My Reports** and create a new report with the **Category** attribute and the **Sales Dollar Amoun**t metric, see image:

Category	Metrics	Sales Dollar Amount
Food		2,208,230,671
Medical		630,868,606
Misc		629,373,169
Non-food		627,390,275

Congratulations, you just created your first Vertica report, and it runs pretty fast for a 5 million fact table.

How it works...

MicroStrategy generates the correct SQL, provided that we import the prefix when selecting the tables in the **Warehouse Catalog** window; other than that, there is no difference from other systems.

There's more...

In the download section of the Vertica Community Edition website, in addition to ODBC and JDBC drivers for several platforms, you'll find connectors to work with Hadoop (including Cloudera distribution) and Informatica plugins.

 You can watch screencasts of this recipe at:
- `http://at5.us/AppDV1`
- `http://at5.us/AppDV2`

See also

Well, I think there are no more pages left...

This was the last recipe; I would like to thank you for your attention and endurance. I hope you enjoyed the book as much as I did writing it. I have put all my efforts into being as clear and precise as possible; however, in case you find some inaccuracies I would appreciate your feedback at `cookbook@eurostrategy.net`.

If you liked the book, please tell your friends.

Index

Symbols

B

C

Thank you for buying
Business Intelligence with MicroStrategy Cookbook

About Packt Publishing

Packt, pronounced 'packed', published its first book "*Mastering phpMyAdmin for Effective MySQL Management*" in April 2004 and subsequently continued to specialize in publishing highly focused books on specific technologies and solutions.

Our books and publications share the experiences of your fellow IT professionals in adapting and customizing today's systems, applications, and frameworks. Our solution-based books give you the knowledge and power to customize the software and technologies you're using to get the job done. Packt books are more specific and less general than the IT books you have seen in the past. Our unique business model allows us to bring you more focused information, giving you more of what you need to know, and less of what you don't.

Packt is a modern, yet unique publishing company, which focuses on producing quality, cutting-edge books for communities of developers, administrators, and newbies alike. For more information, please visit our website: www.PacktPub.com.

About Packt Enterprise

In 2010, Packt launched two new brands, Packt Enterprise and Packt Open Source, in order to continue its focus on specialization. This book is part of the Packt Enterprise brand, home to books published on enterprise software – software created by major vendors, including (but not limited to) IBM, Microsoft and Oracle, often for use in other corporations. Its titles will offer information relevant to a range of users of this software, including administrators, developers, architects, and end users.

Writing for Packt

We welcome all inquiries from people who are interested in authoring. Book proposals should be sent to author@packtpub.com. If your book idea is still at an early stage and you would like to discuss it first before writing a formal book proposal, contact us; one of our commissioning editors will get in touch with you.

We're not just looking for published authors; if you have strong technical skills but no writing experience, our experienced editors can help you develop a writing career, or simply get some additional reward for your expertise.

Oracle Business
Intelligence 11*g* R1
Cookbook

Make complex analytical reports simple and deliver valuable
business data using OBIEE 11g with this comprehensive
and practical guide

Cuneyt Yilmaz

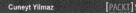

Oracle Business Intelligence 11*g* R1 Cookbook

ISBN: 978-1-84968-600-6   Paperback: 364 pages

Make complex analytical reports simple and deliver
valuable business data using OBIEE 11g with this
comprehensive and practical guide

1. Improve the productivity of business intelligence
   solution to satisfy business requirements with
   real-life scenarios

2. Practical guide on the implementation of OBIEE
   11g from A to Z including best practices

3. Full of useful instructions that can be easily
   adapted to build better business intelligence
   solutions

Business Intelligence Cookbook:
A Project Lifecycle Approach
Using Oracle Technology

Over 80 quick and advanced recipes that focus on real-world
techniques and solutions to manage, design, and build data
warehouse and business intelligence projects

John Heaton

Business Intelligence
Cookbook: A Project
Lifecycle Approach Using
Oracle Technology

ISBN: 978-1-84968-548-1   Paperback: 368 pages

Over 80 quick and advanced recipes that focus on real-
world techniques and solutions to manage, design, and
build data warehouse and business intelligence projects

1. Full of illustrations, diagrams, and tips with clear
   step-by-step instructions and real time examples
   to perform key steps and functions on your project

2. Practical ways to estimate the effort of a data
   warehouse solution based on a standard work
   breakdown structure

Please check **www.PacktPub.com** for information on our titles

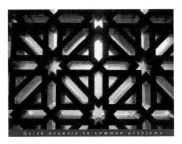

IBM Cognos Business Intelligence 10.1 Dashboarding Cookbook

ISBN: 978-1-84968-582-5   Paperback: 206 pages

Working with dashboards in IBM Cognos BI 10.1: Design, distribute, and collaborate

1. Exploring and interacting with IBM Cognos Business Insight and Business Insight Advanced

2. Creating dashboards in IBM Cognos Business Insight and Business Insight Advanced

3. Sharing and Collaborating on Dashboards using portlets

4. Best practices related to Dashboards in Cognos 10.1

IBM Cognos Business Intelligence 10.1 Dashboarding Cookbook

Working with dashboards in IBM Cognos BI 10.1: Design, distribute, and collaborate

Ankit Garg

Tableau Data Visualization Cookbook

ISBN: 978-1-84968-978-6   Paperback: 172 pages

Over 70 recipes for creating visual stories with your data using Tableau

1. Quickly create impressive and effective graphics which would usually take hours in other tools

2. Lots of illustrations to keep you on track

3. Includes examples that apply to a general audience

Tableau Data Visualization Cookbook

Over 70 recipes for creating visual stories with your data using Tableau

Ashutosh Nandeshwar

Please check **www.PacktPub.com** for information on our titles

27161221R00197

Printed in Great Britain
by Amazon